The Complete Living Will Kit

(+ CD-ROM)

The Complete Living Will Kit

(+ CD-ROM)

Edward A. Haman

Attorney at Law

SPHINX® PUBLISHING
AN IMPRINT OF SOURCEBOOKS, INC.®
NAPERVILLE, ILLINOIS
www.SphinxLegal.com

First Edition: 2006

Published by: **Sphinx® Publishing, An Imprint of Sourcebooks, Inc.®**

Naperville Office
P.O. Box 4410
Naperville, Illinois 60567-4410
630-961-3900
Fax: 630-961-2168
www.sourcebooks.com
www.SphinxLegal.com

This publication is designed to provide accurate and authoritative information in regard to the subject matter covered. It is sold with the understanding that the publisher is not engaged in rendering legal, accounting, or other professional service. If legal advice or other expert assistance is required, the services of a competent professional person should be sought.

From a Declaration of Principles Jointly Adopted by a Committee of the
American Bar Association and a Committee of Publishers and Associations

This product is not a substitute for legal advice.

Disclaimer required by Texas statutes.

Library of Congress Cataloging-in-Publication Data
Haman, Edward A.
   The complete living will kit / by Edward A. Haman. -- 1st ed.
      p. cm.
   Includes index.
   ISBN-13: 978-1-57248-542-6 (pbk. : alk. paper)
   ISBN-10: 1-57248-542-6 (pbk. : alk. paper)
   1. Right to die--Law and legislation--United States--Popular works. I.
Title.

KF3827.E87H355 2006
344.7304'197--dc22
                                                                2006018566

Printed and bound in the United States of America.
SB — 10 9 8 7 6 5 4 3 2 1

Contents

How to Use the CD-ROM

Thank you for purchasing *The Complete Living Will Kit*. In this book, we have worked hard to compile exactly what you need to write your own living will. To make this material even more useful, we have included every document in the book on the CD-ROM in the back of the book.

You can use these forms just as you would the forms in the book. Print them out, fill them in, and use them however you need. You can also fill in the forms directly on your computer. Just identify the form you need, open it, click on the space where the information should go, and input your information. Customize each form for your particular needs. Use them over and over again.

The CD-ROM is compatible with both PC and Mac operating systems. (While it should work with either operating system, we cannot guarantee that it will work with your particular system and we cannot provide technical assistance.) To use the forms on your computer, you will need to use Microsoft Word or another word processing program that can read Word files. The CD-ROM does not contain any such program.

Insert the CD-ROM into your computer. Double-click on the icon representing the disc on your desktop or go through your hard drive to identify the drive that contains the disc and click on it.

Once opened, you will see the files contained on the CD-ROM listed as "Form #: [Form Title]." Open the file you need. You may print the form to fill it out manually at this point, or you can click on the appropriate line to fill it in using your computer.

Any time you see bracketed information [ ] on the form, you can click on it and delete the bracketed information from your final form. This information is only a reference guide to assist you in filling in the forms and should be removed from your final version. Once all your information is filled in, you can print your filled-in form.

*   *   *   *   *

Purchasers of this book are granted a license to use the forms contained in it for their own personal use. By purchasing this book, you have also purchased a limited license to use all forms on the accompanying CD-ROM. The license limits you to personal use only and all other copyright laws must be adhered to. No claim of copyright is made in any government form reproduced in the book or on the CD-ROM. You are free to modify the forms and tailor them to your specific situation.

The author and publisher have attempted to provide the most current and up-to-date information available. However, the courts, Congress, and your state's legislatures review, modify, and change laws on an ongoing basis, as well as create new laws from time to time. Due to the very nature of the information and the continual changes in our legal system, to be sure that you have the current and best information for your situation, you should consult a local attorney or research the current laws yourself.

This publication is designed to provide accurate and authoritative information in regard to the subject matter covered. It is sold with the understanding that the publisher is not engaged in rendering legal, accounting, or other professional service. If legal advice or other expert assistance is required, the services of a competent professional person should be sought.

—From a Declaration of Principles Jointly Adopted by a Committee of the American Bar Association and a Committee of Publishers and Associations

This product is not a substitute for legal advice.

—Disclaimer required by Texas statutes

Using Self-Help Law Books

Before using a self-help law book, you should realize the advantages and disadvantages of doing your own legal work and understand the challenges and diligence that this requires.

The Growing Trend

Rest assured that you won't be the first or only person handling your own legal matter. For example, in some states, more than seventy-five percent of the people in divorces and other cases represent themselves. Because of the high cost of legal services, this is a major trend and many courts are struggling to make it easier for people to represent themselves. However, some courts are not happy with people who do not use attorneys and refuse to help them in any way. For some, the attitude is, "Go to the law library and figure it out for yourself."

We write and publish self-help law books to give people an alternative to the often complicated and confusing legal books found in most law libraries. We have made the explanations of the law as simple and easy to understand as possible. Of course, unlike an attorney advising an individual client, we cannot cover every conceivable possibility.

Cost/Value Analysis

Whenever you shop for a product or service, you are faced with various levels of quality and price. In deciding what product or service to buy, you make a cost/value analysis on the basis of your willingness to pay and the quality you desire.

When buying a car, you decide whether you want transportation, comfort, status, or sex appeal. Accordingly, you decide among such choices as a Neon, a Lincoln, a Rolls Royce, or a Porsche. Before making a decision, you usually weigh the merits of each option against the cost.

When you get a headache, you can take a pain reliever (such as aspirin) or visit a medical specialist for a neurological examination. Given this choice, most people, of course, take a pain reliever, since it costs only pennies; whereas a medical examination costs hundreds of dollars and takes a lot of time. This is usually a logical choice because it is rare to need anything more than a pain reliever for a headache. But in some cases, a headache may indicate a brain tumor and failing to see a specialist right away can result in complications. Should everyone with a headache go to a specialist? Of course not, but people treating their own illnesses must realize that they are betting on the basis of their cost/value analysis of the situation. They are taking the most logical option.

The same cost/value analysis must be made when deciding to do one's own legal work. Many legal situations are very straight forward, requiring a simple form and no complicated analysis. Anyone with a little intelligence and a book of instructions can handle the matter without outside help.

But there is always the chance that complications are involved that only an attorney would notice. To simplify the law into a book like this, several legal cases often must be condensed into a single sentence or paragraph. Otherwise, the book would be several hundred pages long and too complicated for most people. However, this simplification necessarily leaves out many details and nuances that would apply to special or unusual situations. Also, there are many ways to interpret most legal questions. Your case may come before a judge who disagrees with the analysis of our authors.

Therefore, in deciding to use a self-help law book and to do your own legal work, you must realize that you are making a cost/value analysis. You have decided that the money you will save in doing it yourself outweighs the chance that your case will not turn out to your satisfaction. Most people handling their own simple legal matters never have a problem, but occasionally people find that it ended up costing them more to have an attorney straighten out the situation than it would have if they had hired an attorney in the beginning. Keep this in mind while handling your case, and be sure to consult an attorney if you feel you might need further guidance.

Local Rules

The next thing to remember is that a book which covers the law for the entire nation, or even for an entire state, cannot possibly include every procedural difference of every jurisdiction. Whenever possible, we provide the exact form needed; however, in some areas, each county, or even each judge, may require unique forms and procedures. In our state books, our forms usually cover the majority of counties in the state, or provide examples of the type of form which will be required. In our national books, our forms are sometimes even more general in nature but are designed to give a good idea of the type of form that will be needed in most locations. Nonetheless, keep in mind that your state, county, or judge may have a requirement, or use a form, that is not included in this book.

You should not necessarily expect to be able to get all of the information and resources you need solely from within the pages of this book. This book will serve as your guide, giving you specific information whenever possible and helping you to find out what else you will need to know. This is just like if you decided to build your own backyard deck. You might purchase a book on how to build decks. However, such a book would not include the building codes and permit requirements of every city, town, county, and township in the nation; nor would it include the lumber, nails, saws, hammers, and other materials and tools you would need to actually build the deck. You would use the book as your guide, and then do some work and research involving such matters as whether you need a permit of some kind, what type and grade of wood are available in your area, whether to use hand tools or power tools, and how to use those tools.

Before using the forms in a book like this, you should check with your court clerk to see if there are any local rules of which you should be aware, or local forms you will need to use. Often, such forms will require the same information as the forms in the book but are merely laid out differently or use slightly different language. They will sometimes require additional information.

Changes in the Law

Besides being subject to local rules and practices, the law is subject to change at any time. The courts and the legislatures of all fifty states are constantly revising the laws. It is possible that while you are reading this book, some aspect of the law is being changed.

In most cases, the change will be of minimal significance. A form will be redesigned, additional information will be required, or a waiting period will be extended. As a result, you might need to revise a form, file an extra form, or wait out a longer time period; these types of changes will not usually affect the outcome of your case. On the other hand, sometimes a major part of the law is changed, the entire law in a particular area is rewritten, or a case that was the basis of a central legal point is overruled. In such instances, your entire ability to pursue your case may be impaired.

Again, you should weigh the value of your case against the cost of an attorney and make a decision as to what you believe is in your best interest.

Introduction

This book is designed to enable you to prepare your own living will without hiring a lawyer. It explains the law regarding living wills, guides you in deciding which form you need, and gives you the information you need to prepare it. If you have not already done so, be sure to read the section on "Using Self-Help Law Books" starting on page ix.

The difficulty in covering any area of law on a national scale is that the law is different in each state. However, the general type of information found in most living wills is very similar in all states. Appendix A of this book gives you some information about your state's specific laws. Many states have officially approved living will forms. These forms are found in Appendix B, along with general forms for use in any state that does not have its own form. In addition to living wills, this book also discusses some related forms, such as the *health care power of attorney* and the *do not resuscitate order*.

Before beginning to read Chapter 1, you may find it helpful to familiarize yourself with some terminology by reviewing the terms defined in the glossary.

Then, read this entire book (including the listing for your state in Appendix A) before you prepare any papers. This will give you the information you need to decide what form to use and how to complete it. You may also want to visit your local law library to get more information or make sure the law has not changed since this book was published. The section on "Legal Research" in Chapter 2 will help you with further searches.

To complete the necessary form (or forms), you will need to use the general information in the main part of this book, consult the listing for your state in Appendix A, read any instructions on the form itself, and use the information from any additional reading and research.

Chapter 1:
Living Wills and
Related Documents

Thinking about why you might need a living will is not pleasant, but it is a matter that cannot be avoided. With advances in medical science, it is often possible to keep someone technically alive indefinitely. Instead of allowing terminally ill patients to die a natural death, many doctors keep them alive by the use of drugs and machines. A situation can also arise in which a person becomes permanently unconscious, but is not going to die as long as food and water are provided. Either condition can place a burden—both emotionally and financially—upon the person's loved ones.

Some people believe that all human life is sacred and that life should be preserved at all costs. Others believe that certain steps should be taken to preserve life, but some steps should not be taken. Regardless of the view you take, it may one day be important that your family members and doctors know your opinion. You can make your beliefs and desires known through a living will.

The Terri Schiavo case from Florida has pointed out (with vivid clarity) the importance of having a living will. If there is someone whom you trust to make decisions about your medical care if you are unable to do so, you should have a living will and a health care power of attorney. Because of the relentless intervention of the federal and state governments in the Schiavo case, several significant terms have been added to the suggested living will and health care power of attorney documents so your wishes can be made clear and your directions followed.

Living Wills

A *living will* is simply a paper on which you explain your desires in the event medical conditions arise that cause you to be unable to express your wishes. A living will is usually limited to the refusal of, or desire for, medical treatment in the event of:

◆ a terminal illness;

◆ an injury; or,

◆ permanent unconsciousness.

In the event you are unable to communicate your desires in such situations and do not have a living will, doctors or hospitals may decide they are legally obligated to perform certain procedures that you would not desire. If your spouse, adult child, or another relative is called upon to make a decision about your care, he or she will find it helpful if you have expressed your wishes in a living will. A living will tells others what you want to happen in such circumstances.

You may see a living will called by other names, such as:

◆ a declaration regarding life-prolonging procedures;

◆ an advance directive; or,

◆ a declaration.

Traditional Will Compared

It is important not to confuse a living will with a traditional will. A *traditional will* expresses what you want to happen to your property and minor children if you die. A *living will* expresses what you want to happen to your person regarding medical treatment while you are still alive.

Health Care Power of Attorney

In addition to a living will, you should also be aware of another type of document that can be of help in these difficult situations. A *health care power of attorney* gives someone you trust, usually a family member or close friend, the authority to make decisions about your medical treatment. You may also see this referred to as a durable power of attorney for health care, health care proxy, designation of health care surrogate, advance health care directive, or a similar name.

A health care power of attorney goes farther than a living will. A living will simply states, "If I am terminally ill or permanently unconscious and cannot tell my doctors what I want, then this is what I want done." The big restriction with a living will is that it only applies if you are terminally ill or permanently unconscious. If you are only temporarily unconscious or otherwise unable to communicate, but are not terminally ill, a living will is of no use. You need a health care power of attorney to cover such a situation.

With a health care power of attorney, you give another person the power to make decisions about your medical treatment if you are unable to communicate, even if you are not terminally ill or permanently unconscious. This would include approving and giving consent to surgery or other treatment.

A living will may be used along with a health care power of attorney, or the two may be combined into one document. Some of the official state forms combine the two, and may also include various other matters, such as the designation of a primary physician, desires regarding the donation of body organs, and who you would like appointed as your legal guardian if the need arises.

The case of Terri Schiavo demonstrated that having a living will and a health care power of attorney can be crucial. All of the legal, ethical, and religious arguments, the political debate, and the intervention of the various branches of government resulted from the absence of any written direction by Terri. The central question was: What would Terri Schiavo have wanted in her situation? If she had executed a living will, her desires would have been known. Had she executed a health care power of attorney designating her husband as the one she wanted to make decisions on her behalf, her desires would have been known. This would not have been a guarantee that there would have been no court challenge by her parents, but it would have greatly increased the likelihood that her wishes would be followed. It would have also greatly decreased the chances that the matter would linger in the courts and become subject to intervention by the other branches of state and federal government.

Having both a living will and a health care power of attorney can make your wishes known and prevent conflict in your family, since only one person will have the authority to make medical decisions on your behalf.

Living Will Choices

In its most basic form, a living will says, "If I become terminally ill or injured, I do not want any artificial means used that will only delay my death." This is still the basic form used by many of the states that have created living will forms. Over the years, more issues have arisen, resulting in slightly more complex forms being developed. These issues include:

- ◆ conditions of permanent unconsciousness, irreversible coma, or when death is not imminent;
- ◆ conditions in which the burdens of treatment outweigh the expected benefits, but death is not imminent;
- ◆ distinctions between various types of medical procedures;
- ◆ providing food and water through feeding tubes or intravenously;
- ◆ alternative provisions or exceptions if the person is pregnant;

◆ organ donations; and,
◆ covering the situation in which a person does want all possible measures taken to preserve life.

Such provisions have been included in the forms approved by some states. These choices are discussed more fully in later chapters.

Basic Documents for Your Protection

Having a living will is beneficial, but to be better protected, you would be well-advised to have all four of the following basic documents:

1. A *living will,* which tells your health care providers—and your health care agent if you also have a health care power of attorney—what your wishes are if you become terminally ill or permanently unconscious.
2. A *durable power of attorney for health care,* which gives a trusted relative or friend the power to make all types of health care decisions if you are unable to do so.
3. A *durable financial power of attorney*, which gives a trusted relative or friend the ability to handle your financial matters if you become incapacitated.
4. A *will,* which ensures that your property goes to whom you wish to have it and provides for the care and custody of any minor children.

Warning: Great caution must be used with a durable financial power of attorney, because the person you name as your agent could take your money and other property if he or she is dishonest.

Chapter 2:
The Law Concerning
Living Wills

The basics of the law concerning living wills is fairly simple. By signing a living will, you are telling your family, friends, doctors, hospitals, and other health care providers what type of health care you want (or do not want) in certain situations.

The basic reason for having a living will is to get a third party—usually a doctor or hospital—to perform your wishes if you become terminally ill, injured, or permanently unconscious. The concern of the doctor is that he or she may be held liable, either civilly or criminally, for not performing a medical procedure that some could argue would have allowed you to live longer. Many states have passed laws that allow a doctor to honor a living will without being subject to any liability. These laws also provide that other people may rely on your wishes as expressed in your living will and will not be legally responsible for honoring those wishes.

Example: *You state in your living will that you do not want artificial life support procedures used if your condition is terminal. Your doctor will not be subject to a lawsuit by your estate or family for discontinuing life support procedures. Without a living will, the doctor or hospital may be reluctant to discontinue such artificial life support procedures.*

In states that do not have such a law, it may be more difficult to get a doctor to follow your living will instructions. In such cases, it is important that you discuss your wishes with your spouse, family members, or friends, so that someone is fully aware of how you feel. They may then be willing to seek a court order to end artificial life support procedures, and the living will can be used to convince the judge of your wishes.

Some states have laws that authorize certain family members to make these life and death health care decisions even without a living will. However, it will probably be easier for your family members to make such decisions if they are certain how you feel about the subject. A living will can clearly express your desires.

The Law in Your State

Many states have established approved forms for living wills. Some are separate living will forms and others are living will provisions within a health care power of attorney form. First, refer to the listing for your state in Appendix A. It will tell you about the living will laws in your state, which form to use, and where to locate your state's laws if you wish to do further reading. You can then locate the proper form in Appendix B and complete it. (State forms can vary in a few areas.)

Types of Conditions

There are several types of situations that may be covered in a living will. Some state forms refer to only one situation, while others include two or more. The following is a brief explanation of these situations, including where problems occur in the language of some state forms. Where necessary, these matters will be discussed in more detail in each state's listing in Appendix A.

Terminal Conditions

In some states, a *terminal condition* may be called a terminal illness or terminal injury, and may also be accompanied by further language in an attempt to clearly describe the situation. In many state forms, you will find language to the effect that the condition must be *incurable* or *irreversible*, or that death must be likely to occur "within a relatively short period of time." In most cases, there is no definition of what constitutes a relatively short period of time, and in practice, this is left to the doctors to determine.

In a few states, the language of the form requires that it must be determined that the person will die "whether or not life-sustaining procedures are utilized." One of the central purposes of a living will is to allow the person to die when life-sustaining procedures could keep him or her alive indefinitely. To require death to be imminent even if life-sustaining procedures are used defeats the whole purpose of the living will. This is probably just a case of poor drafting of the form. The intent of the legislature was probably to say, as the Texas form provides, that "death is imminent or will result within a relatively short time without the application of life-sustaining procedures." In practice, the poor drafting of these forms will probably be overlooked, and the obvious intent will be recognized. However, if a doctor with a lawyer's mind—or an attorney for the hospital or doctor—ever reads the state form carefully, problems may arise in getting your living will enforced.

It is still advisable to use the official form for your state, as it will probably be quickly recognized and followed by doctors and hospitals. To provide clarification of these poorly drafted forms, you may wish to use form 66 along with the official form for your state. Form 66 gives you options to select that may better explain your desires. This form also states that it is for the purpose of clarifying and detailing your desires, and provides that if it, or any part of it, is determined to be legally invalid, the remainder of the living will remains in effect.

Permanent Unconsciousness

A person in a coma who is not likely to recover consciousness is generally described as being in a state of *permanent unconsciousness*. This may also be called a persistent vegetative state, being permanently comatose, having permanent loss of the ability to communicate concerning medical treatment decisions, or similar language. In several state forms, the language appears to also require the person's condition to be terminal, while in other states, permanent unconsciousness is a sufficient basis on which to invoke the living will—even if the person's condition is not terminal.

Where the Burdens of Treatment Outweigh the Benefits

Only a few states allow as a basis for invoking a living will a condition in which the burdens of treatment outweigh the benefits. This basis does not require a terminal condition.

Oregon Law

Two other situations for invoking a living will are available in Oregon—when the person has an *advanced progressive illness* (this is defined in the official state form) and when the use of life support would cause *permanent and severe pain* and would not help the person's condition.

As a practical matter, except for the Oregon provisions, the factors listed above will usually be connected with a very serious condition that will either be terminal or constitute permanent unconsciousness.

Food and Water

Some state forms have provisions relating to artificially provided food and water, commonly referred to as *nutrition and hydration*. Some forms are silent on this subject, some require it to be provided, others include it as part of the life-sustaining procedures that will be withheld or withdrawn, and others give various types of options to select. If your state's form does not include a provision about food and water, or if you do not like the choices available in your state's form, you may want to complete form 67 (see p.247) and attach it to your state's form. Form 67 will give you more options in this area. (This subject is discussed in more detail in Chapter 3.)

Doctor Certification

A question may arise as to when a person meets the qualifications to invoke his or her living will. For example, if a person must be either in a terminal condition or permanently unconscious, how is it determined whether he or she is in a terminal condition or permanently unconscious?

Some states are silent on this subject and others require one or more doctors to certify that the circumstances exist. See your state's listing in Appendix A for the certification requirements of your state.

Witnesses and Notaries

States differ as to their requirements for how the living will must be signed. All states require the person making the living will to sign and date it. What differs is who must witness the person signing. Depending upon the state, the required witnesses may be:

- ◆ two or more witnesses;
- ◆ two witnesses and a notary public; or,
- ◆ either two witnesses or a notary public.

When both witnesses and a notary are required, some states only require the maker's signature to be notarized, while others require notarization of the signatures of the maker and both witnesses.

Regardless of what may be required in your state, it is strongly suggested that you have two witnesses and that your signature and your witnesses' signatures all be notarized. This is an extra precaution if it is not legally required in your state, but it may make doctors and hospitals more likely to honor your living will without question. It may also be helpful in the event that your living will needs to be invoked while you are in another state. See your state's listing in Appendix A for the requirements of your particular state.

Pregnancy

Another issue may arise when a woman is pregnant and she develops a medical condition that would call for the implementation of her living will. Many state forms do not address this situation. Most states that do address this situation provide that the living will is temporarily invalid, or suspended, for the duration of the pregnancy. In such states, all efforts are made to keep the woman alive until the child can be born, regardless of the wishes of the woman. The forms for Arizona and Maryland have optional provisions to cover pregnancy.

Other Variations

Other various matters that may be covered in living will forms include:

- ◆ designating a person to see that your living will is honored;
- ◆ authorizing organ donation;

◆ expressing wishes regarding an autopsy;

◆ requesting that all efforts be made to preserve life;

◆ designating which procedures are, or are not, desired;

◆ specific revocation provisions;

◆ designating a primary physician; and,

◆ designating a guardian.

Where appropriate, such matters will be mentioned in the listing for your state in Appendix A or described in the form for your state in Appendix B.

Legal Research

Generally, you should not need to go beyond the information in this book. However, if you wish to study your state's law on living wills or health care powers of attorney, this section gives you more information about using the law library and Internet sources. After reading this book, you may want to visit your local law library to do some additional research. One can usually be found at your county courthouse or at a law school. Do not hesitate to ask the law librarian to help you find what you need. The librarian cannot give you legal advice, but he or she can show you where to find your state's laws and other books on living wills.

Statutes or Code

The main source of information is the set of books containing your state's laws. These are the statutes, or code, of your state (e.g., Florida Statutes, Mississippi Code, etc.). The title of the books may also include words such as *Revised* or *Annotated* (e.g., Annotated California Code, Kentucky Revised Statutes, etc.). *Revised* means updated and *annotated* means the books contain information that explains and interprets the laws. Titles may also include the publisher's name, such as Purdon's Pennsylvania Consolidated Statutes Annotated. The listing in Appendix A gives the title of the set of laws for your state.

Each year, the legislatures in all states meet and change the law. Therefore, it is important to be sure you have the most current version. The most common way to update laws is with a softcover supplement, which is found in the back of each volume. There will be a date on the cover to tell you when it was published. Laws can be updated in other ways, including with:

◆ a supplement volume, which is found at the end of the regular set of volumes;

◆ a looseleaf binding, in which pages are removed and replaced; or,

◆ a supplement section added as the law changes.

Checking the most current law is probably all you will need. The following sources may be helpful if you want to go further.

Internet Research

Another place to find statutes and other legal materials is on the Internet. The statutes or codes for all fifty states and the District of Columbia can be found at **www.findlaw.com**. Once you get to the Findlaw site, click on the box titled "For Legal Professionals," then click on "US Laws: Cases & Codes." Scroll down to the heading "US Statutes and Cases" and click on the desired state. Next, click on the state's code or statutes. From this point, navigating your state's website will vary depending upon how that site operates. Generally, you will either be able to enter a specific statute section number, go to a list of the various titles or chapters of the statutes, or do a search by statute number or keyword.

Practice Manuals

A *practice manual* is a book or set of books containing detailed information about various areas of the law. They usually include forms for all different situations.

Digests

A *digest* is a set of books that gives summaries of appeals court cases. A digest for your state is best (such as Florida Digest or Texas Digest), as the national digest is difficult to use. Look in the index of the digest for the subject you want, such as "Living Wills," "Advance Directives," "Life-Prolonging Procedures," "Health Care Power of Attorney," and so on.

Case Reporters

Sets of books called *case reporters*, or *reporters*, contain the full written opinions of the appeals court cases. The cases in the reporters are arranged according to dates they were decided, not according to subject matter. Therefore, you will need to use another source, such as a digest or a legal encyclopedia, to find relevant cases in the reporters.

Legal Encyclopedia

A *legal encyclopedia* is used just like a regular encyclopedia. Look up the subject you want (such as "Living Wills" or "Health Care Power of Attorney") in alphabetical order. *American Jurisprudence* and *Corpus Juris Secundum* are the names of the major sets. Some states have their own, such as Florida Jurisprudence.

Chapter 3:
Writing Your Living Will

A *living will* is a written statement that expresses your wishes to others regarding the use of specifically defined *life-prolonging procedures* in the event you become terminally ill, injured, or permanently unconscious.

Living wills only relate to certain situations—usually when a person has an injury or illness that is fairly certain to result in death, or when the person is in a persistent vegetative state. They typically provide that one or two doctors must determine that death is fairly certain or that the person is in a persistent vegetative state with no hope of recovery. Once this determination is made, the living will tells your family, doctors, hospitals, and other health care providers—and your health care agent, if you have one—what types of medical procedures you do or do not want.

Living Wills and Specific Situations

Originally, living will forms were merely statements that a person did not want life-prolonging procedures if he or she became terminally ill or injured. All that was needed was for the person to fill in his or her name, then sign and date the form. Sometimes they were also signed by witnesses, and sometimes they were notarized. Some of the forms approved by state legislatures are still of this simple nature.

Over the years it became apparent that people were often facing complicated situations, and forms were developed to cover a wider range of possibilities. Many forms now allow you to make choices on matters such as:

- including coverage for a persistent vegetative state, even if your condition is not terminal;
- specifying which medical procedures you do or do not want;

◆ determining the use of artificial nutrition and hydration (i.e., the use of gastric tubes and intravenous feeding);

◆ stating that you *do* want life-prolonging procedures; and,

◆ having spaces for you to write in any other specific instructions or wishes regarding your medical treatment.

Some forms approved by state legislatures have one or more of these features. If your state's form does not include a provision you would like, you can either write it in on the state form, attach a sheet of paper with the additional provision, use form 67 in Appendix B, or use the forms in this book as guides for preparing your own custom form. Just be sure to use the signature, witness, and notary formats found on the form for your state (or use form 65, p.243, if there is no form for your state).

Artificial Nutrition and Hydration

The most common question when these situations arise is whether to provide the person with food and water. If the person will quickly die without artificial means to maintain heart or lung function, then providing food and water will not be an issue. However, this may become important if the person is not likely to die or not likely to die soon.

Most people want to be as comfortable as possible, even if they want to be allowed to die. Withholding food or water can cause additional pain. Some people are willing to accept this pain in order to hasten death (and overall relief). Others would rather live a little longer if it means avoiding pain. You will find this option in many of the forms in Appendix B. To decide which option is best for you, discuss the matter with your doctor, a nurse, or some other health care professional.

Living Will Forms

Every state except New York, Massachusetts, Michigan, and New Jersey has adopted specific living will forms, which are usually very similar.

Forms specific for these states are found in Appendix B. Many of these forms have instructions right on the form, so be sure to read through the form carefully. If your state is one of the four listed above, you may want to check the most current version of your state's statutes or code, because your state legislature could adopt a form at any time. Some states have very simple living will forms, where all you need to do is fill in the date and sign the form before witnesses or a notary public. Other states have specific living will provisions within a statutory health care power of attorney form. Still others just have spaces for you to write in any wishes you may have regarding life-prolonging procedures.

For those states that have no separate living will form, but do have a living will provision within a power of attorney form, the entire state power of attorney/living will form has been included in Appendix B. If all you want is a living will, you can just complete the living will portions of the form and the section for signatures, witnesses, and notary. For those states with separate living will and power of attorney forms, both are provided in Appendix B.

If you live in one of the states that has a living will form, refer to Appendix B for your particular state form. The state **LIVING WILL** forms found in this appendix are basically as simple as form 1 (discussed later in the chapter), so the instructions given for form 1 will help you complete your state form. (As indicated, many state forms also have instructions on the forms themselves.) All of them are simple to complete.

For further help, see the sample completed form for Minnesota beginning on page 14 in this chapter. (The Minnesota form was selected because it is not a simple check-the-box form like those for most states, and it requires the most work to complete.)

HEALTH CARE LIVING WILL

Notice:

This is an important legal document. Before signing this document, you should know these important facts:

(a) This document gives your health care providers or your designated proxy the power and guidance to make health care decisions according to your wishes when you are in a terminal condition and cannot do so. This document may include what kind of treatment you want or do not want and under what circumstances you want these decisions to be made. You may state where you want or do not want to receive any treatment.

(b) If you name a proxy in this document and that person agrees to serve as your proxy, that person has a duty to act consistently with your wishes. If the proxy does not know your wishes, the proxy has the duty to act in your best interests. If you do not name a proxy, your health care providers have a duty to act consistently with your instructions or tell you that they are unwilling to do so.

(c) This document will remain valid and in effect until and unless you amend or revoke it. Review this document periodically to make sure it continues to reflect your preferences. You may amend or revoke the living will at any time by notifying your health care providers.

(d) Your named proxy has the same right as you have to examine your medical records and to consent to their disclosure for purposes related to your health care or insurance unless you limit this right in this document.

(e) If there is anything in this document that you do not understand, you should ask for professional help to have it explained to you.

TO MY FAMILY, DOCTORS, AND ALL THOSE CONCERNED WITH MY CARE:

I, _____Mary L. Jones_____, born on ___April 1_____, 19_48_ (birthdate), being an adult of sound mind, willfully and voluntarily make this statement as a directive to be followed if I am in a terminal condition and become unable to participate in decisions regarding my health care. I understand that my health care providers are legally bound to act consistently with my wishes, within the limits of reasonable medical practice and other applicable law. I also understand that I have the right to make medical and health care decisions for myself as long as I am able to do so and to revoke this living will at any time.

(1) The following are my feelings and wishes regarding my health care (you may state the circumstances under which this living will applies):

I do not want my life prolonged by life-sustaining treatment if it is determined by 2 physicians who have examined me that I have a terminal condition, or that I am in a permanently unconscious state.

(2) I particularly want to have all appropriate health care that will help in the following ways (you may give instructions for care you do want):

Any type of care or treatment that will provide me with comforts and alleviate pain, even if such care or treatment hastens my death.

(3) I particularly do not want the following (you may list specific treatment you do not want in   certain circumstances):

   See paragraph (5) below.

(4) I particularly want to have the following kinds of life-sustaining treatment if I am diagnosed to have a terminal condition (you may list the specific types of life-sustaining treatment that you do want if you have a terminal condition):

      None.

(5) I particularly do not want the following kinds of life-sustaining treatment if I am diagnosed to have a terminal condition (you may list the specific types of life-sustaining treatment that you do not want if you have a terminal condition):

   Any type of life-sustaining treatment, including but not limited to, CPR, artificial breathing, kidney dialysis, drugs or antibiotics, surgery or other invasive procedures, or transfusions of blood or blood products.

(6) I recognize that if I reject artificially administered sustenance, then I may die of dehydration or malnutrition rather than from my illness or injury. The following are my feelings and wishes regarding artificially administered sustenance should I have a terminal condition (you may indicate whether you wish to receive food and fluids given to you in some other way than be mouth if you have a terminal condition):

   I do not want artificially administered sustenance unless it is the opinion of my attending physician that withholding or withdrawing such sustenance would cause me undue pain that cannot be alleviated with medication.

(7) Thoughts I feel are relevant to my instructions. (You may, but need not, give your religious beliefs, philosophy, or other personal values that you feel are important. You may also state preferences concerning the location of your care.):

(8) **Proxy Designation.** (If you wish, you may name someone to see that your wishes are carried out, but you do not have to do this. You may also name a proxy without including specific instructions regarding your care. If you name a proxy, you should discuss your wishes with that person.)

If I become unable to communicate my instructions, I designate the following person(s) to act on my behalf consistently with my instructions, if any, as stated in this document. Unless I write instructions that limit my proxy's authority, my proxy has full power and authority to make health care decisions for me. If a guardian or conservator of the person is to be appointed for me, I nominate my proxy named in this document to act as guardian or conservator of my person.

Name: <u>Joseph P. Jones</u>
Address: <u>123 Main Street, Minneapolis, MN   55401</u>
Phone Number: <u>(505) 555-5155</u>
Relationship: (If any) <u>Husband</u>

If the person I have named above refuses or is unable or unavailable to act on my behalf, or if I revoke that person's authority to act as my proxy, I authorize the following person to do so:

Name: <u>Janet A. Smith</u>
Address: <u>1431 Elm Street, St. Paul, MN   55101</u>
Phone Number: <u>(505) 555-1155</u>
Relationship: (If any) <u>Sister</u>

I understand that I have the right to revoke the appointment of the persons named above to act on my behalf at any time by communicating that decision to the proxy or my health care provider.

(9) **Organ Donation After Death.** (If you wish, you may indicate whether you want to be an organ donor upon your death.) Initial the statement which expresses your wish:

<u>M L J</u>   In the event of my death, I would like to donate my organs. I understand that to become an organ donor, I must be declared brain dead. My organ function may be maintained artificially on a breathing machine, (i.e., artificial ventilation), so that my organs can be removed.

Limitations or special wishes: (If any) <u>I would like to donate organs for any purpose, but I do not wish to donate my body for research or education purposes.</u>

I understand that, upon my death, my next of kin may be asked permission for donation. Therefore, it is in my best interests to inform my next of kin about my decision ahead of time and ask them to honor my request.

I (have) (have not) agreed in another document or on another form to donate some or all of my organs when I die.

_____ I do not wish to become an organ donor upon my death.

DATE: <u>April 21, 2007</u>   SIGNED: *Mary L. Jones*

STATE OF <u>Minnesota</u>

COUNTY OF <u>Hennepin</u>

Subscribed, sworn to, and acknowledged before me by <u>Mary L. Jones</u> on this <u>21st</u> day of <u>April</u>, 200<u>7</u>.

C. U. Sine
NOTARY PUBLIC

OR

(Sign and date here in the presence of two adult witnesses, neither of whom is entitled to any part of your estate under a will or by operation of law, and neither of whom is your proxy.)

I certify that the declarant voluntarily signed this living will in my presence and that the declarant is personally known to me. I am not named as a proxy by the living will, and to the best of my knowledge, I am not entitled to any part of the estate of the declarant under a will or by operation of law.

Witness ___*Bob Smith*___   Address ___123 Main Street___

___St. Paul, MN   55101___

Witness ___*Mary Wilson*___   Address ___456 Oak Street___

___St. Paul, MN   55101___

Reminder: *Keep the signed original with your personal papers. Give signed copies to your doctor, family, and proxy.*

Living Will (form 1)

If you do not live in one of the states with its own living will form in Appendix B, you may use form 1. Follow these instructions to complete the **LIVING WILL.** (form 1, p.74.)

◆ Type your name on the line in the first, unnumbered paragraph.

◆ Include your complete date of birth on the next line found in that paragraph.

◆ Read paragraphs 1, 2, and 3. Initial the line before the paragraph or paragraphs that agree with your wishes. Paragraph 1 concerns terminal illnesses or injuries. Paragraph 2 concerns irreversible coma, permanent unconsciousness, and persistent vegetative states. Paragraph 3 concerns the situation in which the burdens of treatment outweigh the expected benefits.

◆ Initial paragraph 4 *only* if you *do want* life-prolonging procedures. If you initial paragraph 4, do not initial any of the paragraphs 1 through 3.

NOTE: *As to paragraphs 1 through 3, you may initial any one paragraph, two of these paragraphs, or all three of these paragraphs. If you initial any of these three paragraphs, do not initial paragraph 4. If you initial paragraph 4, do not initial any of the paragraphs 1 through 3.*

If you initial any of the paragraphs 1 through 3, you must also initial the line before all of the medical treatments listed that you do not want. For most people, this will probably be all of them. There is also item "g" for you to indicate any other specific treatments you do not want that are not already listed.

◆ Paragraph 5 provides a place for you to specify that you do not want government interference in your health care decisions. You can also specify any individuals you do not want making decisions about your health care.

◆ Paragraph 6 provides space to type in any special instructions. (You are not required to fill in anything here.)

◆ Fill in the date.

◆ Type in your address where indicated below the signature line.

◆ Take the form and your two witnesses to a notary public (you can probably find a notary at your bank). Sign your name on the signature line, before two witnesses and a notary public. Also have the two witnesses sign before the notary on the lines marked "Witness," and type in the witnesses' names and addresses below their signatures. (Not all states require a notary, but it will not hurt to have a notary attest to the signatures. This will also make the form appear more official to a doctor or hospital, and make them more likely to honor it.)

Witnesses

Many states prohibit certain people from serving as a witness to a living will. Some of the state forms spell out who may or may not serve as a witness, so be sure to read the form carefully. The list contained in this section covers most of the types of people who *may not* serve as a witness in at least one state. By avoiding the types of people listed, you will most likely avoid using an improper witness. However, to be certain of exactly who may or may not serve as a witness in your state, you should check the most current version of your state's laws.

Generally, it is *not* a good idea to have a witness who is:

- ◆ your spouse;
- ◆ your parent;
- ◆ your child;
- ◆ related to you by blood, adoption, or marriage;
- ◆ your physician or an employee of your physician;
- ◆ a provider of health care to you, or an employee, agent, or patient of such a health care provider;

NOTE: *This includes places such as hospitals and nursing homes, and their administrators, operators, and employees. It generally only applies to persons connected with a facility where you reside or that provides services to you. So, if you have a friend who happens to work at a nursing home, but you are not a resident of that nursing home, that friend may act as your witness.*

- ◆ entitled to any part of your estate—either by law or through your will—or who has any kind of claim against your estate;
- ◆ a beneficiary on your life insurance policy;
- ◆ directly financially responsible for your medical care;
- ◆ under the age of 18; or,
- ◆ the person named as your agent in a health care power of attorney.

Notarized Signatures

Even if your state does not require a living will to be notarized, it is a good idea to have it notarized. This is just one more thing that may make it more likely for a health care provider to honor the living will without question. It will also be helpful if you are traveling to a state where living wills must be notarized.

Form 65 (see p. 243) is a notary page that you can attach to your living will (of course, this is not necessary if you are in a state with an approved form that already has a notary provision).

NOTE: *Some states have specific requirements as to the form of a notarization statement (which can also be changed by the legislature at any time). Check with the notary you intend to use to be sure the notary format is valid for your state.*

Chapter 4:
Using Your Living Will

Knowing what to do with a living will is just as important as having one. Take the following two examples of common circumstances in which a living will had little effect because the person writing it did not tell his or her family about it.

Example 1: *Betty reads a magazine article telling her she needs a living will. She has one prepared, stating that she does not want any artificial life support provided if she is ever in a terminal condition, and signs it. Figuring that she should keep it with her other important papers, she puts it in her safe-deposit box. She never mentions the living will to anyone. Eight months later, Betty is in a serious car accident. She is brought to the hospital unconscious and it quickly becomes obvious to the emergency room doctor that her injuries are so severe that she will never regain consciousness. She will die soon unless she is hooked up to machines to keep her heart and lungs working. Her living will clearly states that she does not want to be hooked up to the machines, but since her living will is locked up in her safe-deposit box, no one is aware of her wishes. Betty is hooked up to the machines with the permission of her daughter.*

Example 2: *Alternately, Betty's living will states that she wants all efforts made to pre-serve her life. Betty lives in a state that allows a spouse or an adult child to make this type of decision for a person who cannot communicate his or her desires. Again, her living will is locked in her safe-deposit box, and no one knows her wishes. Betty's daughter tells the doctor not to connect Betty to the machines, believing this to be what Betty would want.*

As you can see, it is important that certain people are aware of your living will and have access to it. Exactly who you provide with a copy will depend on whether you also have a health care power of attorney.

Copies of Your Living Will

Due to the Schiavo case, a significant change is recommended regarding the manner in which you use a living will if you also have a health care power of attorney. Initially, your health care agent should use only the health care power of attorney form. The health care power of attorney should be provided to your health care providers, but your living will should not be given to health care providers. The living will should only be given to your health care agent, who should be instructed that it should only to be used in the event someone raises a question as to whether your agent is following your desires or intentions.

In most cases, the health care power of attorney will be honored by health care providers, and your agent's instructions will be followed. The assumption here is that your agent is well aware of your beliefs and desires, and will act in your best interests. Only in the event of a challenge (by either a health care provider or a family member) will it be necessary for your agent to produce the living will to reinforce his or her decision about what you would want. This may allow your agent greater freedom to make decisions while taking into account the complexity of your medical situation. Health care providers will not be comparing your agent's instructions with statements in the living will, which cannot possibly cover all possible scenarios.

Some may disagree with this advice. They would argue that the living will is the clearest expression of your wishes, and having your health care providers aware of this might prevent your health care agent from having a change of heart and going against what you would really want. This may be true. However, if you do not have full trust that the person you intend to name as your health care agent will follow your desires, perhaps you should select someone else.

Therefore, an original of both your LIVING WILL and your HEALTH CARE POWER OF ATTORNEY should be given to the person you designate as your health care agent. Copies of your health care power of attorney should be given to:

- your spouse, adult children, or other close relatives or friends who may be contacted in the event you suffer a terminal illness or injury;
- your regular primary care physician;
- any specialist physician who is treating you;
- any assisted living facility or nursing home in which you reside; and,
- any hospital, outpatient surgery center, or other health care facility where you will be receiving treatment (this is normally done at the time of admission).

If You Only Have a Living Will

As stated earlier, it is very important that you only give a power of attorney to someone in whom you have complete trust to act in your best interests and according to what you would want. If there is no such person, you should not have a health care power of attorney. You will be relying on the living will to express your desires. If all you have is a living will, you should give a copy to all of those listed above.

NOTE: *Carry copies of your living will and health care power of attorney with you whenever you travel, so that you will always be prepared.*

Living Wills and Emergency Medical Care

There have been a few horror stories of an emergency medical technician (EMT) refusing to provide emergency care to a person once it is learned the person has a living will. An EMT has no business making a decision as to whether a person is in a terminal condition, permanently unconscious, or in any other state that would bring a living will into effect. Such determinations need to be made by a physician.

For purposes of emergency medical services, it is not necessary for the technician to know if the patient has a living will. If you are ever asked by an EMT if you have a living will, the safest response may be, "no." If asked if another person has a living will, the safest response may be, "not that I know of." (This should not be confused with a *do not resuscitate order*, which is briefly discussed in Chapter 5.)

Chapter 5:
Other Health Care Forms

In addition to a living will, many other health care forms exist and should be part of your overall consideration. These additional forms include:

- ◆ health care power of attorney;
- ◆ directives for specific medical procedures;
- ◆ do not resuscitate orders;
- ◆ revocation of living will; and,
- ◆ statement of desires and location of property and documents.

This chapter discusses these forms and explains when and how to use them.

Health Care Power of Attorney

The *health care power of attorney* has been briefly discussed throughout this book. It is a document in which you designate someone to be your representative in the event you are unable to make or communicate decisions about all aspects of your health care. In the most basic form, a health care power of attorney merely says, "I want this person to make decisions about my health care if I am unable to do so." The more recent trend is to either have a separate living will to give your agent some guidance, or to incorporate living will provisions in the health care power of attorney. A health care power of attorney can be as broad as possible, or it can limit the type of decisions the person can make. If you do not have a living will, or do not make any type of statements in your health care power of attorney about your desires, it will be up to the person you designate to determine what you would want in a certain situation. It can be a great help to your agent if you also have a living will or living will provisions in the power of attorney to provide some guidance as to what you would like.

Some of the official state forms have a provision where you can designate someone to carry out your wishes or to make all health care decisions on your behalf. Particularly as a result of the Shiavo case in Florida discussed in Chapter 1, it is becoming apparent that a health care power of attorney is as valuable as a living will. If your state's form does not have such a provision, a **DURABLE POWER OF ATTORNEY FOR HEALTH CARE** (form 68, p.249) has been included in Appendix B. Of course, keep in mind that you should only use a health care power of attorney if there is someone whom you trust to make health care decisions on your behalf.

Directives for Specific Medical Procedures

A living will is generally executed well in advance of the need for medical procedures. However, when someone knows he or she will be going in the hospital for surgery, a specific form can be signed just for that particular hospital stay. Such a form can be more detailed and specific than a living will. Many hospitals have such forms for patients to complete prior to the procedure. If you are facing a situation like this, ask your doctor about obtaining and filling out such a form.

Do Not Resuscitate Orders

A *do not resuscitate order* (DNR) is a written order of a physician informing health care providers that no resuscitation efforts are to be made in the event the patient's heart or breathing stops. This type of order is sometimes called a *no code order*.

Traditionally, a DNR order was issued by the attending physician when he or she believed that resuscitating the patient would do nothing but delay death and prolong pain. A DNR order was typically just a notation in the patient's medical record or a simple form posted near the patient's bed. This was often done without the knowledge of the patient or the patient's family members. More recently, some states have passed laws giving family members rights to make decisions about DNR orders. Some states also have laws that allow a person to make an advance directive for a DNR order that is applicable to emergency medical technicians (EMTs).

NOTE: *This is different from an EMT refusing to treat because of the existence of a living will.*

Such laws are currently on the books in Alaska, Arizona, Arkansas, Colorado, Connecticut, Idaho, Maryland, Montana, New York, Rhode Island, South Carolina, Tennessee, Utah, Virginia, and West Virginia.

Revoking a Living Will

If you execute a living will and then change your mind, there are two things you can do. First, you can execute a new living will that expresses your current desires. This has the effect of canceling your previous living will. Second, you can simply revoke your living will without making a new one.

Revocation of Living Will (form 2)

Most state laws provide that you may revoke your living will by simply telling your doctor. However, to be certain your doctor understands that you have changed your mind, it would be better to put your revocation in writing. To do this, use the REVOCATION OF LIVING WILL. (form 2, p.76.)

Complete the REVOCATION OF LIVING WILL as follows.

- ◆ Type in your name and address on the first line in the main paragraph.
- ◆ Type in the title of the living will you are revoking on the second line. This will be the title as it appears on the document, such as "Living Will," "Declaration," "Advance Directive," etc.
- ◆ Type in the date of the living will you are revoking on the third line.
- ◆ Type in the date on the line indicated, and sign on the signature line (sign before a notary if the living will you are revoking was also signed before a notary).

The form for Missouri (form 3, p.155) contains a revocation provision. If you live in Missouri, you do not need to use form 2 to revoke your DECLARATION, but can complete the revocation provision on form 30.

Statement of Desires

In addition to a living will and a traditional will, you may want to have another document informing your family of certain things that you wish to have done. This can be accomplished with a STATEMENT OF DESIRES AND LOCATION OF PROPERTY & DOCUMENTS. (form 66, p.244.) This is not a legally binding document, but merely a statement of your wishes that you hope your family will follow.

In the event of death, many people have certain desires regarding the type of funeral, final interment, and other matters that cannot be taken care of in a will. A will may not be discovered until after burial, so it would do no good to include funeral and final interment instructions in your will.

Another thing that can be done with such a document is to give your family members important information that will assist them in taking care of your estate. The following matters may be included:

◆ the location of your will;

◆ a list of your assets;

NOTE: *It is not always easy for the person handling your estate to find everything that you own, especially things like stocks, bonds, and similar investments. Things stored somewhere other than at your home, such as a coin collection in a safe-deposit box, a boat at a docking facility, a recreational vehicle in a storage lot, furniture at a self-storage company, etc., are often difficult to locate. Your list should include a detailed description of the item and where it is located.*

◆ a list of your life insurance policies, including the name, address, and telephone number of the insurance company (and of your insurance agent), and the policy number;

◆ a list of relatives, friends, and any other people you would like to be notified of your death (include their names, addresses, and telephone numbers);

◆ any desires you may have regarding the education and upbringing of your minor children;

◆ provisions for the custody and care of pets (You do not want your pets to go unfed while you are in the hospital, so be sure you discuss pet care with the relative or friend who will be notified in the event of an emergency. Your will should also state who you want to have your pets, and possibly include giving money to that person for food, veterinary care, etc.); and,

◆ instructions regarding your funeral. (This should include information about any cemetery plot you may own; any prepaid funeral plan; whether you want a traditional burial, burial at sea, cremation, etc.; and, any personal desires, such as the type of music you want played. You may specify a lavish funeral or state that you wish the least expensive burial in order to save assets for your heirs.)

In order for such a document to be of any use, it must be in a place where it can easily be found by a family member. Therefore, it is not a good idea to put it in your safe-deposit box. Once the bank finds out about your death, it may seal your safe-deposit box and only permit it to be opened with a court order. Because it takes time to obtain a court order, it may be well after the funeral that the contents of the safe-deposit box become available.

Chapter 6:
Lawyers

The law regarding living wills is fairly simple. There are very few variables to living will forms. The purpose of a living will is to express your desires. A living will needs to accurately reflect your wishes and meet certain legal requirements for it to be honored by health care providers (as is discussed in Chapter 2). Living will forms are often available from various senior citizen and other activist groups. However, these may not follow the form approved by the legislature of your state.

The way a lawyer would approach this is to first consult your state laws to see if there is an approved form. If not, he or she would possibly consult a book such as this one, look at examples of other living wills, and prepare a document to fit your situation. That is what this book enables you to do for yourself.

However, you may still decide to hire a lawyer. If so, the remainder of this chapter helps you to select and work with your attorney more effectively.

Selecting a Lawyer

Selecting a lawyer is a two-step process. First, you need to decide which attorney to make an appointment with, and then you need to decide if you want to hire that attorney.

Finding Lawyers

Some suggestions to help you find a lawyer include the following.

- ◆ Ask a friend or family member to recommend a lawyer he or she has hired, and with whom he or she was happy.
- ◆ Use a lawyer referral service. You can find a lawyer by looking in the Yellow Pages phone directory under "Attorney Referral Services" or "Attorneys." This is a service, usually

operated by a bar association, that is designed to match a client with an attorney handling cases in the area of law the client needs. The referral service does not guarantee the quality of work, the level of experience, or the ability of the attorney.

◆ Check under the heading for "Attorneys" in the Yellow Pages phone directory for display ads indicating attorneys' areas of practice.

◆ Ask another lawyer you know, or have used in the past for some other matter, if he or she handles living wills or could refer you to an attorney who does.

Evaluating a Lawyer

You should select three to five lawyers worthy of further consideration from your search. Your first step will be to call each attorney's office, explain that you are interested in having a living will prepared, and ask the following questions.

◆ Does the attorney (or firm) handle preparation of a living will?

◆ How much can you expect it to cost?

◆ How soon can you get an appointment?

If you like the answers you receive, ask if you can speak to the attorney. Some offices will permit this, but others will require you to make an appointment. Make the appointment if required. Once you get in contact with the attorney (either on the phone or at the appointment), ask the following questions.

◆ How much will it cost to prepare a living will, and how will the fee be paid?

◆ How long has the attorney been in practice?

◆ Has the attorney handled this type of matter before?

◆ How long will it take to get a document prepared?

If you get acceptable answers to these questions, it is time to ask yourself the following questions about the lawyer.

◆ Do you feel comfortable talking to the lawyer?

◆ Is the lawyer friendly toward you?

◆ Does the lawyer seem confident in him- or herself?

◆ Does the lawyer seem to be straightforward with you and able to explain things so that you understand?

If you get satisfactory answers to all of these questions, you probably will be able to work with this lawyer. Most clients are happiest using an attorney with whom they feel comfortable.

Working with a Lawyer

In general, you will work best with your attorney if you keep an open, honest, and friendly attitude. Following are a few suggestions you could use to help the situation.

Ask Questions

If you want to know something or if you do not understand something, ask your attorney. If you do not understand the answer, tell your attorney and ask him or her to explain it again. You should not be embarrassed to ask questions. Many people who say they had a bad experience with a lawyer either did not ask enough questions or had a lawyer who would not take the time to explain things to them. If your lawyer is not taking the time to explain what he or she is doing, it may be time to look for a new lawyer.

Give Complete Information

Anything you tell your attorney is confidential. An attorney can lose his or her license to practice if he or she reveals information without your permission. So do not hold back information.

Be Patient

Do not expect your lawyer to return your phone calls within an hour. He or she may not be able to return your calls the same day. Most lawyers are very busy and overworked. It is rare that an attorney can maintain a full caseload and still make each client feel as if he or she is the only client.

Keep Your Case Moving

Many lawyers operate on the old principle of *the squeaking wheel gets the oil*. Work on a case tends to get put off until a deadline is near, an emergency develops, or the client calls. The reason for this is that many lawyers take more cases than can be effectively handled in order to earn the income they desire. Your task is to become a squeaking wheel that does not squeak so much that the lawyer wants to avoid you. Whenever you talk to your lawyer, ask the following questions.

- ◆ What is the next step?
- ◆ When do you expect it to be done?
- ◆ When should I talk to you next?

If you do not hear from your lawyer when you expect to, call him or her the following day. Do not remind him or her of the missed phone call—just ask how things are going.

How to Save Money

One of the first concerns you may have about a lawyer is cost. For a very rough estimate, you can probably expect an attorney to charge anywhere from $75 to $300 per hour. Most will prepare a living will for a flat fee—probably between $20 and $75. If you and your spouse each want a living will, the cost will double. A lawyer may then also suggest that you have a health care power of attorney and update your will, which could involve considerably higher costs.

Of course, you do not want to spend unnecessary money for an attorney. The following are a few things you can do to avoid excess legal fees.

♦ Do not make unnecessary phone calls to your lawyer.

♦ Give information to the secretary whenever possible.

♦ Direct your question to the secretary first. He or she will refer it to the attorney if he or she cannot answer it.

♦ Plan your phone calls so you can get to the point and take less of your attorney's time. Write down an outline if necessary.

♦ Do some of the legwork yourself. For example, pick up and deliver papers yourself. Ask your attorney what you can do to assist.

♦ Be prepared for appointments. Have all related papers with you, plan your visit to get to the point, and make an outline of what you want to discuss and what questions you want to ask.

Pay Your Attorney Bill When It is Due

No client gets prompt attention like a client who pays on time. Keep in mind that you are entitled to an itemized bill, showing what the attorney did and how much time it took. If your attorney asks for money in advance, you should be sure that you and the lawyer agree on what is to be done for the fee.

Firing Your Lawyer

If you find that you can no longer work with your lawyer or do not trust your lawyer, it is time to either prepare a living will alone or get a new attorney. You will need to send your lawyer a letter stating that you no longer desire his or her services and are discharging him or her from your case. Also state that you will be coming by his or her office the following day to pick up your file. The attorney does not have to give you his or her own notes or other work he or she has in progress, but he or she must give you the essential contents of your file (such as copies of papers already prepared and billed for and any documents you provided). If he or she refuses to give your file to you for any reason, contact your state's bar association about filing a complaint or grievance against the lawyer. Of course, you will need to settle any remaining fees owed.

Conclusion

The importance of having a living will and the other documents discussed in this book cannot be over-emphasized. End-of-life medical decisions in the absence of such documents raise more problems with each passing year, and with each case to come before the courts. You need to act now to get a living will in place, and discuss these issues with your family, close friends, and physicians.

No one will know what you want if you do not tell them. Having read this book, you now have the knowledge and tools for preparing the necessary documents to make sure your desires are known and carried out if an unfortunate situation arises. Hopefully, your living will and health care power of attorney will never be used, but having them will certainly give you some peace of mind. They will also be of help to those who love you in the event they need to make difficult decisions.

Glossary

It is helpful to know some commonly used terms in order to understand living wills. The definitions in this glossary are not technical legal definitions, since the words and phrases may be defined differently in various states or not defined at all. Nor are they technical medical definitions. Rather, they are general definitions to help you understand the ideas they express, regardless of how they may be specifically defined legally or medically.

A

agent. A person who is given authority to act on behalf of another by a power of attorney.

artificial hydration. The use of feeding tubes (either through the mouth, nose, or intravenously) to provide water to a person who is unable to drink in a normal manner.

artificial nutrition. The use of feeding tubes (either through the mouth, nose, or intravenously) to provide food to a person who is unable to eat in a normal manner.

attorney-at-law. A person licensed to practice law before state or federal courts. The term has no relationship to a power of attorney or an attorney-in-fact.

attorney-in-fact. The person given authority by a power of attorney. This is another term for agent that is used in many statutes. An attorney-in-fact does not have the power to represent anyone in court or to give legal advice.

D

declarant. A person who signs a living will, usually when the living will document is titled "Declaration."

do not resuscitate order (DNR). A physician's written instruction that a patient not be resuscitated in the event the patient's heart stops beating or in the event breathing stops.

durable power of attorney. This is a power of attorney that continues to be effective after the principal becomes incapacitated.

E

execute. To sign a legal document in the legally required manner, thereby making it valid and effective.

H

health care power of attorney. A specific type of power of attorney that gives your agent (usually a family member or close friend) the authority to make decisions about your medical treatment. You may also see this referred to as a durable power of attorney for health care, health care proxy, designation of health care surrogate, advance health care directive, or some similar name.

L

living will. A document that states what treatment a person does or does not desire in certain circumstances.

life-prolonging procedures. Medical procedures applied to a person with a terminal illness or injury in order to delay death. Examples are machines used to maintain respiration and blood circulation. These are sometimes also referred to as life sustaining procedures.

N

no code order. *See do not resuscitate order.*

P

persistent vegetative state. The situation in which a person is unconscious or in a coma, and has virtually no hope of regaining consciousness. It may also be referred to by other terms, such as permanently unconscious or permanently comatose.

power of attorney. A document that gives one person (the agent or attorney-in-fact) authority to act on behalf of another person (the principal). Traditionally, a power of attorney related to financial matters, but now there are also health care powers of attorney.

principal. This is another name for the person who signs a living will or power of attorney.

proxy. *See agent.*

S

surrogate. Another term for the agent in a health care power of attorney.

T

terminal illness, injury, or condition. An illness or injury that is extremely likely to result in death. Some states require that death is likely to occur within a relatively short time, but do not say what constitutes a relatively short time.

W

will. A will expresses what you want to happen to your property (and any minor children) if you die. It should not be confused with a living will, which expresses what medical treatment you want (or do not want) while you are still alive.

your state does not have a health care power of attorney form, form 68 is listed as an optional form. (See page 25 for more information about the health care power of attorney.)

Types of Conditions

The "Types of Conditions" section tells you the various circumstances covered by the state's form. For the exact language and definition of terms, see your state's statutes or code. Words in quotation marks are direct quotes from either the state's form or the state's statute or code section. The most common types of situations covered by living wills follow.

- ◆ *Terminal conditions.* This is an illness or injury that is fairly certain to result in death. Many of the forms require death to be likely to occur "within a relatively short time," or some similar language. In most states, it is not certain what is meant by a relatively short time.
- ◆ *Persistent vegetative state.* This may also be referred to as *permanently unconscious, permanently comatose, in a coma,* etc. The idea is that the person is not aware of his or her surroundings and not able to communicate, and the condition is unlikely to change (the person's condition need not be terminal).
- ◆ *Where the burdens of treatment outweigh the benefits.* This is where treatment will cause pain or discomfort, without appreciable benefits for the person or improvement of the condition (the person's condition need not be terminal).

Doctor Certification

The "Doctor Certification" section tells you if there are any requirements for one or more physicians to officially certify the existence of the condition required for the living will to take effect. In some states, the person's doctor makes this determination informally. In other states, the physician must verify the condition in writing (usually by making a notation in the patient's medical record). In still other states, there must be a written certification by two physicians. Occasionally, the number or types of physicians certifying depends upon the nature of the condition being verified. (For example, only one physician needs to certify to a terminal condition, but two must certify to permanent unconsciousness.)

Food & Water

The "Food & Water" section tells you whether the state's form has any provisions regarding providing food and water to a patient by artificial means (i.e., by feeding tube through the mouth, nose, or intravenously). Some forms include this as a treatment to be withheld or withdrawn, others allow the person to choose whether this is to be included, and other forms do not say anything at all about this subject.

Witnesses

The "Witnesses" section tells you how many people need to witness your signature, and whether the signing needs to be notarized. As mentioned earlier in this book, it is a good idea to have signatures notarized, even if your state does not require it. (see Chapter 3.)

Miscellaneous

The "Miscellaneous" section gives any information that does not relate to one of the other categories. Most frequently noted will be optional provisions in the form and whether the form includes a pregnancy exception. In some states, a living will may not be enforced if the person is pregnant. In such states, treatment is given to keep the person alive until the child can be born. Once the child is delivered, the living will goes back into effect and further treatment can be stopped. These notes will mention where possible problems may arise.

ALABAMA

THE LAW

"Natural Death Act," *Code of Alabama*, Title 22, Chapter 8A, Section 22-8A-1 (C.A. § 22-8A-1). Form at C.A. § 22-8A-4 allows you to designate a person to serve as your *proxy* for assuring that your living will is carried out. You may also find the Code in a set of books titled *Michie's Alabama Code*.

FORM(S)

ADVANCE DIRECTIVE FOR HEALTH CARE (form 3); includes provision for acceptance by the proxy, which is required. Optional: forms 65 and 66.

TYPES OF CONDITIONS

Applies to terminal condition and permanent unconsciousness.

DOCTOR CERTIFICATION

Two physicians, one of whom is the attending physician.

FOOD & WATER

May not be withheld or withdrawn unless specified in the living will.

WITNESSES

Two witnesses; no notary.

MISCELLANEOUS

Form has pregnancy exception.

ALASKA

THE LAW

Alaska Statutes, Title 13, Chapter 52, Section 13.52.010 (A.S. §13.52.010). Titled "Health Care Decisions Act. No separate living will form. Health care power of attorney form, which includes living will provisions, is found at A.S. §13.52.300. DNR: A.S. §13.52.300.

FORM(S)

ADVANCE HEALTH CARE DIRECTIVE (form 4). Includes living will, mental health power of attorney, and other donor provisions. Optional: form 66.

TYPES OF CONDITIONS

Applies to a "condition of permanent unconsciousness," or a "terminal condition."

DOCTOR CERTIFICATION

Not required.

FOOD & WATER

Has optional provision.

WITNESSES

Two witnesses OR notary.

MISCELLANEOUS

Cards, necklaces, bracelets, etc., identifying a person as having a living will or do not resuscitate order are available from the Department of Health and Social Services.

ARIZONA

THE LAW

Arizona Revised Statutes, Section 36-3261 (A.R.S. § 36-3261). Form at A.R.S. § 36-3262. (There is also a "Prehospital Medical Care Directive," which is basically a DNR signed by the patient, A.R.S. § 36-3251.) For health care powers of attorney, see A.R.S. § 36-3224. For mental health power of attorney, see A.R.S. § 36-3286.

FORM(S)

HEALTH CARE POWER OF ATTORNEY (form 5). Optional: form 66.

TYPES OF CONDITIONS

Has options to cover terminal condition or irreversible coma and persistent vegetative state that doctor believes to be irreversible or incurable.

DOCTOR CERTIFICATION

Not required.

FOOD & WATER

Has optional provision.

WITNESSES

One witness OR notary. Form 5 has space for two witnesses, which are recommended. If there is only one witness, that person may not be related to the principal by blood, marriage, or adoption and may not be entitled to any part of the principal's estate by law or under a will at the time the living will is executed. No witness or notary may be designated to make medical decisions for the principal nor be directly involved in providing health care to the principal at the time the living will is executed.

MISCELLANEOUS

Form has optional pregnancy exception provision.

ARKANSAS

THE LAW

"Arkansas Rights of the Terminally Ill or Permanently Unconscious Act," *Arkansas Code of 1987 Annotated*, Title 20, Chapter 17, Section 20-17-201 (A.C.A. § 20-17-201). Form at A.C.A. § 20-17-202. DNR: A.C.A. §§ 20-13-901 to 908.

FORM(S)

DECLARATION (form 6). In both main paragraphs, you must cross out one of the two statements in brackets "[ ]," whichever does *not* express your wishes. One is a statement that you want treatment withheld or withdrawn; the other appoints a person (called a *health care proxy*) to provide instructions. If you cross out the first option, you will need to fill in the name of the person you want as your health care proxy. Optional: forms 65, 66, 67, and 68.

TYPES OF CONDITIONS

Applies to an "incurable or irreversible condition" that will cause death "within a relatively short time," and to being "permanently unconscious."

DOCTOR CERTIFICATION

Attending physician and another physician must determine the conditions are met and attending physician must record it in the patient's medical record.

FOOD & WATER

Optional provisions.

WITNESSES

Two witnesses; no notary.

DISTRICT OF COLUMBIA

THE LAW:

No specific provisions for living wills. (Health care power of attorney provisions found in *District of Columbia Code*, Title 21, Section 2201 (D.C.C. § 21-2201), titled "Health-Care Decisions." The books have "D.C. Code" on the spine and "District of Columbia Code" on the front cover. Health care power of attorney form at D.C.C. § 21-2207.)

FORM(S)

LIVING WILL (form 1) together with **POWER OF ATTORNEY FOR HEALTH CARE** (form 11). Optional: forms 65 and 66.

WITNESSES

For statutory power of attorney, two witnesses; no notary.

FLORIDA

THE LAW

Florida Statutes, Chapter 765, Section 765.301 (F.S. § 765.301). Living will form at F.S. § 765.303. (A health care power of attorney form called "Health Care Surrogate" may be found at F.S. § 765.203.) The law also contains provisions for family members to make health care decisions in the absence of a living will or health care power of attorney, F.S. § 765.401.

FORM(S)

LIVING WILL (form 12). **DESIGNATION OF HEALTH CARE SURROGATE** (form 13). Optional: forms 65, 66, and 67.

TYPES OF CONDITIONS

Applies to a terminal condition with "no medical probability" of recovery, an end-stage condition, or a persistent vegetative state.

DOCTOR CERTIFICATION

The "attending or treating" physician and one other.

FOOD & WATER

No provision.

WITNESSES

Two witnesses; no notary.

MISCELLANEOUS

Has space to designate a *surrogate* to carry out desires as expressed (i.e., give consent to terminate or withhold treatment).

GEORGIA

THE LAW

Official Code of Georgia Annotated, Title 31, Chapter 32, Section 31-32-1 (O.C.G.A. §31-32-1), titled "Living Wills." Living will form found at O.C.G.A. §31-32-3. Health care power of attorney provisions found in the "Durable Power of Attorney for Health Care Act," O.C.G.A. §31-36-1. Health care power of attorney form found at O.C.G.A. §31-36-10, and includes living will provisions.

FORM(S)

GEORGIA STATUTORY SHORT FORM DURABLE POWER OF ATTORNEY FOR HEALTH CARE (form 14). Optional: forms 65 and 66.

TYPES OF CONDITIONS

Applies to a coma, a persistent vegetative state, or when "the burdens of the treatment outweigh the expected benefits."

DOCTOR CERTIFICATION

Not required.

FOOD & WATER

Has space to fill in desires.

WITNESSES

Two witnesses; no notary.

MISCELLANEOUS

Form has pregnancy exception that can be negated only if fetus is not viable and you initial the line in paragraph 5.

HAWAII

THE LAW

Hawaii Revised Statutes, Section 327E-1 (H.R.S. § 327E-1), titled "Uniform Health-Care Decisions Act (Modified)." Living will is part of health care power of attorney form found at H.R.S. § 327E-16. A physician's form for certifying disability may be found at H.R.S. § 327D-10. Form for a mental health care power of attorney found at H.R.S. §327G-14.

FORM(S)

ADVANCE HEALTH-CARE DIRECTIVE (form 15). Optional: form 66.

TYPES OF CONDITIONS

Applies to a terminal condition or the "permanent loss of the ability to communicate concerning medical treatment decisions."

DOCTOR CERTIFICATION

Not required.

FOOD & WATER

Has optional provisions.

WITNESSES

Two witnesses OR notary.

IDAHO

THE LAW

"Medical Consent and Natural Death Act." Idaho Code, Title 39, Chapter 45, Section 39-4501 (I.C. §39-4501). Health care power of attorney form found at I.C. §39-4510, and includes living will provisions. DNR: I.C. §§39-151 to 165.

FORM(S)

Living Will and Durable Power of Attorney for Health Care (form 16). Optional: forms 65 and 66.

TYPES OF CONDITIONS

Applies to a terminal condition or being in a "persistent vegetative state."

DOCTOR CERTIFICATION

Two "medical doctors."

FOOD & WATER

Has optional provisions.

WITNESSES

Form does not provide for witnesses or notary.

MISCELLANEOUS

Form has pregnancy exception.

ILLINOIS

THE LAW

"Illinois Living Will Act," *West's Smith Hurd Illinois Compiled Statutes Annotated*, Chapter 755, Section 35/1 (755 ILCS 35/1). Form found at 755 ILCS 35/3. (Health care power of attorney covered in 755 ILCS 45/4-1. Health care power of attorney form at 755 ILCS 45/4-10. Also see "Health Care Surrogate Act," 755 ILCS 40/1.)

FORM(S)

Illinois Statutory Short Form Power of Attorney for Health Care (form 17) (the last two pages are the Illinois statutory provisions, which must be a part of the form). Optional: forms 65 and 66.

TYPES OF CONDITIONS

Applies to a coma, a persistent vegetative state, or when "the burdens of the treatment outweigh the expected benefits."

DOCTOR CERTIFICATION

Not required.

FOOD & WATER

Has space to fill in desires.

WITNESSES

One witness; no notary.

INDIANA

THE LAW

West's Annotated Indiana Code, Title 16, Article 36, Chapter 4, Section 16-36-4-1 (A.I.C. § 16-36-4-1). Indiana has one form for refusing (A.I.C. § 16-36-4-10) and one for requesting (A.I.C. § 16-36-4-11) life-prolonging procedures. (Information about health care powers of attorney found at A.I.C. § 16-36-1-1, but no form is provided. General power of attorney form under A.I.C. § 30-5-5-1, includes a provision for health care powers.)

FORM(S)

LIVING WILL DECLARATION (form 18), if you do *not* want life-prolonging procedures. Optional: forms 65, 66, and 68. **LIFE PROLONGING PROCEDURES DECLARATION** (form 19) if you *do want* life-prolonging procedures. Optional: forms 65, 66, and 68.

TYPES OF CONDITIONS

Form for refusing treatment applies to a terminal condition when "death will occur within a short time."

DOCTOR CERTIFICATION

Refusal of treatment requires certification by the attending physician.

FOOD & WATER

Refusal of treatment still requires the provision of food and water (i.e., there is no option on the form to refuse food and water).

WITNESSES

Two witnesses; no notary.

IOWA

THE LAW

"Life-sustaining Procedures Act," *Iowa Code Annotated*, Section 144A.1 (I.C.A. § 144A.1); form at I.C.A. § 144A.3. (Health care power of attorney form at I.C.A. § 144B.5.)

FORM(S)

LIVING WILL (form 20). Optional: forms 65, 66, and 67. You should also use the **DURABLE POWER OF ATTORNEY FOR HEALTH CARE** (form 21), with optional form 65.

TYPES OF CONDITIONS

Applies to "incurable or irreversible condition" that will result in "death within a relatively short time or a state of permanent unconsciousness."

DOCTOR CERTIFICATION

Not required.

FOOD & WATER

No specific provision.

WITNESSES

Two witnesses; no notary.

KANSAS

THE LAW

Kansas Statutes Annotated, Section 65-28,101 (K.S.A. §65-28,101). Living will form found at K.S.A. §65-28,103. Health care power of attorney provisions found at K.S.A. §58-625; form found at K.S.A. §58-632. You may find these volumes as either "Vernon's Kansas Statutes Annotated," or "Kansas Statutes Annotated, Official." The supplement is a pocket part in Vernon's, and a separate soft-cover volume in the "Official." Both sets have very poor indexing systems.

FORM(S)

DECLARATION (form 22), for living will only. If you want both a living will and power of attorney, use both form 22 and the **DURABLE POWER OF ATTORNEY FOR HEALTH CARE DECISIONS** (form 23). Optional: form 66.

TYPES OF CONDITIONS

Applies to terminal conditions.

DOCTOR CERTIFICATION

Certification required by two physicians, both of whom must have examined the patient, and one of whom must be the attending physician.

FOOD & WATER

No specific provision.

WITNESSES

Two witnesses and notary.

KENTUCKY

THE LAW

"Kentucky Living Will Directive Act," *Kentucky Revised Statutes*, Chapter 311, Section 311.620 (K.R.S. § 311.620). Form at K.R.S. § 311.625. Look for volume 12.

Form(s)

LIVING WILL DIRECTIVE (form 24). Optional: form 66.

TYPES OF CONDITIONS

Applies to terminal condition or if "permanently unconscious."

DOCTOR CERTIFICATION

Not required.

FOOD & WATER

Optional provisions.

WITNESSES

Two witnesses OR notary.

MISCELLANEOUS

Form has pregnancy exception.

LOUISIANA

THE LAW

"Natural Death Act," *West's Louisiana Statutes Annotated, Revised Statutes*, Section 40.1299.58.1 (LSA Rev. Stat. § 40:1299.58.1). Living will form at LSA Rev. Stat. § 40:1299.58.3. The set is divided into topics, such as "Civil Code," "Revised Statutes," etc. Be sure you have the volumes titled "West's LSA Revised Statutes" on the spine, and "West's Louisiana Revised Statutes" on the front cover. You may also designate a living will on your Louisiana driver's license according to LSA Revised Statutes § 32:410.

FORM(S)

Declaration (form 25). Optional: forms 65, 66, and 68.

TYPES OF CONDITIONS

This statutory form is confusing. In an apparent attempt to make it comprehensive, the legislature has drafted a document that contains so much verbiage that it isn't clear what it means. Many questions arise. For example, does the comatose state need to be accompanied by a terminal condition? If so, why even mention comatose states? Or, the form also states that death must "occur whether or not life-sustaining procedures are utilized." This goes against a central purpose of a living will, which is to avoid situations in which life is maintained indefinitely by life-sustaining procedures.

DOCTOR CERTIFICATION

Certification required by two physicians, one of whom is the attending physician.

FOOD & WATER

No provision.

WITNESSES

Two witnesses; no notary.

MAINE

THE LAW

Living will is part of a health care power of attorney under the "Uniform Health-Care Decisions Act," *Maine Revised Statutes Annotated*, Title 18-A, Section 5-801 (18-A M.R.S.A. § 5-801). Form at 18-A M.R.S.A. § 5-804.

FORM(S)

Advance Health-Care Directive (form 26). You will note that this is a form that also includes provisions for a health care power of attorney, organ donation, and designating a primary physician. This form also has an optional provision for a pregnancy exception. Part 2 is the living will portion of this form. If you only want a living will, then only complete Part 2 and the signature/witness/notary sections. Optional: forms 65 and 66.

TYPES OF CONDITIONS

Applies to: (1) an incurable and irreversible condition that will result in death within a relatively short time; (2) unconsciousness with a reasonable degree of medical certainty that consciousness will not be regained; and, (3) where the likely risks and burdens of treatment outweigh the expected benefits.

DOCTOR CERTIFICATION

Not required.

FOOD & WATER

Optional provisions.

WITNESSES

Two witnesses; no notary.

MARYLAND

THE LAW

Annotated Code of Maryland, Health-General, Section 5-601 (A.C.M., HG § 5-601). Living will and health care power of attorney forms at A.C.M., HG § 5-603. These volumes are arranged by subject, so be sure you have the volume marked "Health-General." Advance directive for DNR: A.C.M., HG § 5-608.

FORM(S)

HEALTH CARE DECISION MAKING FORMS (form 27). Optional: forms 65 and 66.

TYPES OF CONDITIONS

Applies in the case of a terminal condition and a persistent vegetative state with no expectation of recovery "within a medically appropriate period."

DOCTOR CERTIFICATION

Not required.

FOOD & WATER

Optional provisions.

WITNESSES

Two witnesses; no notary.

MISCELLANEOUS

Space is provided to fill in any instructions to be followed in the event of pregnancy.

MASSACHUSETTS

THE LAW

No specific provisions for living wills. (Health care power of attorney is discussed in *Annotated Laws of Massachusetts*, Chapter 201D, Section 1 (A.L.M., C. 201D, § 1).)

FORM(S)

LIVING WILL (form 1). Optional: forms 66 and 68.

MICHIGAN

THE LAW

No specific provisions for living wills. The index listing for "living wills" refers you to the provisions titled "Designation of patient advocate," which authorizes such a designation, but does not provide a form for either a living will or a health care power of attorney. *Michigan Compiled Laws Annotated*, Section 700.5506 (M.C.L.A. § 700.5506).

FORM(S)

LIVING WILL (form 1). Optional: forms 66 and 68.

WITNESSES

Two witnesses; no notary.

MINNESOTA

THE LAW

"Minnesota Living Will Act," *Minnesota Statutes Annotated*, Section 145B.01 (M.S.A. § 145B.01). Living will form at M.S.A. § 145B.04. Living will can also be noted on a driver's license, M.S.A. § 171.07. (Health care power of attorney found at M.S.A. § 145C.01, titled "Durable Power of Attorney for Health Care," form at M.S.A. § 145C.05.)

FORM(S)

HEALTH CARE LIVING WILL (form 28). This is not a check-the-box type of form or one that takes a certain position on various issues. You will need to fill in your wishes for each numbered paragraph. These include topics such as treatment options, food and water, organ donation, and designating a proxy and an alternate proxy. See pages 14 through 17 for a sample completed Minnesota form. Optional: form 66.

TYPES OF CONDITIONS

Applies to a terminal condition, but also has a space to fill in specific circumstances.

DOCTOR CERTIFICATION

Not required.

FOOD & WATER

Optional provisions.

WITNESSES

Notary OR two witnesses.

MISSISSIPPI

THE LAW

"Uniform Health-Care Decisions Act," *Mississippi Code 1972 Annotated*, Title 41, Section 41-41-201 (M.C. § 41-41-201). Advance Health-Care Directive form, which includes sections for health care power of attorney, living will, and designation of primary physician, is found at M.C. § 41-41-209.

FORM(S)

ADVANCE HEALTH CARE DIRECTIVE (form 29). Optional: form 66.

TYPES OF CONDITIONS

Applies to: (1) a terminal condition; (2) permanent unconsciousness; or, (3) where "the risks and burdens of treatment would outweigh the expected benefits."

DOCTOR CERTIFICATION

One physician.

FOOD & WATER

Optional provision.

WITNESSES

Two witnesses OR notary.

MISSOURI

THE LAW

Vernon's Annotated Missouri Statutes, Chapter 459, Section 459.010 (A.M.S. § 459.010). Living will form at A.M.S. § 459.015. (Health care powers of attorney provided for in the "Durable Power of Attorney for Health Care Act," A.M.S. § 404.800. No health care power of attorney form provided.)

FORM(S)

DECLARATION (form 30). Optional: forms 65, 66, 67, and 68.

TYPES OF CONDITIONS

Applies to terminal conditions.

DOCTOR CERTIFICATION

Not required.

FOOD & WATER

No provision.

WITNESSES

Two witnesses; no notary.

MISCELLANEOUS

Form has revocation provision.

MONTANA

THE LAW

"Montana Rights of the Terminally Ill Act," *Montana Code Annotated*, Title 50, Chapter 9, Section 50-9-101 (M.C.A. § 50-9-101). Form at M.C.A. § 59-9-103. DNR: M.C.A. § 50-10-101 to 107. The Montana Code is in paperback volumes, with the annotations in a separate set of binders.

FORM(S)

DIRECTIVE TO PHYSICIANS (form 31), for a simple living will. If you want to appoint someone to be sure your wishes are followed, you can use the **DECLARATION** (form 32) instead of form 31. With either form, you may use the optional forms 65, 66, and 67.

TYPES OF CONDITIONS

Applies to an "incurable or irreversible condition" that will cause death "within a relatively short time."

DOCTOR CERTIFICATION

Not required, however, the forms do state that it is to be the opinion of either your physician or attending advanced practice nurse that the conditions are met.

FOOD & WATER

No provision.

WITNESSES

Two witnesses; no notary.

MISCELLANEOUS

The Montana Attorney General maintains a health care declaration registry (see M.C.A. §50-9-501).

NEBRASKA

THE LAW

"Rights of the Terminally Ill Act," *Revised Statutes of Nebraska*, Chapter 20, Section 20-401 (R.S.A. § 20-401). Living will form at R.S.N. § 20-404. (Heath care power of attorney provided for in R.S.N. § 30-3401, titled "Power of Attorney for Health Care," with form at R.S.N. § 30-3408.)

FORM(S)

DECLARATION (form 33), for a simple living will. You can also use the **POWER OF ATTORNEY FOR HEALTH CARE** (form 34) along with form 33. Optional: forms 66, and 67. Note: The warning referred to at the end of the first paragraph of form 34 relates to the all caps paragraph just above the signature line on the same form.

TYPES OF CONDITIONS

Applies to terminal condition or "persistent vegetative state."

DOCTOR CERTIFICATION

Not required.

FOOD & WATER

No provision.

WITNESSES

Two witnesses OR notary.

NEVADA

THE LAW

"Uniform Act on Rights of the Terminally Ill," *Nevada Revised Statutes Annotated*, Chapter 449, Section 449:535 (N.R.S.A. § 449:535). Form for living will at N.R.S.A. § 449.610. (Health care power of attorney form at N.R.S.A. § 449.613, but it only gives authority for living will-type decisions, not for all types of health care decisions. Also see N.R.S.A. § 449.830.)

FORM(S)

DECLARATION (form 35). Optional: forms 65, 66, 67, and 68.

TYPES OF CONDITIONS

Applies to: (1) irreversible coma; (2) incurable or terminal condition or illness, with no reasonable hope of long term recovery or survival; or, (3) the burdens of treatment outweigh the expected benefits.

DOCTOR CERTIFICATION

By attending physician in patient's medical record.

FOOD & WATER

Optional provision.

WITNESSES

Two witnesses OR notary. One of the witnesses must sign in two places.

NEW HAMPSHIRE

THE LAW

New Hampshire Revised Statutes Annotated 1992, Chapter 137-H, Section 137-H:1 (N.H.R.S.A. § 137-H:1). Ignore "title" numbers; look for "chapter" numbers. Living will form at N.H.R.S.A. § 137-H:3. (Health care powers of attorney covered at N.H.R.S.A. § 137-J:1, with form at N.H.R.S.A. § 137-J:15.)

FORM(S)

DECLARATION (form 36). Optional: forms 66, 67, and 68.

TYPES OF CONDITIONS

Applies to a "terminal" or "permanently unconscious" condition.

DOCTOR CERTIFICATION

Two physicians.

FOOD & WATER

Optional provision.

WITNESSES

Two witnesses AND notary of signer and witnesses.

NEW JERSEY

THE LAW

"New Jersey Advance Directives for Health Care Act," NJSA (for New Jersey Statutes Annotated), Title 26, Section 26:2H-53. The law authorizes both a "proxy directive" and an "instructional directive," but does not provide any forms.

FORM(S)

LIVING WILL (form 1). Optional: forms 66 and 68.

TYPES OF CONDITIONS

Applies to a "terminal" or "permanently unconscious" condition.

DOCTOR CERTIFICATION

Attending physician and another must certify person lacks decision making capacity and so note in medical record. If incapacity is due to a mental or psychological condition, "a physician with appropriate special training or experience" must certify.

FOOD & WATER

Included in the definition of "life-sustaining treatment."

WITNESSES

Two witnesses who must attest that the declarant is of sound mind and free of duress or undue influence OR signature before notary, attorney at law, or other person authorized to administer oaths.

MISCELLANEOUS

Statute provides that a living will can be supplemented with an audio or videotape recording. Statute provides that a woman may include any desired instructions in the event of pregnancy.

NEW MEXICO

THE LAW

New Mexico Statutes 1978 Annotated, Chapter 24, Section 24-7A-1 (N.M.S.A. § 24-7A-1), titled "Uniform Health-Care Decisions." Living will is Part 2 of the health care power of attorney form and is titled "Instructions for Health Care." Health care power of attorney form at N.M.S.A. § 24-7A-4. A supplement to the Statutes is found at the end of each chapter.

FORM(S)

OPTIONAL ADVANCE HEALTH-CARE DIRECTIVE (form 37). You will note that this is a form that also includes provisions for a health care power of attorney and designating a primary physician. Part 2 is the living will portion of this form. If you only want a living will, only complete Part 2 and the signature/witness/notary sections. Optional: forms 65 and 66.

TYPES OF CONDITIONS

Applies to: (1) terminal condition; (2) being permanently unconscious; and, (3) where "the likely risks and burdens of treatment would outweigh the expected benefits."

DOCTOR CERTIFICATION

The "physician in charge" and one other physician must certify in writing to the terminal condition or irreversible coma, with a copy placed in the person's medical record.

FOOD & WATER

Optional provisions.

WITNESSES

Statute states it must be executed in the same manner as a will, but the official form just requires signature (and has spaces for two witnesses designated as "Optional").

MISCELLANEOUS

Has optional provision to request all possible procedures.

NEW YORK

THE LAW

No specific provisions for living wills. (*McKinney's Consolidated Laws of New York Annotated*, Public Health § 2980 (C.L.N.Y., Public Health § 2980), called "Health Care Agents and Proxies," relates to health care powers of attorney with form called "Health Care Proxy" found at § 2981(d).) Advance directive for DNR: C.L.N.Y., Public Health § 2960. This set of books is divided according to subject, so be sure you have the volume marked "Public Health."

FORM(S)

LIVING WILL (form 1). Optional: form 66. If you also want a health care power of attorney, you can use the HEALTH CARE PROXY (form 38) in addition to form 1. Form 38 does not have a notary provision, so you may want to use the optional form 65 with it.

NORTH CAROLINA

THE LAW

Living will provisions at *General Statutes of North Carolina*, Chapter 90, Section 90-320 (G.S.N.C. § 90-320), titled "Right to Natural Death; Brain Death." Living will form at G.S.N.C. § 90-321(d). (Health care power of attorney at G.S.N.C. § 32A-15, titled "Health Care Powers of Attorney." Form at G.S.N.C. § 32A-25.) The North Carolina Secretary of State maintains an "Advance Health Care Directive Registry" where living wills can be registered.

FORM(S)

DECLARATION OF A DESIRE FOR A NATURAL DEATH (form 39). Optional: forms 66 and 68.

TYPES OF CONDITIONS

Applies to terminal condition or if "in a persistent vegetative state."

DOCTOR CERTIFICATION

By attending physician and one other physician.

FOOD & WATER

Optional provisions.

WITNESSES

Two witnesses AND acknowledgment of notary, court clerk, or assistant court clerk of signatures of the signer and witnesses.

NORTH DAKOTA

THE LAW

North Dakota Century Code Annotated, Title 23, Chapter 23-06.5-01 (N.D.C.C. §23-06.5-01), titled "Health Care Decisions." Form at N.D.C.C. §23-06.5-17, which includes health care power of attorney, living will, and other provisions.

FORM(S)

HEALTH CARE DIRECTIVE (form 40). The North Carolina legislature changed the form in 2005, and it appears the intent was to discourage people from making end-of-life directives, by requiring that you write out your beliefs and desires on a number of matters, rather than allow you to simply check optional boxes to indicate your wishes. Optional: form 66.

TYPES OF CONDITIONS

None specifiec.

DOCTOR CERTIFICATION

Not required.

FOOD & WATER

No specific provisions.

WITNESSES

Notary OR two witnesses.

OHIO

THE LAW

"Modified Uniform Rights of the Terminally Ill Act," *Page's* Ohio Revised Code Annotated, Section 2133.01 (O.R.S. § 2133.01) authorizes living wills (referred to as a "declaration" regarding "life-sustaining treatment") and gives some guidelines, but no statutory form is provided. This is a lengthy chapter of the Ohio Revised Code, placing all kinds of obligations and burdens on the physician, and includes matters such as procedures to be followed if a family member objects to terminating treatment. (Health care power of attorney at *Page's* Ohio Revised Code Annotated, Section 1337.11 (O.R.S. § 1337.11, but no form is provided. Also see O.R.S. § 2133.01, titled "Modified Uniform Rights of the Terminally Ill Act.") DNR: See O.R.S. § 2133.21.

FORM(S)

There is no official living will form. However, the **DECLARATION** (form 41) is designed to meet the statutory requirements. Optional: form 66. If you also want a health care power of attorney, use the **DURABLE POWER OF ATTORNEY FOR HEALTH CARE** (form 68) and attach it to the **NOTICE TO ADULT EXECUTING THIS DOCUMENT** (form 42). The state form is form 41, and the optional forms are forms 65, 66, 67, and 68.

TYPES OF CONDITIONS

Applies to terminal condition or a "permanently unconscious state." The definition of these terms must be on the declaration in all capital letters.

DOCTOR CERTIFICATION

Attending physician and one other physician must certify that the person is terminally ill or in a permanently unconscious state; but only the attending physician must certify the person is unable to make an informed decision regarding the administration of life-sustaining treatment. These certifications must be noted in the patient's medical record.

FOOD & WATER

Optional provisions.

(continued)

WITNESSES

Two witnesses OR notary. Witnesses or notary must attest that the declarant "appears to be of sound mind and not under or subject to duress, fraud, or undue influence."

MISCELLANEOUS

May include list of people to be notified by the attending physician if the living will is to be invoked. May include specific instructions regarding CPR.

OKLAHOMA

THE LAW

Living will is part of health care power of attorney form. *Oklahoma Statutes Annotated*, Title 63, Section 3101 (63 O.S.A. § 3101), titled "Oklahoma Rights of the Terminally Ill or Persistently Unconscious Act." Form at 63 O.S.A. § 3101.4.

FORM(S)

ADVANCE DIRECTIVE FOR HEALTH CARE (form 43). This form also includes provisions for a health care power of attorney (*proxy*) and anatomical gifts. Part I is the living will portion of this form. If you only want a living will, then only complete Part I and the signature and witness sections. Optional: form 66.

TYPES OF CONDITIONS

Applies to a terminal condition (must be determined that death will result within six months) or when the person is persistently unconscious.

DOCTOR CERTIFICATION

Two physicians.

FOOD & WATER

Optional provision.

WITNESSES

Two witnesses; no notary.

MISCELLANEOUS

Form has pregnancy exception.

OREGON

THE LAW

Living will is a part of the health care power of attorney form. *Oregon Revised Statutes Annotated*, Chapter 127, Section 127.505 (O.R.S. § 127.505). The required health care power of attorney form found at O.R.S. § 127.531.

FORM(S)

ADVANCE DIRECTIVE (form 44). You will note that this is a form that also includes provisions for a health care power of attorney (health care representative). If you only want a living will, then only complete Part C and the signature/witness/notary sections. Optional: forms 65 and 66.

TYPES OF CONDITIONS

Applies if the person: (1) is close to death and life support would only postpone the moment of death; (2) is permanently unconscious; or, (3) has an advanced progressive illness (as described in the form), or (4) if life support would cause "permanent and severe pain" and would not help the person's condition.

DOCTOR CERTIFICATION

Not required.

FOOD & WATER

Optional provisions.

WITNESSES

Two witnesses; no notary.

MISCELLANEOUS

Of special and unique interest is the Oregon Death With Dignity Act, O.R.S. § 127.800. This act allows a resident of Oregon to make a written "request for medication for the purpose of ending his or her life in a humane and dignified manner." The form is provided at O.R.S. § 127.897.

PENNSYLVANIA

THE LAW

"Advance Directive for Health Care Act," *Purdon's Pennsylvania Consolidated Statutes Annotated*, Title 20, Section 20-5401 (20 Pa.C.S.A. § 5401). Form is found at 20 Pa.C.S.A. § 5404.

FORM(S)

DECLARATION (form 45). Optional: forms 65, 66, and 68.

TYPES OF CONDITIONS

Applies if the person is in a terminal condition or a "state of permanent unconsciousness."

DOCTOR CERTIFICATION

Attending physician.

FOOD & WATER

Optional provision.

WITNESSES

Two witnesses; no notary.

MISCELLANEOUS

Pregnancy exception, unless: (1) the woman will not be maintained so as to permit the growth and birth of the child; (2) it would be physically harmful to the woman; or, (3) it would cause pain that can't be alleviated by medication.

RHODE ISLAND

THE LAW

"Rights of the Terminally Ill Act," *General Laws of Rhode Island*, Section 23-4.11-1 (G.L.R.I. § 23-4.11-1). ("Health Care Power of Attorney Act" may be found beginning at G.L.R.I. § 23-4.10-1. Required health care power of attorney form at G.I.R.I. § 23-4.10-2.) DNR: G.L.R.I. § 23-4.11-14. Ignore "Title" and "Chapter" numbers.

FORM(S)

DECLARATION (form 46), for a simple living will. Optional: forms 65, 66, and 67. For health care power of attorney, use the **STATUTORY DURABLE POWER OF ATTORNEY FOR HEALTH CARE** (form 47). Optional: form 65.

TYPES OF CONDITIONS

Applies if the person has an "incurable or irreversible condition" that will cause death "within a relatively short time."

DOCTOR CERTIFICATION

Not required.

FOOD & WATER

Optional provision.

WITNESSES

Two witnesses; no notary.

SOUTH CAROLINA

THE LAW

"Death With Dignity Act," *Code of Laws* of *South Carolina*, Title 44, Section 44-77-10 (C.L.S.C. § 44-77-10). (Health care power of attorney form at § 44-77-50. "Adult Health Care Consent Act" at C.L.S.C. § 44-66-10, discusses consent for medical treatment and states that this subject can be included in a durable power of attorney, but no form is provided.) DNR: C.L.S.C. §§ 44-78-10 to 65.

FORM(S)

DECLARATION OF A DESIRE FOR A NATURAL DEATH (form 48), which is a living will with an option to designate someone to revoke or enforce your living will. Optional: form 66. If you want to give someone more broad authority to make all kinds of medical decisions, you should also complete the **HEALTH CARE POWER OF ATTORNEY** (form 49). Optional: form 65 (to go with form 49 only).

TYPES OF CONDITIONS

Applies to terminal conditions or permanent unconsciousness. The determination of permanent unconsciousness may only be made after ninety consecutive days of unconsciousness.

DOCTOR CERTIFICATION

Two physicians.

FOOD & WATER

Optional provisions.

WITNESSES

Two witnesses AND notary of signer and witnesses.

SOUTH DAKOTA

THE LAW

South Dakota Codified Laws, Title 34, Section 34-12D-1 (S.D.C.L. §34-12D-1), titled "Living Wills." Living will form found at S.D.C.L. §34-12D-3. Health care power of attorney provisions are also authorized by S.D.C.L. §§59-7-2.5 and 34-12C-3, but no form is provided.

FORM(S)

Living Will Declaration (form 50). Optional: forms 66 and 68.

TYPES OF CONDITIONS

Applies to terminal conditions.

DOCTOR CERTIFICATION

Not required.

FOOD & WATER

Optional provisions.

WITNESSES

Two witnesses; no notary required—however, the statutory form has space for notary to verify signature of signer and witnesses.

TENNESSEE

THE LAW

"Tennessee Right to Natural Death Act," *Tennessee Code Annotated*, Title 32, Section 32-11-101 (T.C.A. § 32-11-101). Form at T.C.A. § 32-11-105. DNR: T.C.A. § 68-140-601.

FORM(S)

Living Will (form 51), for a simple living will. Optional: form 66 and 67. If you also want a health care power of attorney, in addition to form 51 use the **Durable Power of Attorney for Health Care** (form 52).

TYPES OF CONDITIONS

Applies to terminal conditions.

DOCTOR CERTIFICATION

Not required.

FOOD & WATER

Optional provisions.

WITNESSES

Two witnesses; no notary required; however, the statutory form has space for notary to verify signature of signer and witnesses.

MISCELLANEOUS

Also has option for organ donations.

TEXAS

THE LAW

"Advance Directives Act," *Vernon's Texas Codes Annotated*, Health and Safety Code, Section 166.001 (T.C.A., Health and Safety Code § 166.001). Living will form at T.C.A., Health and Safety Code, § 166.033. [Medical Power of Attorney form at T.C.A., Health and Safety Code §§ 166.163 and 166.164.] The T.C.A. is divided into subjects, so be sure you have the proper subject volume. Also, be sure you have the volumes marked "*Vernon's* Texas Codes Annotated," not those marked "*Vernon's* Texas Civil Statutes," which have a volume marked "Health." DNR: T.C.A., Health and Safety Code § 166.081.

FORM(S)

DIRECTIVE TO PHYSICIANS AND FAMILY OR SURROGATES (form 53), which includes both living will and health care power of attorney provisions. Optional: forms 65 and 66.

TYPES OF CONDITIONS

Applies to terminal conditions and irreversible conditions.

DOCTOR CERTIFICATION

Attending physician must certify condition is terminal and death is expected "within six months," or that there is an "irreversible condition" and death is expected.

FOOD & WATER

No provision, but space is provided to state desires.

WITNESSES

Two witnesses; no notary.

MISCELLANEOUS

Form has pregnancy exception.

UTAH

THE LAW

"Personal Choice and Living Will Act," *Utah Code Annotated* 1953, Title 75, Chapter 2, Section 75-2-1101 (U.C.A. § 75-2-1101). Form at U.C.A. § 75-2-1104. DNR: U.C.A. § 75-2-1105.5.

FORM(S)

DIRECTIVE TO PHYSICIANS AND PROVIDERS OF MEDICAL SERVICES (form 54), which is a basic living will. Optional: forms 65, 66, and 67. If you also want a health care power of attorney, in addition to form 54 you should also complete the **SPECIAL POWER OF ATTORNEY** (form 55).

TYPES OF CONDITIONS

Applies to terminal condition or persistent vegetative state.

DOCTOR CERTIFICATION

Two physicians.

FOOD & WATER

Provides that food and water *will* be withheld (the only way to designate otherwise is to cross out this provision).

WITNESSES

Two witnesses; no notary.

VERMONT

THE LAW

Vermont Statutes Annotated, Title 18, Section 9700 (18 V.S.A. §9700). Ignore "Chapter" numbers. Living will form is referred to as a "Terminal Care Document," form found at 18 V.S.A. §9703. Health care power of attorney is provided for in 18 V.S.A. §5263; form and required notices are found at 18 V.S.A. §§5276 and 5277.

FORM(S)

Durable Power of Attorney for Health Care (form 56), which includes a living will under the heading "Terminal Care Document." Optional: forms 65 and 66.

TYPES OF CONDITIONS

Applies to "terminal state."

DOCTOR CERTIFICATION

Not required.

FOOD & WATER

No provision.

WITNESSES

Two witnesses; no notary.

VIRGINIA

THE LAW

Living will is part of health care power of attorney (called an "Advance Medical Directive"), under the "Health Care Decision Act," Code of Virginia 1950, Title 54.1, Section 54.1-2981 (C.V. § 54.1-2981). Form at C.V. § 54.1-2984. DNR: C.V. § 54.1-2987.1. Ignore "Chapter" numbers and look for "Title" and "Section" numbers.

FORM(S)

Advance Medical Directive (form 57). Has option to appoint health care agent. Optional: forms 65, 66, and 67.

TYPES OF CONDITIONS

Applies to terminal conditions.

DOCTOR CERTIFICATION

(1) Attending physician must determine the condition is terminal. (2) If a health care agent has been appointed, there must be written verification that the person is unable to make informed decisions by the attending physician and either another physician or a licensed clinical psychologist.

FOOD & WATER

No provision.

WITNESSES

Two witnesses; no notary.

MISCELLANEOUS

Living will directive can be made orally before the attending physician and two witnesses.

WASHINGTON

THE LAW

"Natural Death Act," *West's Revised Code of Washington Annotated*, Title 70, Chapter 122, Section 70.122.010 (R.C.W.A. § 70.122.010). Form called "Health Care Directive" is found at R.C.W.A. § 70.122.030. (Health care power of attorney is authorized by R.C.W.A. §§ 11.94.010 and 11.94.046, but no form is provided.)

FORM(S)

HEALTH CARE DIRECTIVE (form 58). Optional: forms 65, 66, 67, and 68.

TYPES OF CONDITIONS

Applies to terminal or permanent unconscious conditions (these are further defined in the form).

DOCTOR CERTIFICATION

The attending physician must certify a terminal condition; two physicians must certify to permanent unconsciousness.

FOOD & WATER

Optional provision.

WITNESSES

Two witnesses; no notary.

MISCELLANEOUS

Form has pregnancy exception.

WEST VIRGINIA

THE LAW

"West Virginia Natural Death Act," *West Virginia Code*, Chapter 16, Article 30, Section 16-30-1 (W.V.C. § 16-30-1). Living will and health care power of attorney forms found at W.V.C. § 16-30-4. DNR: "Do Not Resuscitate Act," W.V.C. § 16-30C-1; form at W.V.C. § 16-30C-6.

FORM(S)

STATE OF WEST VIRGINIA LIVING WILL (form 59), which is a basic living will. Optional: forms 66 and 67. If you also want a health care power of attorney, you should also complete the **STATE OF WEST VIRGINIA MEDICAL POWER OF ATTORNEY** (form 60).

TYPES OF CONDITIONS

Applies to terminal condition or persistent vegetative state.

DOCTOR CERTIFICATION

Two physicians, one of whom is attending physician.

FOOD & WATER

No provision. However, you can insert your own provision in the paragraph for listing any special directives or limitations.

WITNESSES

Two witnesses AND notary of signer and witnesses.

WYOMING

THE LAW

Wyoming Statutes Annotated, Title 35, Chapter 22, Section 35-22-101 (W.S.A. § 35-22-101), titled "Living Will." Living will form found at W.S.A. § 35-22-102. Health care powers of attorney are provided for by the "Wyoming Health Care Decisions Act," W.S.A. §35-22-401; form found at W.S.A. §35-22-405. Authorization for psychiatric advance directives found at W.S.A. §35-22-301, but no form is provided.

FORM(S)

DECLARATION (form 63), which is a fairly basic living will. Optional: forms 65, 66, and 67. If you also want a health care power of attorney, instead of using form 63, use the **ADVANCE HEALTH CARE DIRECTIVE** (form 64), which also contains living will provisions. Optional: form 66.

TYPES OF CONDITIONS

Applies to terminal conditions where "death will occur whether or not life-sustaining procedures are utilized." If you think this is confusing, you are right. Here is a prime example of a legislature trying to be so comprehensive in explaining something, that it makes the law unclear. As written, this form fails to accomplish a central purpose of having a living will, which is to cover the situation in which a person can be kept alive indefinitely with machines or other life-sustaining procedures.

DOCTOR CERTIFICATION

Two physicians, one of whom is the attending physician.

FOOD & WATER

No provision.

WITNESSES

Two witnesses; no notary. Form states who may not serve as a witness.

WISCONSIN

THE LAW

West's Wisconsin Statutes Annotated, Section 154.01 (W.S.A. § 154.01). Ignore "Chapter" numbers. Health care power of attorney authorized by W.S.A. § 155.01, but no form provided.

FORM(S)

DECLARATION TO PHYSICIANS (form 61), which is a fairly basic living will. Optional: forms 65, 66, and 67. If you also want a health care power of attorney, you should also complete the **POWER OF ATTORNEY FOR HEALTH CARE** (form 62). Optional: form 65.

TYPES OF CONDITIONS

Applies to terminal condition and persistent vegetative state.

DOCTOR CERTIFICATION

Two physicians.

FOOD & WATER

Optional provisions.

WITNESSES

Two witnesses; no notary.

MISCELLANEOUS

Form has pregnancy exception.

WYOMING

THE LAW

Wyoming Statutes Annotated, Title 35, Chapter 22, Section 35-22-101 (W.S.A. § 35-22-101), titled "Living Will." Living will form found at W.S.A. § 35-22-102. Health care powers of attorney are provided for by the "Wyoming Health Care Decisions Act," W.S.A. §35-22-401; form found at W.S.A. §35-22-405. Authorization for psychiatric advance directives found at W.S.A. §35-22-301, but no form is provided.

FORM(S)

DECLARATION (form 63), which is a fairly basic living will. Optional: forms 65, 66, and 67. If you also want a health care power of attorney, instead of using form 63, use the **ADVANCE HEALTH CARE DIRECTIVE** (form 64), which also contains living will provisions. Optional: form 66.

TYPES OF CONDITIONS

Applies to terminal conditions where "death will occur whether or not life-sustaining procedures are utilized." If you think this is confusing, you are right. Here is a prime example of a legislature trying to be so comprehensive in explaining something, that it makes the law unclear. As written, this form fails to accomplish a central purpose of having a living will, which is to cover the situation in which a person can be kept alive indefinitely with machines or other life-sustaining procedures.

DOCTOR CERTIFICATION

Two physicians, one of whom is the attending physician.

FOOD & WATER

No provision.

WITNESSES

Two witnesses; no notary. Form states who may not serve as a witness.

Appendix B:
Forms

This appendix includes two types of living will forms: (1) statutory living will forms approved by various states and (2) generic forms for any state not having an approved statutory form or to supplement a state form that does not have provisions you want.

The *Table of Forms* on pages 71–73 gives you the number of the form, indicates if it is for a particular state, gives the title of the form, and provides the page number where that form may be found. Form numbers and state names are found at the upper, outside edge of each form. If you want, you can copy the forms you need and delete the form and page numbers at the top of the page. (Remember, the law and forms may change at any time.)

You can look up your state in Appendix A to find out which forms your state requires and which optional forms you can use.

If you want to provide your family with more guidance on what your health care wishes are and where your important documents are located, use form 66 (**STATEMENT OF DESIRES AND LOCATION OF PROPERTY DOCUMENTS**).

If the official form for your state does not have a provision for signature before a notary, you may want to attach form 65 (**STANDARD NOTARY PAGE**) to your state form and have the signatures of yourself and your witnesses notarized.

If your state's form does not have all of the provisions you would like, you may want to complete form 67 (**ADDENDUM TO LIVING WILL**) and attach it to the state form. You may attach both form 65 and form 67 to your state form if necessary.

To complete form 67, follow the instructions for form 1 on page 18. The only difference is that, in addition to filling in your name in the first, unnumbered paragraph, you will also need to fill in the title of the living will form used in your state, and the date you signed it.

Example: *If you live in Maine, the title of Maine's form is* ADVANCE HEALTH-CARE DIRECTIVE *and that title will go in the space on the second line of form 67.*

Table of Forms

Living Will

I, _____, _____ (d/o/b) being of sound mind, willfully and voluntarily make known my desires regarding my medical care and treatment under the circumstances as indicated below:

_____ 1.   If I should have an incurable or irreversible condition that will cause my death within a relatively short time, and if I am unable to make decisions regarding my medical treatment, I direct my attending physician to withhold or withdraw procedures that merely prolong the dying process and are not necessary to my comfort or to alleviate pain. This authorization includes, but is not limited to, the withholding or the withdrawal of the following types of medical treatment (subject to any special instructions in paragraph 5 below):

   _____ a.   Artificial feeding and hydration.
   _____ b.   Cardiopulmonary resuscitation (this includes, but is not limited to, the use of drugs, electric shock, and artificial breathing).
   _____ c.   Kidney dialysis.
   _____ d.   Surgery or other invasive procedures.
   _____ e.   Drugs and antibiotics.
   _____ f.   Transfusions of blood or blood products.
   _____ g.   Other: _____
   _____

_____ 2.   If I should be in an irreversible coma or persistent vegetative state that my attending physician reasonably believes to be irreversible or incurable, I direct my attending physician to withhold or withdraw medical procedures and treatment other than such medical procedures and treatment necessary to my comfort or to alleviate pain. This authorization includes, but is not limited to, the withholding or withdrawal of the following types of medical treatment (subject to any special instructions in paragraph 5 below):

   _____ a.   Artificial feeding and hydration.
   _____ b.   Cardiopulmonary resuscitation (this includes, but is not limited to, the use of drugs, electric shock, and artificial breathing).
   _____ c.   Kidney dialysis.
   _____ d.   Surgery or other invasive procedures.
   _____ e.   Drugs and antibiotics.
   _____ f.   Transfusions of blood or blood products.
   _____ g.   Other: _____
   _____

_____ 3.   If I have a medical condition where I am unable to communicate my desires as to treatment and my physician determines that the burdens of treatment outweigh the expected benefits, I direct my attending physician to withhold or withdraw medical procedures and treatment other than such medical procedures and treatment necessary to my comfort or to alleviate pain. This authorization includes, but is not limited to, the withholding or withdrawal of the following types of medical treatment (subject to any special instructions in paragraph 5 below):

_____ a. Artificial feeding and hydration.

_____ b. Cardiopulmonary resuscitation (this includes, but is not limited to, the use of drugs, electric shock, and artificial breathing).

_____ c. Kidney dialysis.

_____ d. Surgery or other invasive procedures.

_____ e. Drugs and antibiotics.

_____ f. Transfusions of blood or blood products.

_____ g. Other: _____

_____

_____ 4. I want my life prolonged to the greatest extent possible (subject to any special instructions in paragraph 5 below).

_____ 5. I specifically DO NOT want the governor, state legislature, President of the United States, United States Congress, or any other individual, group, body, or agency of any local, state, or federal legislative or executive branch of government to be involved in any manner in the decision-making regarding my medical treatment, or the withholding or withdrawal of medical treatment. I specifically DO NOT want the following person(s) to be involved in any manner in the decision-making regarding my medical treatment, or the withholding or withdrawal of medical treatment: _____.

_____ 6. Special instructions (if any) _____

_____

_____

_____

Signed this _____ day of _____, 200____.

_____

Signature

Address: _____

_____

The declarant is personally known to me and voluntarily signed this document in my presence.

Witness: _____   Witness: _____
Name: _____   Name: _____
Address:_____   Address: _____
_____   _____

State of _____)
County of _____)

On this _____ day of _____, 200_____, before me, personally appeared _____, principal, and _____and _____ witnesses, who are personally known to me or who provided _____ as identification, and signed the foregoing instrument in my presence.

_____

Notary Public

Revocation of Living Will

I, _____
_____(name and address of principal), hereby revoke
the _____, which was executed
by me on _____. This revocation is effective immediately.

Date:_____

_____
Signature

State of _____   )
County of _____   )

On this _____ day of _____, 20___, before me, personally
appeared _____, who is personally known to
me or who provided _____ as identification,
and signed the foregoing instrument in my presence.

_____
Notary Public

My Commission expires:

Advance Directive for Health Care
(Living Will and Health Care Proxy)

This form may be used in the State of Alabama to make your wishes known about what medical treatment or other care you would or would not want if you become too sick to speak for yourself. You are not required to have an advance directive. If you do have an advance directive, be sure that your doctor, family, and friends know you have one and know where it is located.

Section 1. Living Will.

I, _____, being of sound mind and at least 19 years old, would like to make the following wishes known. I direct that my family, my doctors and health care workers, and all others follow the directions I am writing down. I know that at any time I can change my mind about these directions by tearing up this form and writing a new one. I can also do away with these directions by tearing them up and by telling someone at least 19 years of age of my wishes and asking him or her to write them down.

I understand that these directions will only be used if I am not able to speak for myself.

IF I BECOME TERMINALLY ILL OR INJURED:

Terminally ill or injured is when my doctor and another doctor decide that I have a condition that cannot be cured and that I will likely die in the near future from this condition.

Life sustaining treatment—Life sustaining treatment includes drugs, machines, or medical procedures that would keep me alive but would not cure me. I know that even if I choose not to have life sustaining treatment, I will still get medicines and treatments that ease my pain and keep me comfortable.

Place your initials by either "yes" or "no":

I want to have life sustaining treatment if I am terminally ill or injured.
_____ Yes _____ No

Artificially provided food and hydration (Food and water through a tube or an IV)—I understand that if I am terminally ill or injured I may need to be given food and water through a tube or an IV to keep me alive if I can no longer chew or swallow on my own or with someone helping me.

Place your initials by either "yes" or "no":

I want to have food and water provided through a tube or an IV if I am terminally ill or injured.
_____ Yes _____ No

IF I BECOME PERMANENTLY UNCONSCIOUS:

Permanent unconsciousness is when my doctor and another doctor agree that within a reasonable degree of medical certainty I can no longer think, feel anything, knowingly move, or be aware of being alive. They believe this condition will last indefinitely without hope for improvement and have watched me long enough to make that decision. I understand that at least one of these doctors must be qualified to make such a diagnosis.

Life sustaining treatment—Life sustaining treatment includes drugs, machines, or other medical procedures that would keep me alive but would not cure me. I know that even if I choose not to have life sustaining treatment, I will still get medicines and treatments that ease my pain and keep me comfortable.

Place your initials by either "yes" or "no":

I want to have life-sustaining treatment if I am permanently unconscious.
_____ Yes _____No

Artificially provided food and hydration (Food and water through a tube or an IV)—I understand that if I become permanently unconscious, I may need to be given food and water through a tube or an IV to keep me alive if I can no longer chew or swallow on my own or with someone helping me.

Place your initials by either "yes" or "no":

I want to have food and water provided through a tube or an IV if I am permanently unconscious.
_____ Yes _____ No

OTHER DIRECTIONS:

Please list any other things you want done or not done.

In addition to the directions I have listed on this form, I also want the following:
_____
_____

If you do not have other directions, place your initials here: _____ No, I do not have any other directions.

Section 2. If I need someone to speak for me.

This form can be used in the State of Alabama to name a person you would like to make medical or other decisions for you if you become too sick to speak for yourself. This person is called a health care proxy. You do not have to name a health care proxy. The directions in this form will be followed even if you do not name a health care proxy.

Place your initials by only one answer:

_____ I do not want to name a health care proxy. (If you check this answer, go to Section 3)

_____ I do want the person listed below to be my health care proxy. I have talked with this person about my wishes.

First choice for proxy: _____

Relationship to me: _____

Address: _____

City: _____ State: _____ Zip: _____

Day-time phone number: _____ Night-time phone number: _____

If this person is not able, not willing, or not available to be my health care proxy, this is my next choice:

Second choice for proxy: _____

Health Care Power of Attorney

1. Health Care Power of Attorney

I, _____, as principal, designate _____
_____ as my agent for all matters relating to my health care, including, without limitation, full power to give or refuse consent to all medical, surgical, hospital and related health care. This power of attorney is effective on my inability to make or communicate health care decisions. All of my agent's actions under this power during any period when I am unable to make or communicate health care decisions or when there is uncertainty whether I am dead or alive have the same effect on my heirs, devisees and personal representatives as if I were alive, competent and acting for myself.

If my agent is unwilling or unable to serve or continue to serve, I hereby appoint _____
_____ as my agent.

I have _____ I have not _____ completed and attached a living will for purposes of providing specific direction to my agent in situations that may occur during any period when I am unable to make or communicate health care decisions or after my death. My agent is directed to implement those choices I have initialed in the living will.

I have _____ I have not _____ completed a prehospital medical directive pursuant to § 36-3251, Arizona Revised Statutes.

This health care directive is made under § 36-3221, Arizona Revised Statutes, and continues in effect for all who may rely on it except those to whom I have given notice of its revocation.

2. Autopsy (under Arizona law, an autopsy may be required)

If you wish to do so, reflect your desires below:
_____ 1. I do not consent to an autopsy.
_____ 2. I consent to an autopsy.
_____ 3. My agent may give consent to an autopsy.

3. Organ Donation (Optional)

(Under Arizona law, you may make a gift of all or part of your body to a bank or storage facility or a hospital, physician or medical or dental school for transplantation, therapy, medical or dental evaluation or research or for the advancement of medical or dental science. You may also authorize your agent to do so or a member of your family to make a gift unless you give them notice that you do not want a gift made. In the space below you may make a gift yourself or state that you do not want to make a gift. If you do not complete this section, your agent will have the authority to make a gift of a part of your body pursuant to law. Note: The donation elections you make in this health care power of attorney survive your death.)

If any of the statements below reflects your desire, initial on the line next to that statement. You do not have to initial any of the statements.

If you do not check any of the statements, your agent and your family will have the authority to make a gift of all or part of your body under Arizona law.

_____ I do not want to make an organ or tissue donation and do not want my
agent or family to do so.
_____ I have already signed a written agreement or donor card regarding organ and tissue
donation with the following individual or institution:_____
_____ Pursuant to Arizona law, I hereby give, effective on my death:
[   ] Any needed organ or parts.
[   ] The following part or organs listed:

_____
_____
_____

for (check one):
[   ] Any legally authorized purpose.
[   ] Transplant or therapeutic purposes only.

4. <u>Physician Affidavit</u> (Optional)

(Before initialing any choices above you may wish to ask questions of your physician regarding a particular treatment alternative. If you do speak with your physician it is a good idea to ask your physician to complete this affidavit and keep a copy for his file.)

I, Dr. _____, have reviewed this guidance document and have discussed with _____ any questions regarding the probable medical consequences of the treatment choices provided above. This discussion with the principal occurred on _____(date). I have agreed to comply with the provisions of this directive.

_____
Signature of physician

5. <u>Living Will</u> (Optional)

(Some general statements concerning your health care options are outlined below. If you agree with one of the statements, you should initial that statement. **Read all of these statements carefully before you initial your selection**. You can also write your own statement concerning life-sustaining treatment and other matters relating to your health care. You may initial any combination of paragraphs 1, 2, 3 and 4, but if you initial paragraph 5 the others should not be initialed.)

_____ 1. If I have a terminal condition I **do not** want my life to be prolonged and I **do not** want life-sustaining treatment, beyond comfort care, that would serve **only** to artificially delay the moment of my death.

_____ 2. If I am in a terminal condition or an irreversible coma or a persistent vegetative state that my doctors reasonably feel to be irreversible or incurable, I **do** want the medical treatment necessary to provide care that would keep me comfortable, but I **do not** want the following:

    _____ (a) Cardiopulmonary resuscitation, for example, the use of drugs, electric shock and artificial breathing.

    _____ (b) Artificially administered food and fluids.

    _____ (c) To be taken to a hospital if at all avoidable.

_____ 3. Notwithstanding my other directions, if I am known to be pregnant, I do not want life-sustaining treatment withheld or withdrawn if it is possible that the embryo/fetus will develop to the point of live birth with the continued application of life-sustaining treatment.

_____ 4. Notwithstanding my other directions I **do** want the use of all medical care necessary to treat my condition until my doctors reasonably conclude that my condition is terminal or is irreversible and incurable or I am in a persistent vegetative state.

_____ 5. I **want** my life to be prolonged to the greatest extent possible.

Other or additional statement of desires

I have _____ I have not _____ attached additional special provisions or limitations to this document to be honored in the absence of my being able to give health care directions.

_____
Signature of Principal

Witness: _____   Date: _____
_____   Time: _____
Address: _____   _____
_____   Address of Agent
Witness: _____   _____
_____   _____
Address: _____   Telephone of Agent_____

(Note: This document may be notarized instead of being witnessed.)

State of Arizona _____)
County of _____)

    On this _____ day of _____, _____ before me, personally appeared _____ (name of principal), who is personally known to me or provided _____ as identification, and acknowledged that he or she executed it.

    [NOTARY SEAL]

_____
(signature of notary public)

DECLARATION

Initial and complete one or both of the following:

_____ If I should have an incurable or irreversible condition that will cause my death within a relatively short time, and I am no longer able to make decisions regarding my medical treatment, I direct my attending physician, pursuant to Arkansas Rights of the Terminally Ill or Permanently Unconscious Act, to [withhold or withdraw treatment that only prolongs the process of dying and is not necessary to my comfort or to alleviate pain] [follow the instructions of _____ _____, whom I appoint as my health care proxy to decide whether life-sustaining treatment should be withheld or withdrawn].

_____ If I should become permanently unconscious I direct my attending physician, pursuant to Arkansas Rights of the Terminally Ill or Permanently Unconscious Act, to [withhold or withdraw treatment that only prolongs the process of dying and is not necessary to my comfort or to alleviate pain] [follow the instructions of _____ whom I appoint as my health care proxy to decide whether life-sustaining treatment should be withheld or withdrawn].

Initial and complete one of the following:

_____ It is my specific directive that nutrition may be withheld after consultation with my attending physician.
_____ It is my specific directive that nutrition may not be withheld.

Initial and complete one of the following:

_____ It is my specific directive that hydration may be withheld after consultation with my attending physician.
_____ It is my specific directive that hydration may not be withheld.

Signed this _____ day of _____, 20___.

Signature _____
Address _____
_____

The declarant voluntarily signed this writing in my presence.

Witness _____   Witness _____
Address _____   Address _____
_____   _____

Advance Health Care Directive
(California Probate Code Section 4701)

Explanation
You have the right to give instructions about your own health care. You also have the right to name someone else to make health care decisions for you. This form lets you do either or both of these things. It also lets you express your wishes regarding donation of organs and the designation of your primary physician. If you use this form, you may complete or modify all or any part of it. You are free to use a different form.

Part 1 of this form is a power of attorney for health care. Part 1 lets you name another individual as agent to make health care decisions for you if you become incapable of making your own decisions or if you want someone else to make those decisions for you now even though you are still capable. You may also name an alternate agent to act for you if your first choice is not willing, able, or reasonably available to make decisions for you. (Your agent may not be an operator or employee of a community care facility or a residential care facility where you are receiving care, or your supervising health care provider or employee of the health care institution where you are receiving care, unless your agent is related to you or is a coworker.)

Unless the form you sign limits the authority of your agent, your agent may make all health care decisions for you. This form has a place for you to limit the authority of your agent. You need not limit the authority of your agent if you wish to rely on your agent for all health care decisions that may have to be made. If you choose not to limit the authority of your agent, your agent will have the right to:

(a) Consent or refuse consent to any care, treatment, service, or procedure to maintain, diagnose, or otherwise affect a physical or mental condition.

(b) Select or discharge health care providers and institutions.

(c) Approve or disapprove diagnostic tests, surgical procedures, and programs of medication.

(d) Direct the provision, withholding, or withdrawal of artificial nutrition and hydration and all other forms of health care, including cardiopulmonary resuscitation.

(e) Make anatomical gifts, authorize an autopsy, and direct disposition of remains.

Part 2 of this form lets you give specific instructions about any aspect of your health care, whether or not you appoint an agent. Choices are provided for you to express your wishes regarding the provision, withholding, or withdrawal of treatment to keep you alive, as well as the provision of pain relief. Space is also provided for you to add to the choices you have made or for you to write out any additional wishes. If you are satisfied to allow your agent to determine what is best for you in making end-of-life decisions, you need not fill out Part 2 of this form.

Part 3 of this form lets you express an intention to donate your bodily organs and tissues following your death.

Part 4 of this form lets you designate a physician to have primary responsibility for your health care.

After completing this form, sign and date the form at the end. The form must be signed by two qualified witnesses or acknowledged before a notary public. Give a copy of the signed and completed form to your physician, to any other health care providers you may have, to any health care institution at which you are receiving care, and to any health care agents you have named. You should talk to the person you have named as agent to make sure that he or she understands your wishes and is willing to take the responsibility.

You have the right to revoke this advance health care directive or replace this form at any time.

* * * * * * * * * * * * * * * * *

PART 1
POWER OF ATTORNEY FOR HEALTH CARE

(1.1) DESIGNATION OF AGENT: I designate the following individual as my agent to make health care decisions for me:

_____
(name of individual you choose as agent)

_____
(address)   (city)   (state)   (ZIP Code)

_____
(home phone)   (work phone)

OPTIONAL: If I revoke my agent's authority or if my agent is not willing, able, or reasonably available to make a health care decision for me, I designate as my first alternate agent:

_____
(name of individual you choose as first alternate agent)

_____
(address)   (city)   (state)   (ZIP Code)

_____
(home phone)   (work phone)

OPTIONAL: If I revoke the authority of my agent and first alternate agent or if neither is willing, able, or reasonably available to make a health care decision for me, I designate as my second alternate agent:

_____
(name of individual you choose as second alternate agent)

_____
(address)   (city)   (state)   (ZIP Code)

_____
(home phone)   (work phone)

(1.2) AGENT'S AUTHORITY: My agent is authorized to make all health care decisions for me, including decisions to provide, withhold, or withdraw artificial nutrition and hydration and all other forms of health care to keep me alive, except as I state here:

_____
_____
(Add additional sheets if needed.)

(1.3) WHEN AGENT'S AUTHORITY BECOMES EFFECTIVE: My agent's authority becomes effective when my primary physician determines that I am unable to make my own health care decisions, unless I mark the following box.

If I mark this box ( ), my agent's authority to make health care decisions for me takes effect immediately.

(1.4) AGENT'S OBLIGATION: My agent shall make health care decisions for me in accordance with this power of attorney for health care, any instructions I give in Part 2 of this form, and my other wishes to the extent known to my agent. To the extent my wishes are unknown, my agent shall make health care decisions for me in accordance with what my agent determines to be in my best interest. In determining my best interest, my agent shall consider my personal values to the extent known to my agent.

(1.5) AGENT'S POSTDEATH AUTHORITY: My agent is authorized to make anatomical gifts, authorize an autopsy, and direct disposition of my remains, except as I state here or in Part 3 of this form:

_____
(Add additional sheets if needed.)

(1.6) NOMINATION OF CONSERVATOR: If a conservator of my person needs to be appointed for me by a court, I nominate the agent designated in this form. If that agent is not willing, able, or reasonably available to act as conservator, I nominate the alternate agents whom I have named, in the order designated.

PART 2
INSTRUCTIONS FOR HEALTH CARE

If you fill out this part of the form, you may strike any wording you do not want.

(2.1) END-OF-LIFE DECISIONS: I direct that my health care providers and others involved in my care provide, withhold, or withdraw treatment in accordance with the choice I have marked below:
☐ (a) Choice Not To Prolong Life. I do not want my life to be prolonged if (1) I have an incurable and irreversible condition that will result in my death within a relatively short time, (2) I become unconscious and, to a reasonable degree of medical certainty, I will not regain consciousness, or (3) the likely risks and burdens of treatment would outweigh the expected benefits, OR
☐ (b) Choice To Prolong Life. I want my life to be prolonged as long as possible within the limits of generally accepted health care standards.

(2.2) RELIEF FROM PAIN: Except as I state in the following space, I direct that treatment for alleviation of pain or discomfort be provided at all times, even if it hastens my death:

_____

(Add additional sheets if needed.)

(2.3) OTHER WISHES: (If you do not agree with any of the optional choices above and wish to write your own, or if you wish to add to the instructions you have given above, you may do so here.) I direct that:

_____

(Add additional sheets if needed.)

PART 3
DONATION OF ORGANS AT DEATH (OPTIONAL)

(3.1) Upon my death (mark applicable box):
☐ (a) I give any needed organs, tissues, or parts, OR
☐ (b) I give the following organs, tissues, or parts only.

_____

☐ (c) My gift is for the following purposes (strike any of the following you do not want):
     (1) Transplant
     (2) Therapy
     (3) Research
     (4) Education

PART 4
PRIMARY PHYSICIAN (OPTIONAL)

_____
(name of physician)

_____
(address)   (city)   (state)   (ZIP Code)

_____
(phone)

OPTIONAL: If the physician I have designated above is not willing, able, or reasonably available to act as my primary physician, I designate the following physician as my primary physician:

_____
(name of physician)

_____
(address)   (city)   (state)   (ZIP Code)

_____
(phone)

PART 5

(5.1) EFFECT OF COPY: A copy of this form has the same effect as the original.

(5.2) SIGNATURE: Sign and date the form here:

_____   _____
(date)   (sign your name)

_____   _____
(address)   (print your name)

_____
(city)   (state)

(5.3) STATEMENT OF WITNESSES: I declare under penalty of perjury under the laws of California (1) that the individual who signed or acknowledged this advance health care directive is personally known to me, or that the individual's identity was proven to me by convincing evidence (2) that the individual signed or acknowledged this advance directive in my presence, (3) that the individual appears to be of sound mind and under no duress, fraud, or undue influence, (4) that I am not a person appointed as agent by this advance directive, and (5) that I am not the individual's health care provider, an employee of the individual's health care provider, the operator of a community care facility, an employee of an operator of a community care facility, the operator of a residential care facility for the elderly, nor an employee of an operator of a residential care facility for the elderly.

First witness	Second witness
(print name)	(print name)
(address)	(address)
(city) (state)	(city) (state)
(signature of witness)	(signature of witness)
(date)	(date)

(5.4) ADDITIONAL STATEMENT OF WITNESSES: At least one of the above witnesses must also sign the following declaration:

I further declare under penalty of perjury under the laws of California that I am not related to the individual executing this advance health care directive by blood, marriage, or adoption, and to the best of my knowledge, I am not entitled to any part of the individual's estate upon his or her death under a will now existing or by operation of law.

(signature of witness)	(signature of witness)

PART 6
SPECIAL WITNESS REQUIREMENT

(6.1) The following statement is required only if you are a patient in a skilled nursing facility--a health care facility that provides the following basic services: skilled nursing care and supportive care to patients whose primary need is for availability of skilled nursing care on an extended basis. The patient advocate or ombudsman must sign the following statement:

STATEMENT OF PATIENT ADVOCATE OR OMBUDSMAN

I declare under penalty of perjury under the laws of California that I am a patient advocate or ombudsman as designated by the State Department of Aging and that I am serving as a witness as required by Section 4675 of the Probate Code.

(date)	(sign your name)
(address)	(print your name)
(city) (state)	

DECLARATION AS TO MEDICAL OR SURGICAL TREATMENT

I, _____ , being of sound mind and at least eighteen years of age, direct that my life shall not be artificially prolonged under the circumstances set forth below and hereby declare that:

1.   If at any time my attending physician and one other qualified physician certify in writing that:

     a.   I have an injury, disease, or illness which is not curable or reversible and which, in their judgment, is a terminal condition, and

     b.   For a period of seven consecutive days or more, I have been unconscious, comatose, or otherwise incompetent so as to be unable to make or communicate responsible decisions concerning my person, then

I direct that, in accordance with Colorado law, life-sustaining procedures shall be withdrawn and withheld pursuant to the terms of this declaration, it being understood that life-sustaining procedures shall not include any medical procedure or intervention for nourishment considered necessary by the attending physician to provide comfort or alleviate pain. However, I may specifically direct, in accordance with Colorado law, that artificial nourishment be withdrawn or withheld pursuant to the terms of this declaration.

2.   In the event that the only procedure I am being provided is artificial nourishment, I direct that one of the following actions be taken:

_____ a.   Artificial nourishment shall not be continued when it is the only procedure being provided; or

_____ b.   Artificial nourishment shall be continued for _____ days when it is the only procedure being provided; or

_____ c.   Artificial nourishment shall be continued when it is the only procedure being provided.

3.   I execute this declaration, as my free and voluntary act, this _____ day of _____ , 200___ .

By_____

Declarant

The foregoing instrument was signed and declared by _____ to be his declaration, in the presence of us, who, in his presence, in the presence of each other, and at his request, have signed our names below as witnesses, and we declare that, at the time of the execution of this instrument, the declarant, according to our best knowledge and belief, was of sound mind and under no constraint or undue influence.

Dated at _____ , Colorado, this _____ day of _____ , 200___ .

_____
Name and Address of Witness

_____
Name and Address of Witness

STATE OF COLORADO   )
) ss.
COUNTY OF _____   )

     SUBSCRIBED and sworn to before me by _____ , the declarant, and _____ and _____ , witnesses, as the voluntary act and deed of the declarant the _____ day of _____ , 200____ . My commission expires:

_____
Notary Public

Health Care Instructions

THESE ARE MY HEALTH CARE INSTRUCTIONS. MY APPOINTMENT OF A HEALTH CARE AGENT, MY APPOINTMENT OF AN ATTORNEY-IN-FACT FOR HEALTH CARE DECISIONS, THE DESIGNATION OF MY CONSERVATOR OF THE PERSON FOR MY FUTURE INCAPACITY AND MY DOCUMENT OF ANATOMICAL GIFT.

To any physician who is treating me: These are my health care instructions including those concerning the withholding or withdrawal of life support systems, together with the appointment of my health care agent and my attorney-in-fact for health care decisions, the designation of my conservator of the person for future incapacity and my document of anatomical gift. As my physician, you may rely on any decision made by my health care agent, attorney-in-fact for health care decisions or conservator of my person, if I am unable to make a decision for myself.

I, _____, the author of this document, request that, if my condition is deemed terminal or if I am determined to be permanently unconscious, I be allowed to die and not be kept alive through life support systems. By terminal condition, I mean that I have an incurable or irreversible medical condition which, without the administration of life support systems, will, in the opinion of my attending physician, result in death within a relatively short time. By permanently unconscious I mean that I am in a permanent coma or persistent vegetative state which is an irreversible condition in which I am at no time aware of myself or the environment and show no behavioral response to the environment. The life support systems which I do not want include, but are not limited to: Artificial respiration, cardiopulmonary resuscitation and artificial means of providing nutrition and hydration. I do want sufficient pain medication to maintain my physical comfort. I do not intend any direct taking of my life, but only that my dying not be unreasonably prolonged.

I appoint _____ to be my health care agent and my attorney-in-fact for health care decisions. If my attending physician determines that I am unable to understand and appreciate the nature and consequences of health care decisions and unable to reach and communicate an informed decision regarding treatment, my health care agent and attorney-in-fact for health care decisions is authorized to:

> (1) Convey to my physician my wishes concerning the withholding or removal of life support systems;

> (2) Take whatever actions are necessary to ensure that any wishes are given effect;

> (3) Consent, refuse, or withdraw consent to any medical treatment as long as such action is consistent with my wishes concerning the withholding or removal of life support systems; and,

> (4) Consent to any medical treatment designed solely for the purpose of maintaining physical comfort.

If _____ is unwilling or unable to serve as my health care agent and my attorney-in-fact for health care decisions, I appoint _____ _____ to be my alternative health care agent and my attorney-in-fact for health care decisions. If a conservator of my person should need to be appointed, I designate _____ be appointed my conservator. If _____ is unwilling or unable to serve as my conservator, I designate _____. No bond shall be required of either of them in any jurisdiction.

I hereby make this anatomical gift, if medically acceptable, to take effect upon my death.

I give: (check one)

     ___ (1) any needed organs or parts

     ___(2) only the following organs or parts _____ to
           be donated for: (check one)
           (1) ___ any of the purposes stated in subsection (a) of section 19a-279f of the
                general statutes
           (2) ___ these limited purposes _____.

These requests, appointments, and designations are made after careful reflection, while I am of sound mind. Any party receiving a duly executed copy or facsimile of this document may rely upon it unless such party has received actual notice of my revocation of it.

Date _____, 20___

                               _____ L.S.

This document was signed in our presence by _____, the author of this document, who appeared to be eighteen years of age or older, of sound mind and able to understand the nature and consequences of health care decisions at the time this document was signed. The author appeared to be under no improper influence. We have subscribed this document in the author's presence and at the author's request and in the presence of each other.

_____   _____
(Witness)   (Witness)

_____   _____
(Number and Street)   (Number and Street)

_____   _____
(City, State and Zip Code)   (City, State and Zip Code)

STATE OF CONNECTICUT   )
)ss.
COUNTY OF _____)

We, the subscribing witnesses, being duly sworn, say that we witnessed the execution of these health care instructions, the appointments of a health care agent and an attorney-in-fact, the designation of a conservator for future incapacity and a document of anatomical gift by the author of this document; that the author subscribed, published and declared the same to be the author's instructions, appointments and designation in our presence; that we thereafter subscribed the document as witnesses in the author's presence, at the author's request, and in the presence of each other; that at the time of the execution of said document the author appeared to us to be eighteen years of age or older, of sound mind, able to understand the nature and consequences of said document, and under no improper influence, and we make this affidavit at the author's request this _____ day of _____, 20_____.

_____   _____
(Witness)   (Witness)

Subscribed and sworn to before me this _____ day of _____, 20_____.

_____
Commissioner of the Superior Court

Notary Public

My commission expires: _____

Advance Health-Care Directive

EXPLANATION

You have the right to give instructions about your own health care. You also have the right to name someone else to make health-care decisions for you. This form lets you do either or both of these things. It also lets you express your wishes regarding anatomical gifts and the designation of your primary physician. If you use this form, you may complete or modify all or any part of it. You are free to use a different form.

Part 1 of this form is a power of attorney for health care. Part 1 lets you name another individual as agent to make health-care decisions for you if you become incapable of making your own decisions. You may also name an alternate agent to act for you if your first choice is not willing, able or reasonably available to make decisions for you. Unless related to you, an agent may not have a controlling interest in or be an operator or employee of a residential long-term health-care institution at which you are receiving care. If you do not have a qualifying condition (terminal illness/injury or permanent unconsciousness), your agent may make all health-care decisions for you except for decisions providing, withholding or withdrawing of a life sustaining procedure. Unless you limit the agent's authority, your agent will have the right to:

(a)   Consent or refuse consent to any care, treatment, service or procedure to maintain, diagnose or otherwise affect a physical or mental condition unless it's a life-sustaining procedure or otherwise required by law.

(b)   Select or discharge health-care providers and health-care institutions.

If you have a qualifying condition, your agent may make all health-care decisions for you, including, but not limited to:

(c)   The decisions listed in (a) and (b).

(d)   Consent or refuse consent to life sustaining procedures, such as, but not limited to, cardiopulmonary resuscitation and orders not to resuscitate.

(e)   Direct the providing, withholding or withdrawal of artificial nutrition and hydration and all other forms of health care.

Part 2 of this form lets you give specific instructions about any aspect of your health care. Choices are provided for you to express your wishes regarding the provision, withholding or withdrawal of treatment to keep you alive, including the provision of artificial nutrition and hydration as well as the provision of pain relief. Space is also provided for you to add to the choices you have made or for you to write out any additional instructions for other than end of life decisions.

Part 3 of this form lets you express an intention to donate your bodily organs and tissues following your death.

Part 4 of this form lets you designate a physician to have primary responsibility for your health care.

After completing this form, sign and date the form at the end. It is required that 2 other individuals sign as witnesses. Give a copy of the signed and completed form to your physician, to any other health-care providers you may have, to any health-care institution at which you are receiving care and to any health-care agents you have named. You should talk to the person you have named as agent to make sure that the person understands your wishes and is willing to take the responsibility.

You have the right to revoke this advance health-care directive or replace this form at any time.

* * * * * * * * * * * * * * * * * * * *

PART 1: POWER OF ATTORNEY FOR HEALTH CARE

(1)   DESIGNATION OF AGENT: I designate the following individual as my agent to make health-care decisions for me:

_____

(name of individual you choose as agent)

_____

(address)   (city)   (state)   (zip code)

_____

(home phone)   (work phone)

OPTIONAL: If I revoke my agent's authority or if my agent is not willing, able or reasonably available to make a health-care decision for me, I designate as my first alternate agent:

_____
(name of individual you choose as first alternate agent)

_____
(address)   (city)   (state)   (zip code)

_____
(home phone)   (work phone)

OPTIONAL: If I revoke the authority of my agent and first alternate agent or if neither is willing, able or reasonably available to make a health-care decision for me, I designate as my second alternate agent:

_____
(name of individual you choose as second alternate agent)

_____
(address)   (city)   (state)   (zip code)

_____
(home phone)   (work phone)

(2)   AGENT'S AUTHORITY: If I am not in a qualifying condition my agent is authorized to make all health-care decisions for me, except decisions about life-sustaining procedures and as I state here; and if I am in a qualifying condition, my agent is authorized to make all health-care decisions for me, except as I state here:
_____
_____
_____
(Add additional sheets if needed.)

(3)   WHEN AGENT'S AUTHORITY BECOMES EFFECTIVE: My agent's authority becomes effective when my primary physician determines I lack the capacity to make my own health-care decisions. As to decisions concerning the providing, withholding, and withdrawal of life-sustaining procedures my agent's authority becomes effective when my primary physician determines I lack the capacity to make my own health-care decisions and my primary physician and another physician determine that I am in a terminal condition or permanently unconscious.

(4)   AGENT'S OBLIGATIONS: My agent shall make health-care decisions for me in accordance with this power of attorney for health care, any instructions I give in Part 2 of this form, and my other wishes to the extent known to my agent. To the extent my wishes are unknown, my agent shall make health-care decisions for me in accordance with what my agent determines to be in my best interest. In determining my best interest, my agent shall consider my personal values to the extent known to my agent.

(5)   NOMINATION OF GUARDIAN: If a guardian of my person needs to be appointed for me by a court, (please check one):

[   ]   I nominate the agent(s) whom I named in this form in the order designated to act as guardian.

[   ]   I nominate the following to be guardian in the order designated:
_____

[   ]   I do not nominate anyone to be guardian.

PART 2: INSTRUCTIONS FOR HEALTH CARE

If you are satisfied to allow your agent to determine what is best for you in making end-of-life decisions, you need not fill out this part of the form. If you do fill out this part of the form, you may strike any wording you do not want.

(6)   END-OF-LIFE DECISIONS: If I am in a qualifying condition, I direct that my health-care providers and others involved in my care provide, withhold, or withdraw treatment in accordance with the choice I have marked below:

Choice Not To Prolong Life

I do not want my life to be prolonged if: (please check all that apply)

_____(i)   I have a terminal condition (an incurable condition caused by injury, disease, or illness which, to a reasonable degree of medical certainty, makes death imminent and from which, despite the application of life-sustaining procedures, there can be no recovery) and regarding artificial nutrition and hydration, I make the following specific directions:

	I want used	I do not want used
Artificial nutrition through a conduit	_____	_____
Hydration through a conduit	_____	_____

_____(ii)   I become permanently unconscious (a medical condition that has been diagnosed in accordance with currently accepted medical standards that has lasted at least 4 weeks and with reasonable medical certainty as total and irreversible loss of consciousness and capacity for interaction with the environment. The term includes, without limitation, a persistent vegetative state or irreversible coma) and regarding artificial nutrition and hydration, I make the following specific directions:

	I want used	I do not want used
Artificial nutrition through a conduit	_____	_____
Hydration through a conduit	_____	_____

Choice To Prolong Life

_____   I want my life to be prolonged as long as possible within the limits of generally accepted health-care standards.

RELIEF FROM PAIN: Except as I state in the following space, I direct treatment for alleviation of pain or discomfort be provided at all times, even if it hastens my death: _____
_____
_____
_____

(7)   OTHER MEDICAL INSTRUCTIONS: (If you do not agree with any of the optional choices above and wish to write you own, or if you wish to add to the instructions you have given above, you may do so here.) I direct that: _____
_____
_____
(Add additional sheets if necessary.)

PART 3: ANATOMICAL GIFTS AT DEATH
(OPTIONAL)

(8)   I am mentally competent and 18 years or more of age.
        I hereby make this anatomical gift to take effect upon my death. The marks in the appropriate squares and words filled into the blanks below indicate my desires.
        I give: [   ] my body; [   ] any needed organs or parts;
               [   ] the following organs or parts: _____
        To the following person or institutions:
               [   ] the physician in attendance at my death;

[   ] the hospital in which I die;
[   ] the following named physician, hospital, storage bank or other medical institution:

_____

[   ] the following individual for treatment:

_____

for the following purposes: [   ] any purpose authorized by law;
                [   ] transplantation;   [   ] therapy;
                [   ] research;   [   ] medical education.

PART 4: PRIMARY PHYSICIAN
(OPTIONAL)

(9)   I designate the following physician as my primary physician:

_____

(name of physician)   (phone)

_____

(address)   (city)   (state)   (zip code)

OPTIONAL: If the physician I have designated above is not willing, able or reasonably available to act as my primary physician, I designate the following physician as my primary physician:

_____

(name of physician)   (phone)

_____

(address)   (city)   (state)   (zip code)

Primary Physician shall mean a physician designated by an individual or the individual's agent or guardian, to have primary responsibility for the individual's health care or, in the absence of a designation or if the designated physician is not reasonably available, a physician who undertakes the responsibility.

* * * * * * * * * * * * * * * * * * * *

(10)   EFFECT OF COPY: A copy of this form has the same effect as the original.

(11)   SIGNATURE: Sign and date the form here: I understand the purposes and effect of this document.

_____   _____

(date)   (sign your name)

_____   _____

(address)   (print your name)

_____

(city)   (state)   (zip code)

(12) SIGNATURE OF WITNESSES:

Statement Of Witnesses

SIGNED AND DECLARED by the above-named declarant as and for his/her written declaration under 16 Del.C. §§ 2502 and 2503, in our presence, who in his/her presence, at his/her request, and in the presence of each other, have hereunto subscribed our names as witnesses, and state:

A.   That the Declarant is mentally competent.

B.   That neither of them:

     1.   Is related to the declarant by blood, marriage or adoption;

     2.   Is entitled to any portion of the estate of the declarant under any will of the declarant or codicil thereto then existing nor, at the time of the executing of the advance health care directive, is so entitled by operation of law then existing;

     3.   Has, at the time of the execution of the advance health-care directive, a present or inchoate claim against any portion of the estate of the declarant;

     4.   Has a direct financial responsibility for the declarant's medical care;

     5.   Has a controlling interest in or is an operator or an employee of a residential long-term health-care institution in which the declarant is a resident; or

     6.   Is under eighteen years of age.

C.   That if the declarant is a resident of a sanitarium, rest home, nursing home, boarding home or related institution, one of the witnesses, _____, is at the time of the execution of the advance health-care directive, a patient advocate or ombudsman designated by the Division of Services for Aging and Adults with Physical Disabilities or the Public Guardian.

First witness	Second witness
_____	_____
(print name)	(print name)
_____	_____
(address)	(address)
_____	_____
(city) (state)	(city) (state)
_____	_____
(signature of witness)	(signature of witness)
_____	_____
(date)	(date)

I am not prohibited by §2503 of
Title 16 of the Delaware Code
from being a witness.

I am not prohibited by §2503 of
Title 16 of the Delaware Code
from being a witness.

Power of Attorney For Health Care

INFORMATION ABOUT THIS DOCUMENT

THIS IS AN IMPORTANT LEGAL DOCUMENT. BEFORE SIGNING THIS DOCUMENT, IT IS VITAL FOR YOU TO KNOW AND UNDERSTAND THESE FACTS:

THIS DOCUMENT GIVES THE PERSON YOU NAME AS YOUR ATTORNEY IN FACT THE POWER TO MAKE HEALTH-CARE DECISIONS FOR YOU IF YOU CANNOT MAKE THE DECISIONS FOR YOURSELF.

AFTER YOU HAVE SIGNED THIS DOCUMENT, YOU HAVE THE RIGHT TO MAKE HEALTH-CARE DECISIONS FOR YOURSELF IF YOU ARE MENTALLY COMPETENT TO DO SO. IN ADDITION, AFTER YOU HAVE SIGNED THIS DOCUMENT, NO TREATMENT MAY BE GIVEN TO YOU OR STOPPED OVER YOUR OBJECTION IF YOU ARE MENTALLY COMPETENT TO MAKE THAT DECISION.

YOU MAY STATE IN THIS DOCUMENT ANY TYPE OF TREATMENT THAT YOU DO NOT DESIRE AND ANY THAT YOU WANT TO MAKE SURE YOU RECEIVE.

YOU HAVE THE RIGHT TO TAKE AWAY THE AUTHORITY OF YOUR ATTORNEY IN FACT, UNLESS YOU HAVE BEEN ADJUDICATED INCOMPETENT, BY NOTIFYING YOUR ATTORNEY IN FACT OR HEALTH-CARE PROVIDER EITHER ORALLY OR IN WRITING. SHOULD YOU REVOKE THE AUTHORITY OF YOUR ATTORNEY IN FACT, IT IS ADVISABLE TO REVOKE IN WRITING AND TO PLACE COPIES OF THE REVOCATION WHEREVER THIS DOCUMENT IS LOCATED.

IF THERE IS ANYTHING IN THIS DOCUMENT THAT YOU DO NOT UNDERSTAND, YOU SHOULD ASK A SOCIAL WORKER, LAWYER, OR OTHER PERSON TO EXPLAIN IT TO YOU.

* * * * *

YOU SHOULD KEEP A COPY OF THIS DOCUMENT AFTER YOU HAVE SIGNED IT. GIVE A COPY TO THE PERSON YOU NAME AS YOUR ATTORNEY IN FACT. IF YOU ARE IN A HEALTH-CARE FACILITY, A COPY OF THIS DOCUMENT SHOULD BE INCLUDED IN YOUR MEDICAL RECORD.

I, _____, hereby appoint:

_____	_____
name	home address
_____	_____
home telephone number	
_____	
work telephone number	

as my attorney in fact to make health-care decisions for me if I become unable to make my own health-care decisions. This gives my attorney in fact the power to grant, refuse, or withdraw consent on my behalf for any health-care service, treatment or procedure. My attorney in fact also has the authority to talk to health-care personnel, get information and sign forms necessary to carry out these decisions.

If the person named as my attorney in fact is not available or is unable to act as my attorney in fact, I appoint the following persons to serve in the order listed below:

1.
_____	_____
name	home address
_____	
home telephone number	
_____	
work telephone number	

2.
_____	_____
name	home address
_____	
home telephone number	
_____	
work telephone number	

With this document, I intend to create a power of attorney for health care, which shall take effect if I become incapable of making my own health-care decisions and shall continue during that incapacity.

My attorney in fact shall make health-care decisions as I direct below or as I make known to my attorney in fact in some other way.

(a) STATEMENT OF DIRECTIVES CONCERNING LIFE-PROLONGING CARE, TREATMENT, SERVICES, AND PROCEDURES:

_____

_____

_____

(b) SPECIAL PROVISIONS AND LIMITATIONS:

_____

_____

_____

BY MY SIGNATURE I INDICATE THAT I UNDERSTAND THE PURPOSE AND EFFECT OF THIS DOCUMENT.

I sign my name to this form on _____
(date)

at: _____
(address)

_____
(Signature)

WITNESSES

I declare that the person who signed or acknowledged this document is personally known to me, that the person signed or acknowledged this durable power of attorney for health care in my presence, and that the person appears to be of sound mind and under no duress, fraud, or undue influence. I am not the person appointed as the attorney in fact by this document, nor am I the health-care provider of the principal or an employee of the health-care provider of the principal.

First Witness

Signature: _____

Home Address: _____

Print Name: _____

Date: _____

Second Witness

Signature: _____

Home Address: _____

Print Name: _____

Date: _____

(AT LEAST 1 OF THE WITNESSES LISTED ABOVE SHALL ALSO SIGN THE FOLLOWING DECLARATION.)

I further declare that I am not related to the principal by blood, marriage or adoption, and, to the best of my knowledge, I am not entitled to any part of the estate of the principal under a currently existing will or by operation of law.

Signature: _____

Signature: _____

LIVING WILL

Declaration made this _____ day of _____, _____ (year) , I, _____, willfully and voluntarily make known my desire that my dying not be artificially prolonged under the circumstances set forth below, and I do hereby declare that, if at any time I am incapacitated and (please only initial one):

    _____ I have a terminal condition

               OR

    _____ I have an end-stage condition

               OR

    _____ I am in a persistent vegetative state

And if my attending or treating physician and another consulting physician have determined that there is no reasonable medical probability of my recovery from such condition, I direct that life-prolonging procedures be withheld or withdrawn when the application of such procedures would serve only to prolong artificially the process of dying, and that I be permitted to die naturally with only the administration of medication or the performance of any medical procedure deemed necessary to provide me with comfort care or to alleviate pain.

It is my intention that this declaration be honored by my family and physician as the final expression of my legal right to refuse medical or surgical treatment and to accept the consequences for such refusal.

In the event that I have been determined to be unable to provide express and informed consent regarding the withholding, withdrawal, or continuation of life-prolonging procedures, I wish to designate, as my surrogate to carry out the provisions of this declaration:

Name: _____

Address: _____

_____

_____

Zip Code: _____

Phone: _____

I understand the full import of this declaration, and I am emotionally and mentally competent to make this declaration.

Additional Instructions (optional):

Signed _____

Witness 1	Witness 2
Address: _____	Address: _____
_____	_____
_____	_____
Phone: _____	Phone: _____

Designation of Health Care Surrogate

Name: _____(Last)_____(First)_____(Middle Initial)

In the event that I have been determined to be incapacitated to provide informed consent for medical treatment and surgical and diagnostic procedures, I wish to designate as my surrogate for health care decisions:

Name: _____

Address: _____

Phone: _____   Zip Code: _____

If my surrogate is unwilling or unable to perform his or her duties, I wish to designate as my alternate surrogate:

Name: _____

Address: _____

Phone: _____   Zip Code: _____

I fully understand that this designation will permit my designee to make health care decisions, except for anatomical gifts, unless I have executed an anatomical gift declaration pursuant to law, and to provide, withhold, or withdraw consent on my behalf; to apply for public benefits to defray the cost of health care; and to authorize my admission to or transfer from a health care facility.

Additional instructions (optional): _____
_____
_____

I further affirm that this designation is not being made as a condition of treatment or admission to a health care facility. I will notify and send a copy of this document to the following persons other than my surrogate, so they may know who my surrogate is.

Name: _____

Name: _____

Signed: _____

Date: _____

Witnesses:

1. _____

2. _____

Georgia Statutory Short Form Durable Power of Attorney for Health Care

NOTICE: THE PURPOSE OF THIS POWER OF ATTORNEY IS TO GIVE THE PERSON YOU DESIGNATE (YOUR AGENT) BROAD POWERS TO MAKE HEALTH CARE DECISIONS FOR YOU, INCLUDING POWER TO REQUIRE, CONSENT TO, OR WITHDRAW ANY TYPE OF PERSONAL CARE OR MEDICAL TREATMENT FOR ANY PHYSICAL OR MENTAL CONDITION AND TO ADMIT YOU TO OR DISCHARGE YOU FROM ANY HOSPITAL, HOME, OR OTHER INSTITUTION; BUT NOT INCLUDING PSYCHOSURGERY, STERILIZATION, OR INVOLUNTARY HOSPITALIZATION OR TREATMENT COVERED BY TITLE 37 OF THE OFFICIAL CODE OF GEORGIA ANNOTATED. THIS FORM DOES NOT IMPOSE A DUTY ON YOUR AGENT TO EXERCISE GRANTED POWERS; BUT, WHEN A POWER IS EXERCISED, YOUR AGENT WILL HAVE TO USE DUE CARE TO ACT FOR YOUR BENEFIT AND IN ACCORDANCE WITH THIS FORM. A COURT CAN TAKE AWAY THE POWERS OF YOUR AGENT IF IT FINDS THE AGENT IS NOT ACTING PROPERLY. YOU MAY NAME CO-AGENTS AND SUCCESSOR AGENTS UNDER THIS FORM, BUT YOU MAY NOT NAME A HEALTH CARE PROVIDER WHO MAY BE DIRECTLY OR INDIRECTLY INVOLVED IN RENDERING HEALTH CARE TO YOU UNDER THIS POWER. UNLESS YOU EXPRESSLY LIMIT THE DURATION OF THIS POWER IN THE MANNER PROVIDED BELOW OR UNTIL YOU REVOKE THIS POWER OR A COURT ACTING ON YOUR BEHALF TERMINATES IT, YOUR AGENT MAY EXERCISE THE POWERS GIVEN IN THE POWER THROUGHOUT YOUR LIFETIME, EVEN AFTER YOU BECOME DISABLED, INCAPACITATED, OR INCOMPETENT. THE POWERS YOU GIVE YOUR AGENT, YOUR RIGHT TO REVOKE THOSE POWERS, AND THE PENALTIES FOR VIOLATING THE LAW ARE EXPLAINED MORE FULLY IN CODE SECTIONS 31-36-6, 31-36-9, AND 31-36-10 OF THE GEORGIA 'DURABLE POWER OF ATTORNEY FOR HEALTH CARE ACT' OF WHICH THIS FORM IS A PART (SEE THE BACK OF THIS FORM). THAT ACT EXPRESSLY PERMITS THE USE OF ANY DIFFERENT FORM OF POWER OF ATTORNEY YOU MAY DESIRE. IF THERE IS ANYTHING ABOUT THIS FORM THAT YOU DO NOT UNDERSTAND, YOU SHOULD ASK A LAWYER TO EXPLAIN IT TO YOU.

DURABLE POWER OF ATTORNEY made this _____ day of _____, _____.

     1.   I, _____,
                       (insert name and address of principal)
hereby appoint _____
                       (insert name and address of agent)
as my attorney in fact (my agent) to act for me and in my name in any way I could act in person to make any and all decisions for me concerning my personal care, medical treatment, hospitalization, and health care and to require, withhold, or withdraw any type of medical treatment or procedure, even though my death may ensue. My agent shall have the same access to my medical records that I have, including the right to disclose the contents to others. My agent shall also have full power to make a disposition of any part or all of my body for medical purposes, authorize an autopsy of my body, and direct the disposition of my remains.

THE ABOVE GRANT OF POWER IS INTENDED TO BE AS BROAD AS POSSIBLE SO THAT YOUR AGENT WILL HAVE AUTHORITY TO MAKE ANY DECISION YOU COULD MAKE TO OBTAIN OR TERMINATE ANY TYPE OF HEALTH CARE, INCLUDING WITHDRAWAL OF NOURISHMENT AND FLUIDS AND OTHER LIFE-SUSTAINING OR DEATH-DELAYING MEASURES, IF YOUR AGENT BELIEVES SUCH ACTION WOULD BE CONSISTENT WITH YOUR INTENT AND DESIRES. IF YOU WISH TO LIMIT THE SCOPE OF YOUR AGENT'S POWERS OR PRESCRIBE SPECIAL RULES TO LIMIT THE POWER TO MAKE AN ANATOMICAL GIFT, AUTHORIZE AUTOPSY, OR DISPOSE OF REMAINS, YOU MAY DO SO IN THE FOLLOWING PARAGRAPHS.

     2.   The powers granted above shall not include the following powers or shall be subject to the following rules or limitations (here you may include any specific limitations you

deem appropriate, such as your own definition of when life-sustaining or death-delaying measures should be withheld; a direction to continue nourishment and fluids or other life-sustaining or death-delaying treatment in all events; or instructions to refuse any specific types of treatment that are inconsistent with your religious beliefs or unacceptable to you for any other reason, such as blood transfusion, electroconvulsive therapy, or amputation):

_____

_____

THE SUBJECT OF LIFE-SUSTAINING OR DEATH-DELAYING TREATMENT IS OF PARTICULAR IMPORTANCE. FOR YOUR CONVENIENCE IN DEALING WITH THAT SUBJECT, SOME GENERAL STATEMENTS CONCERNING THE WITHHOLDING OR REMOVAL OF LIFE-SUSTAINING OR DEATH-DELAYING TREATMENT ARE SET FORTH BELOW. IF YOU AGREE WITH ONE OF THESE STATEMENTS, YOU MAY INITIAL THAT STATEMENT, BUT DO NOT INITIAL MORE THAN ONE:

I do not want my life to be prolonged nor do I want life-sustaining or death-delaying treatment to be provided or continued if my agent believes the burdens of the treatment outweigh the expected benefits. I want my agent to consider the relief of suffering, the expense involved, and the quality as well as the possible extension of my life in making decisions concerning life-sustaining or death-delaying treatment.

Initialed_____

I want my life to be prolonged and I want life-sustaining or death-delaying treatment to be provided or continued unless I am in a coma, including a persistent vegetative state, which my attending physician believes to be irreversible, in accordance with reasonable medical standards at the time of reference. If and when I have suffered such an irreversible coma, I want life-sustaining or death-delaying treatment to be withheld or discontinued.

Initialed_____

I want my life to be prolonged to the greatest extent possible without regard to my condition, the chances I have for recovery, or the cost of the procedures.

Initialed_____

THIS POWER OF ATTORNEY MAY BE AMENDED OR REVOKED BY YOU AT ANY TIME AND IN ANY MANNER WHILE YOU ARE ABLE TO DO SO. IN THE ABSENCE OF AN AMENDMENT OR REVOCATION, THE AUTHORITY GRANTED IN THIS POWER OF ATTORNEY WILL BECOME EFFECTIVE AT THE TIME THIS POWER IS SIGNED AND WILL CONTINUE UNTIL YOUR DEATH AND WILL CONTINUE BEYOND YOUR DEATH IF ANATOMICAL GIFT, AUTOPSY, OR DISPOSITION OF REMAINS IS AUTHORIZED, UNLESS A LIMITATION ON THE BEGINNING DATE OR DURATION IS MADE BY INITIALING AND COMPLETING EITHER OR BOTH OF THE FOLLOWING:

3. (   ) This power of attorney shall become effective on_____ _____(insert a future date or event during your lifetime, such as court determination of your disability, incapacity, or incompetency, when you want this power to first take effect).

4. (   ) This power of attorney shall terminate on_____ _____(insert a future date or event, such as court determination of your disability, incapacity, or incompetency, when you want this power to terminate prior to your death).

IF YOU WISH TO NAME SUCCESSOR AGENTS, INSERT THE NAMES AND ADDRESSES OF SUCH SUCCESSORS IN THE FOLLOWING PARAGRAPH:

5. If any agent named by me shall die, become legally disabled, incapacitated, or incompetent, or resign, refuse to act, or be unavailable, I name the following (each to act successively in the order named) as successors to such agent:

_____

_____

IF YOU WISH TO NAME A GUARDIAN OF YOUR PERSON IN THE EVENT A COURT DECIDES THAT ONE SHOULD BE APPOINTED, YOU MAY, BUT ARE NOT REQUIRED TO, DO SO BY INSERTING THE NAME OF SUCH GUARDIAN IN THE FOLLOWING PARAGRAPH. THE COURT WILL APPOINT THE PERSON NOMINATED BY YOU IF THE COURT FINDS THAT SUCH APPOINTMENT WILL SERVE YOUR BEST INTERESTS AND WELFARE. YOU MAY , BUT ARE NOT REQUIRED TO, NOMINATE AS YOUR GUARDIAN THE SAME PERSON NAMED IN THIS FORM AS YOUR AGENT.

      6.   If a guardian of my person is to be appointed, I nominate the following to serve as such guardian:

_____
(insert name and address of nominated guardian of the person)

      7.   I am fully informed as to all the contents of this form and understand the full import of this grant of powers to my agent.

      Signed_____(Principal)

The principal has had an opportunity to read the above form and has signed the above form in our presence. We, the undersigned, each being over 18 years of age, witness the principal's signature at the request and in the presence of the principal, and in the presence of each other, on the day and year above set out.

Witnesses: Addresses:

_____   _____

_____   _____

Additional witness required when health care agency is signed in a hospital or skilled nursing facility.

I hereby witness this health care agency and attest that I believe the principal to be of sound mind and to have made this health care agency willingly and voluntarily.

Witness:_____   Address:_____
        Attending Physician

YOU MAY, BUT ARE NOT REQUIRED TO, REQUEST YOUR AGENT AND SUCCESSOR AGENTS TO PROVIDE SPECIMEN SIGNATURES BELOW. IF YOU INCLUDE SPECIMEN SIGNATURES IN THIS POWER OF ATTORNEY, YOU MUST COMPLETE THE CERTIFICATION OPPOSITE THE SIGNATURES OF THE AGENTS.

Specimen signatures of agent   I certify that the signature of my agent and
and successor(s)   successor(s) is correct.

_____   _____
(Agent)   (Principal)

_____   _____
(Successor agent)   (Principal)

_____   _____
(Successor agent)   (Principal)

Advance Health-Care Directive

Explanation

You have the right to give instructions about your own health care. You also have the right to name someone else to make health-care decisions for you. This form lets you do either or both of these things. It also lets you express your wishes regarding the designation of your health-care provider. If you use this form, you may complete or modify all or any part of it. You are free to use a different form.

Part 1 of this form is a power of attorney for health care. Part 1 lets you name another individual as agent to make health-care decisions for you if you become incapable of making your own decisions or if you want someone else to make those decisions for you now even though you are still capable. You may name an alternate agent to act for you if your first choice is not willing, able, or reasonably available to make decisions for you. Unless related to you, your agent may not be an owner, operator, or employee of a health-care institution where you are receiving care.

Unless the form you sign limits the authority of your agent, your agent may make all health-care decisions for you. This form has a place for you to limit the authority of your agent. You need not limit the authority of your agent if you wish to rely on your agent for all health-care decisions that may have to be made. If you choose not to limit the authority of your agent, your agent will have the right to:

(1) Consent or refuse consent to any care, treatment, service, or procedure to maintain, diagnose, or otherwise affect a physical or mental condition;

(2) Select or discharge health-care providers and institutions;

(3) Approve or disapprove diagnostic tests, surgical procedures, programs of medication, and orders not to resuscitate; and

(4) Direct the provision, withholding, or withdrawal of artificial nutrition and hydration and all other forms of health care.

Part 2 of this form lets you give specific instructions about any aspect of your health care. Choices are provided for you to express your wishes regarding the provision, withholding, or withdrawal of treatment to keep you alive, including the provision of artificial nutrition and hydration, as well as the provision of pain relief medication. Space is provided for you to add to the choices you have made or for you to write out any additional wishes.

Part 4 of this form lets you designate a physician to have primary responsibility for your health care.
After completing this form, sign and date the form at the end and have the form witnessed by one of the two alternative methods listed below. Give a copy of the signed and completed form to your physician, to any other health-care providers you may have, to any health-care institution at which you are receiving care, and to any health-care agents you have named. You should talk to the person you have named as agent to make sure that he or she understands your wishes and is willing to take the responsibility.
You have the right to revoke this advance health-care directive or replace this form at any time.

PART 1
DURABLE POWER OF ATTORNEY FOR HEALTH-CARE DECISIONS

(1) DESIGNATION OF AGENT: I designate the following individual as my agent to make health-care decisions for me:

_____
(name of individual you choose as agent)

_____
(address)   (city)   (state)   (zip code)

_____
(home phone)   (work phone)

OPTIONAL: If I revoke my agent's authority or if my agent is not willing, able, or reasonably available to make a health-care decision for me, I designate as my first alternate agent:

_____
(name of individual you choose as first alternate agent)

_____
(address)   (city)   (state)   (zip code)

_____
(home phone)   (work phone)

OPTIONAL: If I revoke the authority of my agent and first alternate agent or if neither is willing, able, or reasonably available to make a health-care decision for me, I designate as my second alternate agent:

_____
(name of individual you choose as second alternate agent)

_____
(address)   (city)   (state)   (zip code)

_____
(home phone)   (work phone)

(2) AGENT'S AUTHORITY: My agent is authorized to make all health-care decisions for me, including decisions to provide, withhold, or withdraw artificial nutrition and hydration, and all other forms of health care to keep me alive, except as I state here:

_____
_____
(Add additional sheets if needed.)

(3) WHEN AGENT'S AUTHORITY BECOMES EFFECTIVE: My agent's authority becomes effective when my primary physician determines that I am unable to make my own health-care decisions unless I mark the following box. If I mark this box [ ], my agent's authority to make health-care decisions for me takes effect immediately.

(4) AGENT'S OBLIGATION: My agent shall make health-care decisions for me in accordance with this power of attorney for health care, any instructions I give in Part 2 of this form, and my other wishes to the extent known to my agent. To the extent my wishes are unknown, my agent shall make health-care decisions for me in accordance with what my agent determines to be in my best interest. In determining my best interest, my agent shall consider my personal values to the extent known to my agent.

(5) NOMINATION OF GUARDIAN: If a guardian needs to be appointed for me by a court, I nominate the agent designated in this form. If that agent is not willing, able, or reasonably available to act as guardian, I nominate the alternate agents whom I have named, in the order designated.

PART 2
INSTRUCTIONS FOR HEALTH CARE

If you are satisfied to allow your agent to determine what is best for you in making end-of-life decisions, you need not fill out this part of the form. If you do fill out this part of the form, you may strike any wording you do not want.

(6) END-OF-LIFE DECISIONS: I direct that my health-care providers and others involved in my care provide, withhold, or withdraw treatment in accordance with the choice I have marked below: (Check only one box.)

[ ] (a) Choice Not To Prolong Life

I do not want my life to be prolonged if (i) I have an incurable and irreversible condition that will result in my death within a relatively short time, (ii) I become unconscious and, to a reasonable degree of medical certainty, I will not regain consciousness, or (iii) the likely risks and burdens of treatment would outweigh the expected benefits, OR

[ ] (b) Choice To Prolong Life

I want my life to be prolonged as long as possible within the limits of generally accepted health-care standards.

(7) ARTIFICIAL NUTRITION AND HYDRATION: Artificial nutrition and hydration must be provided, withheld or withdrawn in accordance with the choice I have made in paragraph (6) unless I mark the following box. If I mark this box [ ], artificial nutrition and hydration must be provided regardless of my condition and regardless of the choice I have made in paragraph (6).

(8) RELIEF FROM PAIN: If I mark this box [ ], I direct that treatment to alleviate pain or discomfort should be provided to me even if it hastens my death.

(9) OTHER WISHES: (If you do not agree with any of the optional choices above and wish to write your own, or if you wish to add to the instructions you have given above, you may do so here.) I direct that:

_____

_____

(Add additional sheets if needed.)

PART 3
DONATION OF ORGANS AT DEATH (OPTIONAL)

(10) Upon my death: (mark applicable box)
[ ] (a) I give any needed organs, tissues, or parts, OR
[ ] (b) I give the following organs, tissues, or parts only _____
[ ] (c) My gift is for the following purposes (strike any of the following you do not want)
     (i) Transplant
     (ii) Therapy
     (iii) Research
     (iv) Education

PART 4
PRIMARY PHYSICIAN (OPTIONAL)

(11) I designate the following physician as my primary physician:

_____
(name of physician)

_____
(address)   (city)   (state)   (zip code)

_____
(phone)

OPTIONAL: If the physician I have designated above is not willing, able, or reasonably available to act as my primary physician, I designate the following physician as my primary physician:

_____
(name of physician)

_____
(address)   (city)   (state)   (zip code)

_____
(phone)

(12) EFFECT OF COPY: A copy of this form has the same effect as the original.

(13) SIGNATURES: Sign and date the form here:

_____
(date)   (sign your name)

_____
(address)   (print your name)

_____
(city)   (state)

(14) WITNESSES: This power of attorney will not be valid for making health-care decisions unless it is either (a) signed by two qualified adult witnesses who are personally known to you and who are present when you sign or acknowledge your signature; or (b) acknowledged before a notary public in the State.

ALTERNATIVE NO. 1

Witness

I declare under penalty of false swearing pursuant to section 710-1062, Hawaii Revised Statutes, that the principal is personally known to me, that the principal signed or acknowledged this power of attorney in my presence, that the principal appears to be of sound mind and under no duress, fraud, or undue influence, that I am not the person appointed as agent by this document, and that I am not a health-care provider, nor an employee of a health-care provider or facility. I am not related to the principal by blood, marriage, or adoption, and to the best of my knowledge, I am not entitled to any part of the estate of the principal upon the death of the principal under a will now existing or by operation of law.

(date)	(signature of witness)
(address)	(printed name of witness)
(city)	(state)

Witness

I declare under penalty of false swearing pursuant to section 710-1062, Hawaii Revised Statutes, that the principal is personally known to me, that the principal signed or acknowledged this power of attorney in my presence, that the principal appears to be of sound mind and under no duress, fraud, or undue influence, that I am not the person appointed as agent by this document, and that I am not a health-care provider, nor an employee of a health-care provider or facility.

(date)	(signature of witness)
(address)	(printed name of witness)
(city)	(state)

ALTERNATIVE NO. 2

State of Hawaii
County of _____

On this _____ day of _____, in the year _____, before me, _____ (insert name of notary public) appeared _____, personally known to me (or proved to me on the basis of satisfactory evidence) to be the person whose name is subscribed to this instrument, and acknowledged that he or she executed it.

Notary Seal

_____
(Signature of Notary Public)

LIVING WILL AND DURABLE POWER OF ATTORNEY FOR HEALTH CARE

Date of Directive: _____

Name of person executing Directive: _____

Address of person executing Directive: _____

A LIVING WILL
A Directive to Withhold or to Provide Treatment

1. Being of sound mind, I willfully and voluntarily make known my desire that my life shall not be prolonged artificially under the circumstances set forth below. This Directive shall only be effective if I am unable to communicate my instructions and:

a. I have an incurable injury, disease, illness or condition and two (2) medical doctors who have examined me have certified:

    1. That such injury, disease, illness or condition is terminal; and
    2. That the application of artificial life-sustaining procedures would serve only to prolong artificially my life; and
    3. That my death is imminent, whether or not artificial life-sustaining procedures are utilized; or

b. I have been diagnosed as being in a persistent vegetative state.

In such event, I direct that the following marked expression of my intent be followed, and that I receive any medical treatment or care that may be required to keep me free of pain or distress.

Check one box and initial the line after such box:

☐ I direct that all medical treatment, care and procedures necessary to restore my health, sustain my life, and to abolish or alleviate pain or distress be provided to me. Nutrition and hydration, whether artificial or nonartificial, shall not be withheld or withdrawn from me if I would likely die primarily from malnutrition or dehydration rather than from my injury, disease, illness or condition. _____

OR

☐ I direct that all medical treatment, care and procedures, including artificial life-sustaining procedures, be withheld or withdrawn, except that nutrition and hydration, whether artificial or nonartificial shall not be withheld or withdrawn from me if, as a result, I would likely die primarily from malnutrition or dehydration rather than from my injury, disease, illness or condition, as follows: (If none of the following boxes are checked and initialed, then both nutrition and hydration, of any nature, whether artificial or nonartificial, shall be administered.)

Check one box and initial the line after such box.

☐ Only hydration, of any nature, whether artificial or nonartificial, shall be administered; _____

☐ Only nutrition, of any nature, whether artificial or nonartificial, shall be administered; _____

☐ Both nutrition and hydration, of any nature, whether artificial or nonartificial shall be administered. _____

OR

_____ I direct that all medical treatment, care and procedures be withheld or withdrawn, including withdrawal of the administration of artificial nutrition and hydration.

2. This Directive shall be the final expression of my legal right to refuse or accept medical and surgical treatment, and I accept the consequences of such refusal or acceptance.

3. If I have been diagnosed as pregnant, this Directive shall have no force during the course of my pregnancy.

4. I understand the full importance of this Directive and am mentally competent to make this Directive. No participant in the making of this Directive or in its being carried into effect shall be held responsible in any way for complying with my directions.

A DURABLE POWER OF ATTORNEY FOR HEALTH CARE

1. DESIGNATION OF HEALTH CARE AGENT. None of the following may be designated as your agent: (1) your treating health care provider; (2) a nonrelative employee of your treating health care provider; (3) an operator of a community care facility; or (4) a nonrelative employee of an operator of a community care facility. If the agent or an alternate agent designated in this Directive is my spouse, and our marriage is thereafter dissolved, such designation shall be thereupon revoked.

I do hereby designate and appoint the following individual as my attorney in fact (agent) to make health care decisions for me as authorized in this Directive. (Insert name, address and telephone number of one individual only as your agent to make health care decisions for you.)

Name of Health Care Agent: _____
Address of Health Care Agent: _____
Telephone Number of Health Care Agent: _____

For the purposes of this Directive, "health care decision" means consent, refusal of consent, or withdrawal of consent to any care, treatment, service or procedure to maintain, diagnose or treat an individual's physical condition.

2. CREATION OF DURABLE POWER OF ATTORNEY FOR HEALTH CARE. By this portion of this Directive, I create a durable power of attorney for health care. This power of attorney shall not be affected by my subsequent incapacity. This power shall be effective only when I am unable to communicate rationally.

3. GENERAL STATEMENT OF AUTHORITY GRANTED. Subject to any limitations in this Directive, including as set forth in paragraph 2 immediately above, I hereby grant to my agent full power and authority to make health care decisions for me to the same extent that I could make such decisions for myself if I had the capacity to do so. In exercising this authority, my agent shall make health care decisions that are consistent with my desires as stated in this Directive or otherwise made known to my agent including, but not limited to, my desires concerning obtaining or refusing or withdrawing life-prolonging care, treatment, services and procedures, including such desires set forth in a living will or similar document executed by me, if any. (If you want to limit the authority of your agent to make health care decisions for you, you can state the limitations in paragraph 4 ("Statement of Desires, Special Provisions, and Limitations") below. (You can indicate your desires by including a statement of your desires in the same paragraph.)

4. STATEMENT OF DESIRES, SPECIAL PROVISIONS, AND LIMITATIONS. (Your agent must make health care decisions that are consistent with your known desires. You can, but are not required to, state your desires in the space provided below. You should consider whether you want to include a statement of your desires concerning life-prolonging care, treatment, services and procedures. You can also include a statement of your desires concerning other matters

relating to your health care, including a list of one or more persons whom you designate to be able to receive medical information about you and/or to be allowed to visit you in a medical institution. You can also make your desires known to your agent by discussing your desires with your agent or by some other means. If there are any types of treatment that you do not want to be used, you should state them in the space below. If you want to limit in any other way the authority given your agent by this Directive, you should state the limits in the space below. If you do not state any limits, your agent will have broad powers to make health care decisions for you, except to the extent that there are limits provided by law.) In exercising the authority under this durable power of attorney for health care, my agent shall act consistently with my desires as stated below and is subject to the special provisions and limitations stated in a living will or similar document executed by me, if any. Additional statement of desires, special provisions, and limitations:

_____

_____

(You may attach additional pages or documents if you need more space to complete your statement.)

5. INSPECTION AND DISCLOSURE OF INFORMATION RELATING TO MY PHYSICAL OR MENTAL HEALTH.

A. General Grant of Power and Authority. Subject to any limitations in this Directive, my agent has the power and authority to do all of the following: (1) Request, review and receive any information, verbal or written, regarding my physical or mental health including, but not limited to, medical and hospital records; (2) Execute on my behalf any releases or other documents that may be required in order to obtain this information; (3) Consent to the disclosure of this information; and (4) Consent to the donation of any of my organs for medical purposes. (If you want to limit the authority of your agent to receive and disclose information relating to your health, you must state the limitations in paragraph 4 ("Statement of Desires, Special Provisions, and Limitations") above.)

B. HIPAA Release Authority. My agent shall be treated as I would be with respect to my rights regarding the use and disclosure of my individually identifiable health information or other medical records. This release authority applies to any information governed by the Health Insurance Portability and Accountability Act of 1996 (HIPAA), 42 U.S.C. 1320d and 45 CFR 160 through 164. I authorize any physician, health care professional, dentist, health plan, hospital, clinic, laboratory, pharmacy, or other covered health care provider, any insurance company, and the Medical Information Bureau, Inc. or other health care clearinghouse that has provided treatment or services to me, or that has paid for or is seeking payment from me for such services, to give, disclose and release to my agent, without restriction, all of my individually identifiable health information and medical records regarding any past, present or future medical or mental health condition, including all information relating to the diagnosis of HIV/AIDS, sexually transmitted diseases, mental illness, and drug or alcohol abuse. The authority given my agent shall supersede any other agreement that I may have made with my health care providers to restrict access to or disclosure of my individually identifiable health information. The authority given my agent has no expiration date and shall expire only in the event that I revoke the authority in writing and deliver it to my health care provider.

6. SIGNING DOCUMENTS, WAIVERS AND RELEASES. Where necessary to implement the health care decisions that my agent is authorized by this Directive to make, my agent has the power and authority to execute on my behalf all of the following: (a) Documents titled, or purporting to be, a "Refusal to Permit Treatment" and/or a "Leaving Hospital Against Medical Advice"; and (b) Any necessary waiver or release from liability required by a hospital or physician.

7. DESIGNATION OF ALTERNATE AGENTS. (You are not required to designate any alternate agents but you may do so. Any alternate agent you designate will be able to make the same health care decisions as the agent you designated in paragraph 1 above, in the event that agent

is unable or ineligible to act as your agent. If an alternate agent you designate is your spouse, he or she becomes ineligible to act as your agent if your marriage is thereafter dissolved.) If the person designated as my agent in paragraph 1 is not available or becomes ineligible to act as my agent to make a health care decision for me or loses the mental capacity to make health care decisions for me, or if I revoke that person's appointment or authority to act as my agent to make health care decisions for me, then I designate and appoint the following persons to serve as my agent to make health care decisions for me as authorized in this Directive, such persons to serve in the order listed below:

A. First Alternate Agent:
Name _____
Address _____
Telephone Number _____

B. Second Alternate Agent:
Name _____
Address _____
Telephone Number _____

C. Third Alternate Agent:
Name _____
Address _____
Telephone Number _____

8. PRIOR DESIGNATIONS REVOKED. I revoke any prior durable power of attorney for health care. DATE AND SIGNATURE OF PRINCIPAL. (You must date and sign this Living Will and Durable Power of Attorney for Health Care.)

I sign my name to this Statutory Form Living Will and Durable Power of Attorney for Health Care on the date set forth at the beginning of this Form at _____ (City, State).

_____
Signature

Illinois Statutory Short Form Power of Attorney for Health Care

(NOTICE: THE PURPOSE OF THIS POWER OF ATTORNEY IS TO GIVE THE PERSON YOU DESIGNATE (YOUR "AGENT") BROAD POWERS TO MAKE HEALTH CARE DECISIONS FOR YOU, INCLUDING POWER TO REQUIRE, CONSENT TO OR WITHDRAW ANY TYPE OF PERSONAL CARE OR MEDICAL TREATMENT FOR ANY PHYSICAL OR MENTAL CONDITION AND TO ADMIT YOU TO OR DISCHARGE YOU FROM ANY HOSPITAL, HOME OR OTHER INSTITUTION. THIS FORM DOES NOT IMPOSE A DUTY ON YOUR AGENT TO EXERCISE GRANTED POWERS; BUT WHEN POWERS ARE EXERCISED, YOUR AGENT WILL HAVE TO USE DUE CARE TO ACT FOR YOUR BENEFIT AND IN ACCORDANCE WITH THIS FORM AND KEEP A RECORD OF RECEIPTS, DISBURSEMENTS AND SIGNIFICANT ACTIONS TAKEN AS AGENT. A COURT CAN TAKE AWAY THE POWERS OF YOUR AGENT IF IT FINDS THE AGENT IS NOT ACTING PROPERLY. YOU MAY NAME SUCCESSOR AGENTS UNDER THIS FORM BUT NOT CO-AGENTS, AND NO HEALTH CARE PROVIDER MAY BE NAMED. UNLESS YOU EXPRESSLY LIMIT THE DURATION OF THIS POWER IN THE MANNER PROVIDED BELOW, UNTIL YOU REVOKE THIS POWER OR A COURT ACTING ON YOUR BEHALF TERMINATES IT, YOUR AGENT MAY EXERCISE THE POWERS GIVEN HERE THROUGHOUT YOUR LIFETIME, EVEN AFTER YOU BECOME DISABLED. THE POWERS YOU GIVE YOUR AGENT, YOUR RIGHT TO REVOKE THOSE POWERS AND THE PENALTIES FOR VIOLATING THE LAW ARE EXPLAINED MORE FULLY IN SECTIONS 4-5, 4-6, 4-9 AND 4-10(b) OF THE ILLINOIS "POWERS OF ATTORNEY FOR HEALTH CARE LAW" OF WHICH THIS FORM IS A PART (SEE ATTACHED). THAT LAW EXPRESSLY PERMITS THE USE OF ANY DIFFERENT FORM OF POWER OF ATTORNEY YOU MAY DESIRE. IF THERE IS ANYTHING ABOUT THIS FORM THAT YOU DO NOT UNDERSTAND, YOU SHOULD ASK A LAWYER TO EXPLAIN IT TO YOU.)

POWER OF ATTORNEY made this _____ day of _____

(month)   (year)

1.   I, _____

_____

_____,

(insert name and address of principal)

hereby appoint:

_____

_____

(insert name and address of agent)

as my attorney-in-fact (my "agent") to act for me and in my name (in any way I could act in person) to make any and all decisions for me concerning my personal care, medical treatment, hospitalization and health care and to require, withhold or withdraw any type of medical treatment or procedure, even though my death may ensue. My agent shall have the same access to my medical records that I have, including the right to disclose the contents to others. My agent shall also have full power to make a disposition of any part or all of my body for medical purposes, authorize an autopsy and direct the disposition of my remains.

(THE ABOVE GRANT OF POWER IS INTENDED TO BE AS BROAD AS POSSIBLE SO THAT YOUR AGENT WILL HAVE AUTHORITY TO MAKE ANY DECISION YOU COULD MAKE TO OBTAIN OR TERMINATE ANY TYPE OF HEALTH CARE, INCLUDING WITHDRAWAL OF FOOD AND WATER AND OTHER LIFE-SUSTAINING MEASURES, IF YOUR AGENT BELIEVES SUCH ACTION WOULD BE CONSISTENT WITH YOUR INTENT AND DESIRES. IF YOU WISH TO LIMIT THE SCOPE OF YOUR AGENT'S POWERS OR PRESCRIBE SPECIAL RULES OR LIMIT THE POWER TO MAKE AN ANATOMICAL GIFT, AUTHORIZE AUTOPSY OR DISPOSE OF REMAINS, YOU MAY DO SO IN THE FOLLOWING PARAGRAPHS.)

2.   The powers granted above shall not include the following powers or shall be subject to the following rules or limitations (here you may include any specific limitations you deem appropriate, such as: your own definition of when life-sustaining measures should be withheld; a direction to continue food and fluids or life-sustaining treatment in all events; or instructions to refuse any specific types of treatment that are inconsistent with your religious beliefs or unacceptable to you for any other reason, such as blood transfusion, electro-convulsive therapy, amputation, psychosurgery, voluntary admission to a mental institution, etc.):

_____

_____

(THE SUBJECT OF LIFE-SUSTAINING TREATMENT IS OF PARTICULAR IMPORTANCE. FOR YOUR CONVENIENCE IN DEALING WITH THAT SUBJECT, SOME GENERAL STATEMENTS CONCERNING THE WITHHOLDING OR REMOVAL OF LIFE-SUSTAINING TREATMENT ARE SET FORTH BELOW. IF YOU AGREE WITH ONE OF THESE STATEMENTS, YOU MAY INITIAL THAT STATEMENT; BUT DO NOT INITIAL MORE THAN ONE:)

I do not want my life to be prolonged nor do I want life-sustaining treatment to be provided or continued if my agent believes the burdens of the treatment outweigh the expected benefits. I want my agent to consider the relief of suffering, the expense involved and the quality as well as the possible extension of my life in making decisions concerning life sustaining treatment.

Initialed _____

I want my life to be prolonged and I want life-sustaining treatment to be provided or continued unless I am in a coma which my attending physician believes to be irreversible, in accordance with reasonable medical standards at the time of reference. If and when I have suffered irreversible coma, I want life-sustaining treatment to be withheld or discontinued.

Initialed _____

I want my life to be prolonged to the greatest extent possible without regard to my condition, the chances I have for recovery or the cost of the procedures.

Initialed _____

(THIS POWER OF ATTORNEY MAY BE AMENDED OR REVOKED BY YOU IN THE MANNER PROVIDED IN SECTION 4-6 OF THE ILLINOIS "POWERS OF ATTORNEY FOR HEALTH CARE LAW" (SEE THE END OF THIS FORM). ABSENT AMENDMENT OR REVOCATION, THE AUTHORITY GRANTED IN THIS POWER OF ATTORNEY WILL BECOME EFFECTIVE AT THE TIME THIS POWER IS SIGNED AND WILL CONTINUE UNTIL YOUR DEATH, AND BEYOND IF ANATOMICAL GIFT, AUTOPSY OR DISPOSITION OF REMAINS IS AUTHORIZED, UNLESS A LIMITATION ON THE BEGINNING DATE OR DURATION IS MADE BY INITIALING AND COMPLETING EITHER OR BOTH OF THE FOLLOWING:)

3. (   ) This power of attorney shall become effective on _____ _____ (insert a future date or event during your lifetime, such as court determination of your disability, when you want this power to first take effect).

4. (   ) This power of attorney shall terminate on _____ _____ (insert a future date or event, such as court determination of your disability, when you want this power to terminate prior to your death).

(IF YOU WISH TO NAME SUCCESSOR AGENTS, INSERT THE NAMES AND ADDRESSES OF SUCH SUCCESSORS IN THE FOLLOWING PARAGRAPH.)

5.   If any agent named by me shall die, become incompetent, resign, refuse to accept the office of agent or be unavailable, I name the following (each to act alone and successively, in the order named) as successors to such agent:_____

_____

For purposes of this paragraph 5, a person shall be considered to be incompetent if and while the person is a minor or an adjudicated incompetent or disabled person or the person is unable to give prompt and intelligent consideration to health care matters, as certified by a licensed physician.

(IF YOU WISH TO NAME YOUR AGENT AS GUARDIAN OF YOUR PERSON, IN THE EVENT A COURT DECIDES THAT ONE SHOULD BE APPOINTED, YOU MAY, BUT ARE NOT REQUIRED TO, DO SO BY RETAINING THE FOLLOWING PARAGRAPH. THE COURT WILL APPOINT YOUR AGENT IF THE COURT FINDS THAT SUCH APPOINTMENT WILL SERVE YOUR BEST INTERESTS AND WELFARE. STRIKE OUT PARAGRAPH 6 IF YOU DO NOT WANT YOUR AGENT TO ACT AS GUARDIAN.)

6.   If a guardian of my person is to be appointed, I nominate the agent acting under this power of attorney as such guardian, to serve without bond or security. (insert name and address of nominated guardian of the person)

7.   I am fully informed as to all the contents of this form and understand the full import of this grant of powers to my agent.

Signed _____
                                                              (principal)

The principal has had an opportunity to read the above form and has signed the form or acknowledged his or her signature or mark on the form in my presence.

_____   Residing at_____
                   (witness)
                                                           _____

(YOU MAY, BUT ARE NOT REQUIRED TO, REQUEST YOUR AGENT AND SUCCESSOR AGENTS TO PROVIDE SPECIMEN SIGNATURES BELOW. IF YOU INCLUDE SPECIMEN SIGNATURES IN THIS POWER OF ATTORNEY YOU MUST COMPLETE THE CERTIFICATION OPPOSITE THE SIGNATURES OF THE AGENTS.)

Specimen signatures of agent   I certify that the signatures of my agent (and
(and successors)   successors) are correct.

_____   _____
                   (agent)   (principal)

_____   _____
             (successor agent)   (principal)

_____   _____
             (successor agent)   (principal)

Illinois Statutory Short Form Power of Attorney for Health Care Law

§ 4-5.   Limitations on health care agencies. Neither the attending physician nor any other health care provider may act as agent under a health care agency; however, a person who is not administering health care to the patient may act as health care agent for the patient even though the person is a physician or otherwise licensed, certified, authorized, or permitted by law to administer health care in the ordinary course of business or the practice of a profession.

§4-6. Revocation and amendment of health care agencies.
(a)   Every health care agency may be revoked by the principal at any time, without regard to the principal's mental or physical condition, by any of the following methods:
1.   By being obliterated, burnt, torn or otherwise destroyed or defaced in a manner indicating intention to revoke;
2.   By a written revocation of the agency signed and dated by the principal or person acting at the direction of the principal; or
3.   By an oral or any other expression of the intent to revoke th agency in the presence of a witness 18 years of age or older who signs and dates a writing confirming that such expression of intent was made.
(b)   Every health care agency may be amended at any time by a written amendment signed and dated by the principal or person acting at the direction of the principal.
(c)   Any person, other than the agent, to whom a revocation or amendment is communicated or delivered shall make all reasonable efforts to inform the agent of that fact as promptly as possible.

§4-9.   Penalties. All persons shall be subject to the following sanctions in relation to health care agencies, in addition to all other sanctions applicable under any other law or rule of professional conduct:
(a)   Any person shall be civilly liable who, without the principal's consent, wilfully conceals, cancels or alters a health care agency or any amendment of revocation of the agency or who falsifies or forges a health care agency, amendment or revocation.
(b)   A person who falsifies or forges a health care agency or wilfully conceals or withholds personal knowledge of an amendment or revocation of a health care agency with the intent to cause a withholding or withdrawal of life-sustaining or death-delaying procedures contrary to the intent of the principal and thereby, because of such act, directly causes life-sustaining or death-delaying procedures to be withheld or withdrawn and death to the patient to be hastened shall be subject to prosecution for involuntary manslaughter.
(c)   Any person who requires or prevents execution of a health care agency as a condition of insuring or providing any type of health care services to the patient shall be civilly liable and guilty of a Class A misdemeanor.

§ 4-10(b).   The statutory short form power of attorney for health care (the "statutory health care power") authorizes the agent to make any and all health care decisions on behalf of the principal which the principal could make if present and under no disability, subject to any limitations on the granted powers that appear on the face of the form, to be exercised in such manner as the agent deems consistent with the intent and desires of the principal. The agent will be under no duty to exercise granted powers or to assume control of or responsibility for the principal's health care; but when granted powers are exercised, the agent will be required to use due care to act for the benefit of the principal in accordance with the terms of the statutory health care power and will be liable for negligent exercise. The agent may act in person or through others reasonably employed by the agent for that purpose but may not delegate authority to make health care decisions. The agent may sign and deliver all instruments, negotiate and enter into all agreements and do all other acts reasonably necessary to implement the exercise of the powers granted to the agent. Without limiting the generality of the foregoing, the statutory health care power shall include the following powers, subject to any limitations appearing on the face of the form:

(1)   The agent is authorized to give consent to and authorize or refuse, or to withhold or withdraw consent to, any and all types of medical care, treatment or procedures relating to the physical or mental health of the principal, including any medication program, surgical procedures, life-sustaining treatment or provision of food and fluids for the principal.

(2)   The agent is authorized to admit the principal to or discharge the principal from any and all types of hospitals, institutions, homes, residential or nursing facilities, treatment centers and other health care institutions providing personal care or treatment for any type of physical or mental condition. The agent shall have the same right to visit the principal in the hospital or other institution as is granted to a spouse or adult child of the principal, any rule of the institution to the contrary notwithstanding.

(3)   The agent is authorized to contract for any and all types of health care services and facilities in the name of and on behalf of the principal and to bind the principal to pay for all such services and facilities, and to have an exercise those powers over the principal's property as are authorized under the statutory property power, to the extent the agent deems necessary to pay health care costs; and the agent shall not be personally liable for any services or care contracted for on behalf of the principal.

(4)   At the principal's expense and subject to reasonable rules of the health care provider to prevent disruption of the principal's health care, the agent shall have the same right th principal has to examine and copy and consent to disclosure of all the principal's medical records that the agent deems relevant to the exercise of the agent's powers, whether the records relate to mental health or any other medical condition and whether they are in the possession of or maintained by any physician, psychiatrist, psychologist, therapist, hospital, nursing home or other health care provider.

(5)   The agent is authorized: to direct that an autopsy be made pursuant to Section 2 of "An Act in relation to autopsy of dead bodies," approved August 13, 1965, including all amendments; to make a disposition of any part or all of the principal's body pursuant to the Uniform Anatomical Gift Act, as now or hereafter amended; and to direct the disposition of the principal's remains.

LIVING WILL DECLARATION

Declaration made this _____ day of _____ (month, year). I, _____, being at least eighteen (18) years of age and of sound mind, willfully, and voluntarily make known my desires that my dying shall not be artificially prolonged under the circumstances set forth below, and I declare:

If at any time my attending physician certifies in writing that: (1) I have an incurable injury, disease, or illness; (2) my death will occur within a short time; and (3) the use of life prolonging procedures would serve only to artificially prolong the dying process, I direct that such procedures be withheld or withdrawn, and that I be permitted to die naturally with only the performance or provision of any medical procedure or medication necessary to provide me with comfort care or to alleviate pain, and, if I have so indicated below, the provision of artificially supplied nutrition and hydration. (Indicate your choice by initialing or making your mark before signing this declaration):

_____ I wish to receive artificially supplied nutrition and hydration, even if the effort to sustain life is futile or excessively burdensome to me.

_____ I do not wish to receive artificially supplied nutrition and hydration, if the effort to sustain life is futile or excessively burdensome to me.

_____ I intentionally make no decision concerning artificially supplied nutrition and hydration, leaving the decision to my health care representative appointed under IC 16-36-1-7 or my attorney in fact with health care powers under IC 30-5-5.

In the absence of my ability to give directions regarding the use of life prolonging procedures, it is my intention that this declaration be honored by my family and physician as the final expression of my legal right to refuse medical or surgical treatment and accept the consequences of the refusal.

I understand the full import of this declaration.

Signed _____

_____
City, County, and State of Residence

The declarant has been personally known to me, and I believe (him/her) to be of sound mind. I did not sign the declarant's signature above for or at the direction of the declarant. I am not a parent, spouse, or child of the declarant. I am not entitled to any part of the declarant's estate or directly financially responsible for the declarant's medical care. I am competent and at least eighteen (18) years of age.

Witness _____   Date _____

Witness _____   Date _____

LIFE PROLONGING PROCEDURES DECLARATION

Declaration made this _____ day of _____ (month, year). I, _____, being at least eighteen (18) years of age and of sound mind, willfully and voluntarily make known my desire that if at any time I have an incurable injury, disease, or illness determined to be a terminal condition I request the use of life prolonging procedures that would extend my life. This includes appropriate nutrition and hydration, the administration of medication, and the performance of all other medical procedures necessary to extend my life, to provide comfort care, or to alleviate pain.

In the absence of my ability to give directions regarding the use of life prolonging procedures, it is my intention that this declaration be honored by my family and physician as the final expression of my legal right to request medical or surgical treatment and accept the consequences of the request.

I understand the full import of this declaration.

Signed _____

_____
City, County, and State of Residence

The declarant has been personally known to me, and I believe (him/her) to be of sound mind. I am competent and at least eighteen (18) years of age.

Witness_____ Date_____

Witness_____ Date_____

Living Will

If I should have an incurable or irreversible condition that will result either in death within a relatively short period of time or a state of permanent unconsciousness from which, to a reasonable degree of medical certainty, there can be no recovery, it is my desire that my life not be prolonged by the administration of life-sustaining procedures. If I am unable to participate in my health care decisions, I direct my attending physician to withhold or withdraw life-sustaining procedures that merely prolong the dying process and are not necessary to my comfort or freedom from pain.

Date _____

_____
Signature

Witness: _____

Witness: _____

Durable Power of Attorney for Health Care

I hereby designate _____ as my attorney in fact (my agent) and give to my agent the power to make health care decisions for me. this power exists only when I am unable, in the judgment of my attending physician, to make those health care decisions. The attorney in fact must act consistently with my desires as stated in this document or otherwise made known.

Except as otherwise specified in this document, this document gives my agent the power, where otherwise consistent with the law to this state, to consent to my physician not giving health care or stopping health care which is necessary to keep me alive.

This document gives my agent power to make health care decisions on my behalf, including to consent, to refuse to consent, or to withdraw consent to the provision of any care, treatment, service, or procedure to maintain, diagnose, or treat a physical or mental condition. This power is subject to any statement of my desires and any limitations included in this document.

My agent has the right to examine my medical records and to consent to disclosure of such records.

The powers granted by this document are subject to the following instructions and limitations (if none, type in "none"): _____
_____
_____

In the event my designated agent is unable or unwilling to serve, I designate the following alternative attorneys in fact (agents), to serve in the order stated below:

First Alternative Agent: _____

Second Alternative Agent: _____

Signature: _____

DECLARATION

Declaration made this _____ day of _____ (month, year). I, _____, being of sound mind, willfully and voluntarily make known my desire that my dying shall not be artificially prolonged under the circumstances set forth below, do hereby declare:

If at any time I should have an incurable injury, disease, or illness certified to be a terminal condition by two physicians who have personally examined me, one of whom shall be my attending physician, and the physicians have determined that my death will occur whether or not life-sustaining procedures are utilized and where the application of life-sustaining procedures would serve only to artificially prolong the dying process, I direct that such procedures be withheld or withdrawn, and that I be permitted to die naturally with only the administration of medication or the performance of any medical procedure deemed necessary to provide me with comfort care.

In the absence of my ability to give directions regarding the use of such life-sustaining procedures, it is my intention that this declaration shall be honored by my family and physician(s) as the final expression of my legal right to refuse medical or surgical treatment and accept the consequences from such refusal.

I understand the full import of this declaration and I am emotionally and mentally competent to make this declaration.

Signed _____

City, County and State of Residence _____

The declarant has been personally known to me and I believe the declarant to be of sound mind. I did not sign the declarant's signature above for or at the direction of the declarant. I am not related to the declarant by blood or marriage, entitled to any portion of the estate of the declarant according to the laws of intestate succession or under any will of declarant or codicil thereto, or directly financially responsible for declarant's medical care.

Witness _____

Witness _____

(OR)

STATE OF _____)

_____ss.

COUNTY OF _____)

This instrument was acknowledged before me on _____ (date) by _____ (name of person).

_____
(Signature of notary public)

(Seal, if any)

My appointment expires: _____

Durable Power of Attorney for Health Care Decisions

I, _____ , designate and appoint:

Name _____

Address: _____

_____

Telephone Number: _____

to be my agent for health care decisions and pursuant to the language stated below, on my behalf to:

(1)   consent, refuse consent, or withdraw consent to any care, treatment, service or procedure to maintain, diagnose or treat a physical or mental condition, and to make decisions about organ donation, autopsy and disposition of the body;

(2)   make all necessary arrangements at any hospital, psychiatric hospital or psychiatric treatment facility, hospice, nursing home or similar institution; to employ or discharge health care personnel to include physicians, psychiatrists, psychologists, dentists, nurses, therapists or any other person who is licensed, certified or otherwise authorized or permitted by the laws of this state to administer health care as the agent shall deem necessary for my physical, mental; and emotional well being; and

(3)   request, receive and review any information, verbal or written, regarding my personal affairs or physical or mental health including medical and hospital records and to execute any releases of other documents that may be required in order to obtain such information.

In exercising the grant of authority set forth above my agent for health care decisions shall:

_____

_____

_____

(Here may be inserted any special instructions or statement of the principal's desires to be followed by the agent in exercising the authority granted).

Limitations of Authority

(1)   The powers of the agent herein shall be limited to the extent set out in writing in this durable power of attorney for health care decisions, and shall not include the power to revoke or invalidate any previously existing declaration made in accordance with the natural death act.

(2)   The agent shall be prohibited from authorizing consent for the following items:

_____

(3)   This durable power of attorney for health care decisions shall be subject to the additional following limitations:

_____

_____

Effective Time

This power of attorney for health care decisions shall become effective (check one):

☐   immediately and shall not be affected by my subsequent disability or incapacity.

☐   upon the occurrence of my disability or incapacity.

Revocation

Any durable power of attorney for health care decisions I have previously made is hereby revoked.

This durable power of attorney for health care decisions shall be revoked (check one):

□   by an instrument in writing executed, witnessed or acknowledged in the same manner as required herein.

□   _____

(set out another manner of revocation, if desired.)

Execution

Executed this _____, at _____, Kansas.

_____

Principal

     This document must be: (1) witnessed by two individuals of lawful age who are not the agent, not related to the principal by blood, marriage or adoption, not entitled to any portion of the principal's estate and not financially responsible for principal's health care; OR (2) acknowledged by a notary public.

_____   _____

     Witness   Witness

_____   _____

     Address   Address

(OR)

STATE OF _____)

                                SS.

COUNTY OF _____)

     This instrument was acknowledged before me on _____, by

_____.

_____

Signature of notary public

(Seal, if any)   My appointment expires: _____

Living Will Directive

My wishes regarding life-prolonging treatment and artificially provided nutrition and hydration to be provided to me if I no longer have decisional capacity, have a terminal condition, or become permanently unconscious have been indicated by checking and initialing the appropriate lines below. By checking and initialing the appropriate lines, I specifically:

_____   Designate _____ as my health care surrogate(s) to make health care decisions for me in accordance with this directive when I no longer have decisional capacity. If _____ refuses or is not able to act for me, I designate _____ as my health care surrogate(s).

Any prior designation is revoked.

If I do not designate a surrogate, the following are my directions to my attending physician. If I have designated a surrogate, my surrogate shall comply with my wishes as indicated below:

_____   Direct that treatment be withheld or withdrawn, and that I be permitted to die naturally with only the administration of medication or the performance of any medical treatment deemed necessary to alleviate pain.

_____   DO NOT authorize that life-prolonging treatment be withheld or withdrawn.

_____   Authorize the withholding or withdrawal of artificially provided food, water, or other artificially provided nourishment or fluids.

_____   DO NOT authorize the withholding or withdrawal of artificially provided food, water, or other artificially provided nourishment or fluids.

_____   Authorize my surrogate, designated above, to withhold or withdraw artificially provided nourishment or fluids, or other treatment if the surrogate determines that withholding or withdrawing is in my best interest; but I do not mandate that withholding or withdrawing.

_____   Authorize the giving of all or any part of my body upon death for any purpose specified in KRS 311.185.

_____   DO NOT authorize the giving of all or any part of my body upon death.

In the absence of my ability to give direction regarding the use of life-prolonging treatment and artificially provided nutrition and hydration, it is my intention that this directive shall be honored by my attending physician, my family, and any surrogate designated pursuant to this directive as the final expression of my legal right to refuse medical or surgical treatment and I accept the consequences of the refusal.

If I have been diagnosed as pregnant and that diagnosis is known to my attending physician, this directive shall have no force or effect during the course of my pregnancy.

I understand the full import of this directive and I am emotionally and mentally competent to make this directive.

Signed this _____ day of _____, 200____ .

_____
Signature

_____
Address

In our joint presence, the grantor, who is of sound mind and eighteen (18) years of age, or older, voluntarily dated and signed this writing or directed it to be dated and signed for the grantor.

_____   _____
Signature of witness   Signature of witness

_____   _____
Address   Address

OR

STATE OF KENTUCKY   )

_____ COUNTY)

Before me, the undersigned authority, came the grantor who is of sound mind and eighteen (18) years of age, or older, and acknowledged that he voluntarily dated and signed this writing or directed it to be signed and dated as above.

Done this _____ day of _____, 200____ .

_____
Signature of Notary Public or other officer

Date commission expires: _____

Execution of this document restricts withholding and withdrawing of some medical procedures. Consult Kentucky Revised Statutes or your attorney.

DECLARATION

Declaration made this _____ day of _____, _____ (month, year).

I, _____, being of sound mind, willfully and voluntarily make known my desire that my dying shall not be artificially prolonged under the circumstances set forth below and do hereby declare:

If at any time I should have an incurable injury, disease or illness, or be in a continual profound comatose state with no reasonable chance of recovery, certified to be a terminal and irreversible condition by two physicians who have personally examined me, one of whom shall be my attending physician, and the physicians have determined that my death will occur whether or not life-sustaining procedures are utilized and where the application of life-sustaining procedure would serve only to prolong artificially the dying process, I direct (initial one only):

_____ That all life-sustaining procedures, including nutrition and hydration, be withheld or withdrawn so that food and water will not be administered invasively.

_____ That life-sustaining procedures, except nutrition and hydration, be withheld or withdrawn so that food and water can be administered invasively.

I further direct that I be permitted to die naturally with only the administration of medication or the performance of any medical procedure deemed necessary to provide me with comfort care.

In the absence of my ability to give directions regarding the use of such life-sustaining procedures, it is my intention that this declaration shall be honored by my family and physician(s) as the final expression of my legal right to refuse medical or surgical treatment and accept the consequences from such refusal.

I understand the full import of this declaration and I am emotionally and mentally competent to make this declaration.

Signed _____

City, Parish, and State of Residence _____

The declarant has been personally known to me and I believe him or her to be of sound mind.

Witness _____

Witness _____

Advance Health-Care Directive

Explanation

You have the right to give instructions about your own health care. You also have the right to name someone else to make health-care decisions for you. This form lets you do either or both of these things. It also lets you express your wishes regarding donation of organs and the designation of your primary physician. If you use this form, you may complete or modify all or any part of it. You are free to use a different form.

Part 1 of this form is a power of attorney for health care. Part 1 lets you name another individual as agent to make health-care decisions for you if you become incapable of making your own decisions or if you want someone else to make those decisions for you now even though you are still capable. You may also name an alternate agent to act for you if your first choice is not willing, able or reasonably available to make decisions for you. Unless related to you, your agent may not be an owner, operator or employee of a residential long-term health-care institution at which you are receiving care.

Unless the form you sign limits the authority of your agent, your agent may make all health-care decisions for you. This form has a place for you to limit the authority of your agent. You need not limit the authority of your agent if you wish to rely on your agent for all health-care decisions that may have to be made. If you choose not to limit the authority of your agent, your agent will have the right to:

(a)   Consent or refuse consent to any care, treatment, service or procedure to maintain, diagnose or otherwise affect a physical or mental condition;

(b)   Select or discharge health-care providers and institutions;

(c)   Approve or disapprove diagnostic tests, surgical procedures, programs of medication and orders not to resuscitate; and

(d)   Direct the provision, withholding or withdrawal of artificial nutrition and hydration and all other forms of health care, including life-sustaining treatment.

Part 2 of this form lets you give specific instructions about any aspect of your health care. Choices are provided for you to express your wishes regarding the provision, withholding or withdrawal of treatment to keep you alive, including the provision of artificial nutrition and hydration, as well as the provision of pain relief. Space is also provided for you to add to the choices you have made or for you to write out any additional wishes.

Part 3 of this form lets you express an intention to donate your bodily organs and tissues following your death.

Part 4 of this form lets you designate a physician to have primary responsibility for your health care.

After completing this form, sign and date the form at the end. You must have 2 other individuals sign as witnesses. Give a copy of the signed and completed form to your physician, to any other health-care providers you may have, to any health-care institution at which you are receiving care and to any health-care agents you have named. You should talk to the person you have named as agent to make sure that he or she understands your wishes and is willing to take the responsibility.

You have the right to revoke this advance health-care directive or replace this form at any time.

*   *   *   *   *   *   *   *   *   *   *   *   *   *   *   *   *   *   *   *

PART 1. POWER OF ATTORNEY FOR HEALTH CARE

(1)   DESIGNATION OF AGENT: I designate the following individual as my agent to make health-care decisions for me:

_____
(name of individual you choose as agent)

_____
(address)   (city)   (state)   (zip code)

_____
(home phone)   (work phone)

OPTIONAL: If I revoke my agent's authority or if my agent is not willing, able or reasonably available to make a health-care decision for me, I designate as my first alternate agent:

_____
(name of individual you choose as first alternate agent)

_____
(address)   (city)   (state)   (zip code)

_____
(home phone)   (work phone)

OPTIONAL: If I revoke the authority of my agent and first alternate agent or if neither is willing, able or reasonably available to make a health-care decision for me, I designate as my second alternate agent:

_____
(name of individual you choose as second alternate agent)

_____
(address)   (city)   (state)   (zip code)

_____
(home phone)   (work phone)

(2)   AGENT'S AUTHORITY: My agent is authorized to make all health-care decisions for me, including decisions to provide, withhold or withdraw artificial nutrition and hydration and all other forms of health care to keep me alive, except as I state here:

_____
_____
_____
(Add additional sheets if needed)

(3)   WHEN AGENT'S AUTHORITY BECOMES EFFECTIVE: My agent's authority becomes effective when my primary physician determines that I am unable to make my own health-care decisions unless I mark the following box. If I mark this box [   ], my agent's authority to make health-care decisions for me takes effect immediately.

(4)   AGENT'S OBLIGATION: My agent shall make health-care decisions for me in accordance with this power of attorney for health care, any instructions I give in Part 2 of this form and my other wishes to the extent known to my agent. To the extent my wishes are unknown, my agent shall make health-care decisions for me in accordance with what my agent determines to

be in my best interest. In determining my best interest, my agent shall consider my personal values to the extent known to my agent.

(5)   NOMINATION OF GUARDIAN: If a guardian of my person needs to be appointed for me by a court, I nominate the agent designated in this form. If that agent is not willing, able or reasonably available to act as guardian, I nominate the alternate agents whom I have named, in the order designated.

PART 2. INSTRUCTIONS FOR HEALTH CARE

If you are satisfied to allow your agent to determine what is best for you in making end-of-life decisions, you need not fill out this part of the form. If you do fill out this part of the form, you may strike any wording you do not want.

(6)   END-OF-LIFE DECISIONS: I direct that my health-care providers and others involved in my care provide, withhold or withdraw treatment in accordance with the choice I have marked below:

[ ]   (a)   Choice Not To Prolong Life: I do not want my life to be prolonged if (i) I have an incurable and irreversible condition that will result in my death within a relatively short time, (ii) I become unconscious and, to a reasonable degree of medical certainty, I will not regain consciousness, or (iii) the likely risks and burdens of treatment would outweigh the expected benefits, OR

[ ]   (b)   Choice To Prolong Life: I want my life to be prolonged as long as possible within the limits of generally accepted health-care standards.

(7)   ARTIFICIAL NUTRITION AND HYDRATION: Artificial nutrition and hydration must be provided, withheld or withdrawn in accordance with the choice I have made in paragraph (6) unless I mark the following box. If I mark this box [ ], artificial nutrition and hydration must be provided regardless of my condition and regardless of the choice I have made in paragraph (6).

(8)   RELIEF FROM PAIN: Except as I state in the following space, I direct that treatment for alleviation of pain or discomfort be provided at all times, even if it hastens my death:

_____

_____

(9)   OTHER WISHES: (If you do not agree with any of the optional choices above and wish to write your own, or if you wish to add to the instructions you have given above, you may do so here.) I direct that:

_____

_____

(Add additional sheets if needed)

PART 3. DONATION OF ORGANS AT DEATH (OPTIONAL)

(10)   Upon my death (mark applicable box)

[ ]   (a)   I give needed organs, tissues or parts OR

[ ]   (b)   I give the following organs, tissues or parts only

_____

[ ]   (c)   My gift is for the following purposes (strike any of the following you do not want)

(i)	Transplant	(iii)	Research
(ii)	Therapy	(iv)	Education

PART 4. PRIMARY PHYSICIAN (OPTIONAL)

(11)   I designate the following physician as my primary physician:

_____

(name of physician)   (phone)

_____

(address)   (city)   (state)   (zip code)

OPTIONAL: If the physician I have designated above is not willing, able or reasonably available to act as my primary physician, I designate the following physician as my primary physician:

_____

(name of physician)   (phone)

_____

(address)   (city)   (state)   (zip code)

* * * * * * * * * * * * * * * * * *

(12)   EFFECT OF COPY: A copy of this form has the same effect as the original.

(13)   SIGNATURES: Sign and date the form here:

_____   _____

(date)   (sign your name)

_____   _____

(address)   (print your name)

_____

(city)   (state)

SIGNATURES OF WITNESSES:

          First witness   Second witness

_____   _____

(print name)   (print name)

_____   _____

(address)   (address)

_____   _____

(city)   (state)   (city)   (state)

_____   _____

(signature of witness)   (signature of witness)

_____   _____

(date)   (date)

Health Care Decision Making Forms

The following forms allow you to make some decisions about future health care issues. Form I, called a "Living Will," allows you to make decisions about life-sustaining procedures if, in the future, your death from a terminal condition is imminent despite the application of life-sustaining procedures or you are in a persistent vegetative state. Form II, called an "Advance Directive," allows you to select a health care agent, give health care instructions, or both. If you use the advance directive, you can make decisions about life-sustaining procedures in the event of terminal condition, persistent vegetative state, or end-stage condition. You can also use the advance directive to make any other health care decisions.

These forms are intended to be guides. You can use one form or both, and you may complete all or only part of the forms that you use. Different forms may also be used.

Please note: If you decide to select a health care agent that person may not be a witness to your advance directive. Also, at least one of your witnesses may not be a person who may financially benefit by reason of your death.

Form I
Living Will
(Optional Form)

If I am not able to make an informed decision regarding my health care, I direct my health care providers to follow my instructions as set forth below. (Initial those statements you wish to be included in the document and cross through those statements which do not apply.)

a. If my death from a terminal condition is imminent and even if life-sustaining procedures are used there is no reasonable expectation of my recovery—

_____ I direct that my life not be extended by life-sustaining procedures, including the administration of nutrition and hydration artificially.

_____ I direct that my life not be extended by life-sustaining procedures, except that, if I am unable to take food by mouth, I wish to receive nutrition and hydration artificially.

_____ I direct that, even in a terminal condition, I be given all available medical treatment in accordance with accepted health care standards.

b. If I am in a persistent vegetative state, that is if I am not conscious and am not aware of my environment nor able to interact with others, and there is no reasonable expectation of my recovery within a medically appropriate period—

_____ I direct that my life not be extended by life-sustaining procedures, including the administration of nutrition and hydration artificially.

_____ I direct that my life not be extended by life-sustaining procedures, except that, if I am unable to take food by mouth, I wish to receive nutrition and hydration artificially.

_____ I direct that I be given all available medical treatment in accordance with accepted health care standards.

c. If I am pregnant my agent shall follow these specific instructions: _____
_____
_____
_____

d. Upon my death, I wish to donate:
_____ Any needed organs, tissues, or eyes.
_____ Only the following organs, tissues, or eyes: _____

I authorize the use of my organs, tissues, or eyes:
_____ For transplantation
_____ For therapy
_____ For research
_____ For medical education
_____ For any purpose authorized by law.

I understand that before any vital organ, tissue, or eye may be removed for transplantation, I must be pronounced dead. After death, I direct that all support measures be continued to maintain the viability for transplantation of my organs, tissues, and eyes until organ, tissue, and eye recovery has been completed.

I understand that my estate will not be charged for any costs associated with my decision to donate my organs, tissues, or eyes or the actual disposition of my organs, tissues, or eyes.

By signing below, I indicate that I am emotionally and mentally competent to make this living will and that I understand its purpose and effect.

_____   _____
(Date)   (Signature of Declarant)

The declarant signed or acknowledged signing this living will in my presence and based upon my personal observation the declarant appears to be a competent individual.

_____   _____
(Witness)   (Witness)

(Signature of Two Witnesses)

Form II
Advance Directive

Part A
Appointment of Health Care Agent
(Optional Form)

(Cross through if you do not want to appoint a health care agent to make health care decisions for you. If you do want to appoint an agent, cross through any items in the form that you do not want to apply.)

(1)   I, _____ , residing at _____
_____ , appoint the following individual as my agent to make health care decisions for me_____
_____ .
(Full Name, Address, and Telephone Number)

Optional: If this agent is unavailable or is unable or unwilling to act as my agent, then I appoint the following person to act in this capacity _____
_____ .
(Full Name, Address, and Telephone Number)

(2)   In accordance with the Health Insurance Portability and Accountability Act, a health care agent is a personal representative and is entitled to request and receive protected health information.

(3) My agent has full power and authority to make health care decisions for me, including the power to:

a. In accordance with the Health Insurance Portability and Accountability Act and as mypersonal representative, request, receive, and review any information, oral or written, regarding my physical or mental health, including, but not limited to, medical and hospital records, and other protected health information, and consent to disclosure of this information;

b. Employ and discharge my health care providers;

c. Authorize my admission to or discharge from (including transfer to another facility) any hospital, hospice, nursing home, adult home, or other medical care facility; and

d. Consent to the provision, withholding, or withdrawal of health care, including, in appropriate circumstances, life-sustaining procedures.

(4) The authority of my agent is subject to the following provisions and limitations:_____
_____
_____
_____

(5) My agent's authority becomes operative (initial the option that applies):

_____ When my attending physician and a second physician determine that I am incapable of making an informed decision regarding my health care, provided however, when this document is signed, each individual identified in paragraph (1) is, in accordance with the Health Insurance Portability and Accountability Act, my personal representative for all purposes related to any assessment of my capacity to make an informed decision regarding my health care; or

_____ When this document is signed.

(6) My agent is to make health care decisions for me based on the health care instructions I give in this document and on my wishes as otherwise known to my agent. If my wishes are unknown or unclear, my agent is to make health care decisions for me in accordance with my best interest, to be determined by my agent after considering the benefits, burdens, and risks that might result from a given treatment or course of treatment, or from the withholding or withdrawal of a treatment or course of treatment.

(7) My agent shall not be liable for the costs of care based solely on this authorization.

By signing below, I indicate that I am emotionally and mentally competent to make this appointment of a health care agent and that I understand its purpose and effect.

_____   _____
(Date)   (Signature of Declarant)

The declarant signed or acknowledged signing this appointment of a health care agent in my presence and based upon my personal observation appears to be a competent individual.

_____   _____
(Witness)   (Witness)

(Signature of Two Witnesses)

Part B
Advance Medical Directive
Health Care Instructions
(Optional Form)

(Cross through if you do not want to complete this portion of the form. If you do want to complete this portion of the form, initial those statements you want to be included in the document and cross through those statements that do not apply.)

If I am incapable of making an informed decision regarding my health care, I direct my health care providers to follow my instructions as set forth below.
(Initial all those that apply.)

(1) If my death from a terminal condition is imminent and even if life-sustaining procedures are used there is no reasonable expectation of my recovery—

_____ I direct that my life not be extended by life-sustaining procedures, including the administration of nutrition and hydration artificially.

_____ I direct that my life not be extended by life-sustaining procedures, except that, if I am unable to take food by mouth, I wish to receive nutrition and hydration artificially.

(2) If I am in a persistent vegetative state, that is, if I am not conscious and am not aware of my environment or able to interact with others, and there is no reasonable expectation of my recovery —

_____ I direct that my life not be extended by life-sustaining procedures, including the administration of nutrition and hydration artificially.

_____ I direct that my life not be extended by life-sustaining procedures, except that, if I am unable to take food by mouth, I wish to receive nutrition and hydration artificially.

(3) If I have an end-stage condition, that is a condition caused by injury, disease, or illness, as a result of which I have suffered severe and permanent deterioration indicated by incompetency and complete physical dependency and for which, to a reasonable degree of medical certainty, treatment of the irreversible condition would be medically ineffective—

_____ I direct that my life not be extended by life-sustaining procedures, including the administration of nutrition and hydration artificially.

_____ I direct that my life not be extended by life-sustaining procedures, except that, if I am unable to take food by mouth, I wish to receive nutrition and hydration artificially.

(4) I direct that no matter what my condition, medication not be given to me to relieve pain and suffering, if it would shorten my remaining life.

(5) I direct that no matter what my condition, I be given all available medical treatment in accordance with accepted health care standards.

(6) If I am pregnant, my decision concerning life-sustaining procedures shall be modified as follows: _____

_____

_____

(7) Upon my death, I wish to donate:

_____ Any needed organs, tissues, or eyes.

_____ Only the following organs, tissues, or eyes: _____

I authorize the use of my organs, tissues, or eyes:

_____ For transplantation
_____ For therapy
_____ For research
_____ For medical education
_____ For any purpose authorized by law.

       I understand that before any vital organ, tissue, or eye may be removed for transplantation, I must be pronounced dead. After death, I direct that all support measures be continued to maintain the viability for transplantation of my organs, tissues, and eyes until organ, tissue, and eye recovery has been completed.

       I understand that my estate will not be charged for any costs associated with my decision to donate my organs, tissues, or eyes or the actual disposition of my organs, tissues, or eyes.

(8)   I direct (in the following space, indicate any other instructions regarding receipt or nonreceipt of any health care) _____

_____

_____

       By signing below, I indicate that I am emotionally and mentally competent to make this advance directive and that I understand the purpose and effect of this document.

_____   _____

(Date)   (Signature of Declarant)

       The declarant signed or acknowledged signing the foregoing advance directive in my presence and based upon personal observation appears to be a competent individual.

_____   _____

(Witness)   (Witness)

                 (Signature of Two Witnesses)

HEALTH CARE LIVING WILL

Notice:

This is an important legal document. Before signing this document, you should know these important facts:

(a)   This document gives your health care providers or your designated proxy the power and guidance to make health care decisions according to your wishes when you are in a terminal condition and cannot do so. This document may include what kind of treatment you want or do not want and under what circumstances you want these decisions to be made. You may state where you want or do not want to receive any treatment.

(b)   If you name a proxy in this document and that person agrees to serve as your proxy, that person has a duty to act consistently with your wishes. If the proxy does not know your wishes, the proxy has the duty to act in your best interests. If you do not name a proxy, your health care providers have a duty to act consistently with your instructions or tell you that they are unwilling to do so.

(c)   This document will remain valid and in effect until and unless you amend or revoke it. Review this document periodically to make sure it continues to reflect your preferences. You may amend or revoke the living will at any time by notifying your health care providers.

(d)   Your named proxy has the same right as you have to examine your medical records and to consent to their disclosure for purposes related to your health care or insurance unless you limit this right in this document.

(e)   If there is anything in this document that you do not understand, you should ask for professional help to have it explained to you.

TO MY FAMILY, DOCTORS, AND ALL THOSE CONCERNED WITH MY CARE:

I, _____ , born on _____ , 19_____ (birthdate), being an adult of sound mind, willfully and voluntarily make this statement as a directive to be followed if I am in a terminal condition and become unable to participate in decisions regarding my health care. I understand that my health care providers are legally bound to act consistently with my wishes, within the limits of reasonable medical practice and other applicable law. I also understand that I have the right to make medical and health care decisions for myself as long as I am able to do so and to revoke this living will at any time.

(1)   The following are my feelings and wishes regarding my health care (you may state the circumstances under which this living will applies):

_____
_____
_____

(2)   I particularly want to have all appropriate health care that will help in the following ways (you may give instructions for care you do want):

_____
_____
_____

(3)   I particularly do not want the following (you may list specific treatment you do not want in certain circumstances):

_____
_____

(4) I particularly want to have the following kinds of life-sustaining treatment if I am diagnosed to have a terminal condition (you may list the specific types of life-sustaining treatment that you do want if you have a terminal condition):

_____
_____
_____

(5) I particularly do not want the following kinds of life-sustaining treatment if I am diagnosed to have a terminal condition (you may list the specific types of life-sustaining treatment that you do not want if you have a terminal condition):

_____
_____
_____

(6) I recognize that if I reject artificially administered sustenance, then I may die of dehydration or malnutrition rather than from my illness or injury. The following are my feelings and wishes regarding artificially administered sustenance should I have a terminal condition (you may indicate whether you wish to receive food and fluids given to you in some other way than by mouth if you have a terminal condition):

_____
_____
_____

(7) Thoughts I feel are relevant to my instructions. (You may, but need not, give your religious beliefs, philosophy, or other personal values that you feel are important. You may also state preferences concerning the location of your care.):

_____
_____
_____

(8) Proxy Designation. (If you wish, you may name someone to see that your wishes are carried out, but you do not have to do this. You may also name a proxy without including specific instructions regarding your care. If you name a proxy, you should discuss your wishes with that person.)

If I become unable to communicate my instructions, I designate the following person(s) to act on my behalf consistently with my instructions, if any, as stated in this document. Unless I write instructions that limit my proxy's authority, my proxy has full power and authority to make health care decisions for me. If a guardian or conservator of the person is to be appointed for me, I nominate my proxy named in this document to act as guardian or conservator of my person.

Name: _____
Address: _____
Phone Number: _____
Relationship: (If any) _____

If the person I have named above refuses or is unable or unavailable to act on my behalf, or if I revoke that person's authority to act as my proxy, I authorize the following person to do so:

Name: _____
Address: _____
Phone Number: _____
Relationship: (If any) _____

I understand that I have the right to revoke the appointment of the persons named above to act on my behalf at any time by communicating that decision to the proxy or my health care provider.

(9)   Organ Donation After Death. (If you wish, you may indicate whether you want to be an organ donor upon your death.) Initial the statement which expresses your wish:

_____ In the event of my death, I would like to donate my organs. I understand that to become an organ donor, I must be declared brain dead. My organ function may be maintained artificially on a breathing machine, (i.e., artificial ventilation), so that my organs can be removed.

Limitations or special wishes: (If any) _____
_____
_____

I understand that, upon my death, my next of kin may be asked permission for donation. Therefore, it is in my best interests to inform my next of kin about my decision ahead of time and ask them to honor my request.
I (have) (have not) agreed in another document or on another form to donate some or all of my organs when I die.

_____ I do not wish to become an organ donor upon my death.

DATE: _____   SIGNED: _____

STATE OF _____

COUNTY OF _____

Subscribed, sworn to, and acknowledged before me by _____
on this _____ day of _____, 200____.

_____
NOTARY PUBLIC

OR

(Sign and date here in the presence of two adult witnesses, neither of whom is entitled to any part of your estate under a will or by operation of law, and neither of whom is your proxy.)

I certify that the declarant voluntarily signed this living will in my presence and that the declarant is personally known to me. I am not named as a proxy by the living will, and to the best of my knowledge, I am not entitled to any part of the estate of the declarant under a will or by operation of law.

Witness _____   Address _____
                                                 _____

Witness _____   Address _____
                                                 _____

Reminder: Keep the signed original with your personal papers.
Give signed copies to your doctor, family, and proxy.

ADVANCE HEALTH CARE DIRECTIVE

Explanation

You have the right to give instructions about your own health care. You also have the right to name someone else to make health care decisions for you. This form lets you do either or both of these things. It also lets you express your wishes regarding the designation of your primary physician. If you use this form, you may complete or modify all or any part of it. You are free to use a different form.

Part 1 of this form is a power of attorney for health care. Part 1 lets you name another individual as agent to make health care decisions for you if you become incapable of making your own decisions or if you want someone else to make those decisions for you now even though you are still capable. You may name an alternate agent to act for you if your first choice is not willing, able or reasonably available to make decisions for you. Unless related to you, your agent may not be an owner, operator, or employee of a residential long-term health care institution at which you are receiving care.

Unless the form you sign limits the authority of your agent, your agent may make all health care decisions for you. This form has a place for you to limit the authority of your agent. You need not limit the authority of your agent if you wish to rely on your agent for all health care decisions that may have to be made. If you choose not to limit the authority of your agent, your agent will have the right to:

(a) Consent or refuse consent to any care, treatment, service, or procedure to maintain, diagnose, or otherwise affect a physical or mental condition;

(b) Select or discharge health care providers and institutions;

(c) Approve or disapprove diagnostic tests, surgical procedures, programs of medication, and orders not to resuscitate; and

(d) Direct the provision, withholding, or withdrawal of artificial nutrition and hydration and all other forms of health care.

Part 2 of this form lets you give specific instructions about any aspect of your health care. Choices are provided for you to express your wishes regarding the provision, withholding, or withdrawal of treatment to keep you alive, including the provision of artificial nutrition and hydration, as well as the provision of pain relief. Space is provided for you to add to the choices you have made or for you to write out any additional wishes.

Part 3 of this form lets you designate a physician to have primary responsibility for your health care.

Part 4 of this form lets you authorize the donation of your organs at your death, and declares that this decision will supersede any decision by a member of your family.

After completing this form, sign and date the form at the end and have the form witnessed by one of the two alternative methods listed below. Give a copy of the signed and completed form to your physician, to any other health care providers you may have, to any health care institution at which you are receiving care, and to any health care agents you have named. You should talk to the person you have named as agent to make sure that he or she understands your wishes and is willing to take the responsibility.

You have the right to revoke this advance health care directive or replace this form at any time.

PART 1
POWER OF ATTORNEY FOR HEALTH CARE

(1) DESIGNATION OF AGENT: I designate the following individual as my agent to make health care decisions for me:

_____
(name of individual you choose as agent)

_____
(address)   (city)   (state)   (zip code)

_____
(home phone)   (work phone)

OPTIONAL: If I revoke my agent's authority or if my agent is not willing, able, or reasonably available to make a health care decision for me, I designate as my first alternate agent:

_____
(name of individual you choose as first alternate agent)

_____
(address)   (city)   (state)   (zip code)

_____
(home phone)   (work phone)

OPTIONAL: If I revoke the authority of my agent and first alternate agent or if neither is willing, able, or reasonably available to make a health care decision for me, I designate as my second alternate agent:

_____
(name of individual you choose as second alternate agent)

_____
(address)   (city)   (state)   (zip code)

_____
(home phone)   (work phone)

(2) AGENT'S AUTHORITY: My agent is authorized to make all health care decisions for me, including decisions to provide, withhold, or withdraw artificial nutrition and hydration, and all other forms of health care to keep me alive, except as I state here:

_____
_____
_____

(Add additional sheets if needed.)

(3) WHEN AGENT'S AUTHORITY BECOMES EFFECTIVE: My agent's authority becomes effective when my primary physician determines that I am unable to make my own health care decisions unless I mark the following box. If I mark this box [ ], my agent's authority to make health care decisions for me takes effect immediately.

(4) AGENT'S OBLIGATION: My agent shall make health care decisions for me in accordance with this power of attorney for health care, any instructions I give in Part 2 of this form, and my other wishes to the extent known to my agent. To the extent my wishes are unknown, my agent shall make health care decisions for me in accordance with what my agent determines to be in my best interest. In determining my best interest, my agent shall consider my personal values to the extent known to my agent.

(5) NOMINATION OF GUARDIAN: If a guardian of my person needs to be appointed for me by a court, I nominate the agent designated in this form. If that agent is not willing, able, or reasonably available to act as guardian, I nominate the alternate agents whom I have named, in the order designated.

PART 2
INSTRUCTIONS FOR HEALTH CARE

If you are satisfied to allow your agent to determine what is best for you in making end-of-life decisions, you need not fill out this part of the form. If you do fill out this part of the form, you may strike any wording you do not want.

(6) END-OF-LIFE DECISIONS: I direct that my health care providers and others involved in my care provide, withhold or withdraw treatment in accordance with the choice I have marked below:

[ ] (a) Choice Not To Prolong Life

I do not want my life to be prolonged if (i) I have an incurable and irreversible condition that will result in my death within a relatively short time, (ii) I become unconscious and, to a reasonable degree of medical certainty, I will not regain consciousness, or (iii) the likely risks and burdens of treatment would outweigh the expected benefits, or

[ ] (b) Choice To Prolong Life

I want my life to be prolonged as long as possible within the limits of generally accepted health care standards.

(7) ARTIFICIAL NUTRITION AND HYDRATION: Artificial nutrition and hydration must be provided, withheld or withdrawn in accordance with the choice I have made in paragraph (6) unless I mark the following box. If I mark this box [ ], artificial nutrition and hydration must be provided regardless of my condition and regardless of the choice I have made in paragraph (6).

(8) RELIEF FROM PAIN: Except as I state in the following space, I direct that treatment for alleviation of pain or discomfort be provided at all times, even if it hastens my death:

_____
_____

(9) OTHER WISHES: (If you do not agree with any of the optional choices above and wish to write your own, or if you wish to add to the instructions you have given above, you may do so here.) I direct that:

_____
_____

(Add additional sheets if needed.)

PART 3
PRIMARY PHYSICIAN
(OPTIONAL)

(10) I designate the following physician as my primary physician:

_____

(name of physician)

_____

(address)   (city)   (state)   (zip code)

_____

(phone)

OPTIONAL: If the physician I have designated above is not willing, able, or reasonably available to act as my primary physician, I designate the following physician as my primary physician:

_____

(name of physician)

_____

(address)   (city)   (state)   (zip code)

_____

(phone)

(11) EFFECT OF COPY: A copy of this form has the same effect as the original.

(12) SIGNATURES: Sign and date the form here:

_____   _____

(date)   (sign your name)

_____   _____

(address)   (print your name)

_____

(city)   (state)

PART 4
CERTIFICATION OF AUTHORIZATION FOR ORGAN DONATION
(OPTIONAL)

I, the undersigned, this _____ day of _____, 20_____, desire that my _____ organ(s) be made available after my demise for:

(a) Any licensed hospital, surgeon or physician, for medical education, research, advancement of medical science, therapy or transplantation to individuals;

(b) Any accredited medical school, college or university engaged in medical education or research, for therapy, educational research or medical science purposes or any accredited school of mortuary science;

(c) Any person operating a bank or storage facility for blood, arteries, eyes, pituitaries, or other human parts, for use in medical education, research, therapy or transplantation to individuals;

(d) The donee specified below, for therapy or transplantation needed by him or her, do donate my
_____ for that purpose
to _____ (name) at _____
_____ (address).

I authorize a licensed physician or surgeon to remove and preserve for use my _____
_____ for that purpose.

I specifically provide that this declaration shall supersede and take precedence over any decision by my family to the contrary.

Witnessed this _____ day of _____, 20_____.

_____
(donor)

_____
(address)

_____
(telephone)

_____
(witness)

_____
(witness)

(13) WITNESSES: This power of attorney will not be valid for making health care decisions unless it is either (a) signed by two (2) qualified adult witnesses who are personally known to you and who are present when you sign or acknowledge your signature; or (b) acknowledged before a notary public in the state.

ALTERNATIVE NO. 1

Witness

I declare under penalty of perjury pursuant to Section 97-9-61, Mississippi Code of 1972, that the principal is personally known to me, that the principal signed or acknowledged this power of attorney in my presence, that the principal appears to be of sound mind and under no duress, fraud or undue influence, that I am not the person appointed as agent by this document, and that I am not a health care provider, nor an employee of a health care provider or facility. I am not related to the principal by blood, marriage or adoption, and to the best of my knowledge, I am not entitled to any part of the estate of the principal upon the death of the principal under a will now existing or by operation of law.

_____   _____
(date)   (signature of witness)

_____   _____
(address)   (print name of witness)

_____
(city)   (state)

Witness

I declare under penalty of perjury pursuant to Section 97-9-61, Mississippi Code of 1972, that the principal is personally known to me, that the principal signed or acknowledged this power of attorney in my presence, that the principal appears to be of sound mind and under no duress, fraud or undue influence, that I am not the person appointed as agent by this document, and that I am not a health care provider, nor an employee of a health care provider or facility.

_____   _____
(date)   (signature of witness)

_____   _____
(address)   (print name of witness)

_____
(city)   (state)

ALTERNATIVE NO. 2

State of _____

County of _____

On this _____ day of _____, in the year _____, before me, _____ (insert name of notary public) appeared _____, personally known to me (or proved to me on the basis of satisfactory evidence) to be the person whose name is subscribed to this instrument, and acknowledged that he or she executed it. I declare under the penalty of perjury that the person whose name is subscribed to this instrument appears to be of sound mind and under no duress, fraud or undue influence.

Notary Seal

_____
(Signature of Notary Public)

DECLARATION

I have the primary right to make my own decisions concerning treatment that might unduly prolong the dying process. By this declaration I express to my physician, family and friends my intent. If I should have a terminal condition it is my desire that my dying not be prolonged by administration of death-prolonging procedures. If my condition is terminal and I am unable to participate in decisions regarding my medical treatment, I direct my attending physician to withhold or withdraw medical procedures that merely prolong the dying process and are not necessary to my comfort or to alleviate pain. It is not my intent to authorize affirmative or deliberate acts or omissions to shorten my life rather only to permit the natural process of dying.

Signed this _____ day of _____, 200_____.

Signature _____

City, County and State of residence _____

The declarant is known to me, is eighteen years of age or older, of sound mind and voluntarily signed this document in my presence.

Witness _____
Address _____
_____

Witness _____
Address _____
_____

REVOCATION PROVISION

I hereby revoke the above declaration.

Signed _____
(Signature of Declarant)

Date _____

Directive to Physicians

If I should have an incurable or irreversible condition that, without the administration of life-sustaining treatment, will, in the opinion of my attending physician, cause my death within a relatively short time and I am no longer able to make decisions regarding my medical treatment, I direct my attending physician, pursuant to the Montana Rights of the Terminally III Act, to withhold or withdraw treatment that only prolongs the process of dying and is not necessary to my comfort or to alleviate pain.

Signed this _____ day of _____, 200____.

Signature _____

City, County, and State of Residence _____

_____

The declarant voluntarily signed this document in my presence.

Witness: _____

Address: _____

Witness: _____

Address: _____

DECLARATION

If I should have an incurable and irreversible condition that, without the administration of life-sustaining treatment, will, in the opinion of my attending physician or attending advanced practice registered nurse, cause my death within a relatively short time and I am no longer able to make decisions regarding my medical treatment, I appoint _____ or, if he or she is not reasonably available or is unwilling to serve, _____, to make decisions on my behalf regarding withholding or withdrawal of treatment that only prolongs the process of dying and is not necessary for my comfort or to alleviate pain, pursuant to the Montana Rights of the Terminally Ill Act.

If the individual I have appointed is not reasonably available or is unwilling to serve, I direct my attending physician or attending advanced practice registered nurse, pursuant to the Montana Rights of the Terminally Ill Act, to withhold or withdraw treatment that only prolongs the process of dying and is not necessary for my comfort or to alleviate pain.

Signed this _____ day of _____, _____.

Signature _____

City, County, and State of Residence _____

The declarant voluntarily signed this document in my presence.

Witness

_____

Address

_____

Witness

_____

Address

_____

Name and address of designee.

Name

_____

Address

_____

DECLARATION

If I should lapse into a persistent vegetative state or have an incurable and irreversible condition that, without the administration of life-sustaining treatment, will, in the opinion of my attending physician, cause my death within a relatively short time and I am no longer able to make decisions regarding my medical treatment, I direct my attending physician, pursuant to the Rights of the Terminally Ill Act, to withhold or withdraw life sustaining treatment that is not necessary for my comfort or to alleviate pain.

Signed this _____ day of _____.

Signature _____

Address _____

_____

The declarant voluntarily signed this writing in my presence.

_____   _____

Witness   Witness

_____   _____

Address   Address

_____   _____

OR

The declarant voluntarily signed this writing in my presence.

_____

Notary Public

Power of Attorney for Health Care

I appoint _____, whose address is _____
_____, and whose telephone number is
_____, as my attorney in fact for health care. I appoint
_____, whose address is _____
_____, and whose telephone number is
_____, as my successor attorney in fact for
health care. I authorize my attorney in fact appointed by this document to make health
care decisions for me when I am determined to be incapable of making my own health
care decisions. I have read the warning which accompanies this document and
understand the consequences of executing a power of attorney for health care.

I direct that my attorney in fact comply with the following instructions or
limitations:

_____
_____
_____

I direct that my attorney in fact comply with the following instructions on life-
sustaining treatment: (optional) _____
_____
_____

I direct that my attorney in fact comply with the following instructions on artificially
administered nutrition and hydration: (optional) _____
_____
_____

I HAVE READ THIS POWER OF ATTORNEY FOR HEALTH CARE. I
UNDERSTAND THAT IT ALLOWS ANOTHER PERSON TO MAKE LIFE AND DEATH
DECISIONS FOR ME IF I AM INCAPABLE OF MAKING SUCH DECISIONS. I ALSO
UNDERSTAND THAT I CAN REVOKE THIS POWER OF ATTORNEY FOR HEALTH
CARE AT ANY TIME BY NOTIFYING MY ATTORNEY IN FACT, MY PHYSICIAN, OR
THE FACILITY IN WHICH I AM A PATIENT OR RESIDENT. I ALSO UNDERSTAND
THAT I CAN REQUIRE IN THIS POWER OF ATTORNEY FOR HEALTH CARE THAT
THE FACT OF MY INCAPACITY IN THE FUTURE BE CONFIRMED BY A SECOND
PHYSICIAN.

_____
(Signature of person making designation/date)

DECLARATION OF WITNESSES

We declare that the principal is personally known to us, that the principal signed or acknowledged his or her signature on this power of attorney for health care in our presence, that the principal appears to be of sound mind and not under duress or undue influence, and that neither of us not the principal's attending physician is the person appointed as attorney in fact by this document.

Witnessed By:

_____   _____
(Signature of Witness/Date)   (Printed Name of Witness)

_____   _____
(Signature of Witness/Date)   (Printed Name of Witness)

OR

State of Nebraska,   )
) ss.
County of _____)

On this _____ day of _____, _____, before me, _____
_____, a notary public in and for _____ County, personally came _____, personally to me known to be the identical person whose name is affixed to the above power of attorney for health care as principal, and I declare that he or she appears in sound mind and not under duress or undue influence, that he or she acknowledges the execution of the same to be his or her voluntary act and deed, and that I am not the attorney in fact or successor attorney in fact designated by this power of attorney for health care.

Witness my hand and notarial seal at _____ in such county the day and year last above written.

_____
Seal   Signature of Notary Public

DECLARATION

If I should have an incurable and irreversible condition that, without the administration of life-sustaining treatment, will, in the opinion of my attending physician, cause my death within a relatively short time, and I am no longer able to make decisions regarding my medical treatment, I appoint _____ or, if he or she is not reasonably available or is unwilling to serve, _____, to make decisions on my behalf regarding withholding or withdrawal of treatment that only prolongs the process of dying and is not necessary for my comfort or to alleviate pain, pursuant to NRS 449.535 to 449.690, inclusive. (If the person or persons I have so appointed are not reasonably available or are unwilling to serve, I direct my attending physician, pursuant to those sections, to withhold or withdraw treatment that only prolongs the process of dying and is not necessary for my comfort or to alleviate pain.) Strike language in parentheses if you do not desire it.

If you wish to include this statement in this declaration, you must INITIAL the statement in the box provided:
Withholding or withdrawal of artificial nutrition and hydration may result in death by starvation or dehydration. Initial this box if you want to receive or continue receiving artificial nutrition and hydration by way of the gastro-intestinal tract after all other treatment is withheld pursuant to this declaration. (   )

Signed this _____ day of _____, _____
Signature _____
Address _____

The declarant voluntarily signed this writing in my presence.
Witness _____
Address _____
Witness _____
Address _____

Name and address of each designee.
Name _____
Address _____

DECLARATION

Declaration made this _____ day of _____ (month, year).
I, _____, being of sound mind, willfully and voluntarily make known my desire that my dying shall not be artificially prolonged under the circumstances set forth below, do hereby declare:

If at any time I should have an incurable injury, disease, or illness certified to be a terminal condition or a permanently unconscious condition by 2 physicians who have personally examined me, one of whom shall be my attending physician, and the physicians have determined that my death will occur whether or not life-sustaining procedures are utilized or that I will remain in a permanently unconscious condition and where the application of life-sustaining procedures would serve only to artificially prolong the dying process, I direct that such procedures be withheld or withdrawn, and that I be permitted to die naturally with only the administration of medication, sustenance, or the performance of any medical procedure deemed necessary to provide me with comfort care. I realize that situations could arise in which the only way to allow me to die would be to discontinue artificial nutrition and hydration. In carrying out any instruction I have given under this section, I authorize that artificial nutrition and hydration not be started or, if started, be discontinued.

(yes) (no) (Circle your choice and initial beneath it. If you choose "yes," artificial nutrition and _____ hydration will be provided and will not be removed.)

In the absence of my ability to give directions regarding the use of such life-sustaining procedures, it is my intention that this declaration shall be honored by my family and physicians as the final expression of my right to refuse medical or surgical treatment and accept the consequences of such refusal.

I understand the full import of this declaration, and I am emotionally and mentally competent to make this declaration.

Signed_____

State of _____
_____County

We, the following witnesses, being duly sworn each declare to the notary public or justice of the peace or other official signing below as follows:

1.   The declarant signed the instrument as a free and voluntary act for the purposes expressed, or expressly directed another to sign for him.
2.   Each witness signed at the request of the declarant, in his presence, and in the presence of the other witness.
3.   To the best of my knowledge, at the time of the signing the declarant was at least 18 years of age, and was of sane mind and under no constraint or undue influence.

_____ Witness
_____ Witness

Sworn to and signed before me by _____, declarant, _____ and _____, witnesses on _____.

_____
Signature

_____
Official Capacity

Optional Advance Health-Care Directive

Explanation

You have the right to give instructions about your own health care. You also have the right to name someone else to make health-care decisions for you. This form lets you do either or both of these things. It also lets you express your wishes regarding the designation of your primary physician.

THIS FORM IS OPTIONAL. Each paragraph and word of this form is also optional. If you use this form, you may cross out, complete or modify all or any part of it. You are free to use a different form. If you use this form, be sure to sign it and date it.

PART 1 of this form is a power of attorney for health care. PART 1 lets you name another individual as agent to make health-care decisions for you if you become incapable of making your own decisions or if you want someone else to make those decisions for you now even though you are still capable. You may also name an alternate agent to act for you if your first choice is not willing, able or reasonably available to make decisions for you. Unless related to you, your agent may not be an owner, operator or employee of a health-care institution at which you are receiving care.

Unless the form you sign limits the authority of your agent, your agent may make all health-care decisions for you. This form has a place for you to limit the authority of your agent. You need not limit the authority of your agent if you wish to rely on your agent for all health-care decisions that may have to be made. If you choose not to limit the authority of your agent, your agent will have the right to:

(a) consent or refuse consent to any care, treatment, service or procedure to maintain, diagnose or otherwise affect a physical or mental condition;

(b) select or discharge health-care providers and institutions;

(c) approve or disapprove diagnostic tests, surgical procedures, programs of medication and orders not to resuscitate; and

(d) direct the provision, withholding or withdrawal of artificial nutrition and hydration and all other forms of health care.

PART 2 of this form lets you give specific instructions about any aspect of your health care. Choices are provided for you to express your wishes regarding life-sustaining treatment, including the provision of artificial nutrition and hydration, as well as the provision of pain relief. In addition, you may express your wishes regarding whether you want to make an anatomical gift of some or all of your organs and tissue. Space is also provided for you to add to the choices you have made or for you to write out any additional wishes.

PART 3 of this form lets you designate a physician to have primary responsibility for your health care. After completing this form, sign and date the form at the end. It is recommended but not required that you request two other individuals to sign as witnesses. Give a copy of the signed and completed form to your physician, to any other health-care providers you may have, to any health-care institution at which you are receiving care and to any health-care agents you have named. You should talk to the person you have named as agent to make sure that he or she understands your wishes and is willing to take the responsibility.

You have the right to revoke this advance health-care directive or replace this form at any time.

PART 1
POWER OF ATTORNEY FOR HEALTH CARE

(1) DESIGNATION OF AGENT: I designate the following individual as my agent to make health-care decisions for me:

_____
(name of individual you choose as agent)

_____
(address)   (city)   (state)   (zip code)

_____
(home phone)   (work phone)

If I revoke my agent's authority or if my agent is not willing, able or reasonably available to make a health-care decision for me, I designate as my first alternate agent:

_____
(name of individual you choose as first alternate agent)

_____
(address)   (city)   (state)   (zip code)

_____
(home phone)   (work phone)

If I revoke the authority of my agent and first alternate agent or if neither is willing, able or reasonably available to make a health-care decision for me, I designate as my second alternate agent:

_____
(name of individual you choose as second alternate agent)

_____
(address)   (city)   (state)   (zip code)

_____
(home phone)   (work phone)

(2) AGENT'S AUTHORITY: My agent is authorized to obtain and review medical records, reports and information about me and to make all health-care decisions for me, including decisions to provide, withhold or withdraw artificial nutrition, hydration and all other forms of health care to keep me alive, except as I state here:

_____
(Add additional sheets if needed.)

(3) WHEN AGENT'S AUTHORITY BECOMES EFFECTIVE: My agent's authority becomes effective when my primary physician and one other qualified health-care professional determine that I am unable to make my own health-care decisions. If I initial this box [ ], my agent's authority to make health-care decisions for me takes effect immediately.

(4) AGENT'S OBLIGATION: My agent shall make health-care decisions for me in accordance with this power of attorney for health care, any instructions I give in Part 2 of this form and my other wishes to the extent known to my agent. To the extent my wishes are unknown, my agent shall make health-care decisions for me in accordance with what my agent determines to be in my best interest. In determining my best interest, my agent shall consider my personal values to the extent known to my agent.

(5) NOMINATION OF GUARDIAN: If a guardian of my person needs to be appointed for me by a court, I nominate the agent designated in this form. If that agent is not willing, able or reasonably available to act as guardian, I nominate the alternate agents whom I have named, in the order designated.

PART 2
INSTRUCTIONS FOR HEALTH CARE

If you are satisfied to allow your agent to determine what is best for you in making end-of-life decisions, you need not fill out this part of the form. If you do fill out this part of the form, you may cross out any wording you do not want.

(6) END-OF-LIFE DECISIONS: If I am unable to make or communicate decisions regarding my health care, and IF (i) I have an incurable or irreversible condition that will result in my death within a relatively short time, OR (ii) I become unconscious and, to a reasonable degree of medical certainty, I will not regain consciousness, OR (iii) the likely risks and burdens of treatment would outweigh the expected benefits, THEN I direct that my health-care providers and others involved in my care provide, withhold or withdraw treatment in accordance with the choice I have initialed below in one of the following three boxes:

[ ] I CHOOSE NOT To Prolong Life
I do not want my life to be prolonged.

[ ] I CHOOSE To Prolong Life
I want my life to be prolonged as long as possible within the limits of generally accepted health-care standards.

[ ] I CHOOSE To Let My Agent Decide
My agent under my power of attorney for health care may make life-sustaining treatment decisions for me.

(7) ARTIFICIAL NUTRITION AND HYDRATION: If I have chosen above NOT to prolong life, I also specify by marking my initials below:

[ ] I DO NOT want artificial nutrition OR

[ ] I DO want artificial nutrition.

[ ] I DO NOT want artificial hydration unless required for my comfort OR

[ ] I DO want artificial hydration.

(8) RELIEF FROM PAIN: Regardless of the choices I have made in this form and except as I state in the following space, I direct that the best medical care possible to keep me clean, comfortable and free of pain or discomfort be provided at all times so that my dignity is maintained, even if this care hastens my death: _____
_____

(9) ANATOMICAL GIFT DESIGNATION: Upon my death I specify as marked below whether I choose to make an anatomical gift of all or some of my organs or tissue:

[ ] I CHOOSE to make an anatomical gift of all of my organs or tissue to be determined by medical suitability at the time of death, and artificial support may be maintained long enough for organs to be removed.

[ ] I CHOOSE to make a partial anatomical gift of some of my organs and tissue as specified below, and artificial support may be maintained long enough for organs to be removed.
_____
_____

[ ] I REFUSE to make an anatomical gift of any of my organs or tissue.

[ ] I CHOOSE to let my agent decide.

(10) OTHER WISHES: (If you wish to write your own instructions, or if you wish to add to the instructions you have given above, you may do so here.) I direct that:
_____
_____

(Add additional sheets if needed.)

PART 3
PRIMARY PHYSICIAN

(11) I designate the following physician as my primary physician:

_____
(name of physician)

_____
(address)   (city)   (state)   (zip code)

_____
(phone)

If the physician I have designated above is not willing, able or reasonably available to act as my primary physician, I designate the following physician as my primary physician:

_____
(name of physician)

_____
(address)   (city)   (state)   (zip code)

_____
(phone)

* * * * * * * * * * * * * * * * * * *

(12) EFFECT OF COPY: A copy of this form has the same effect as the original.

(13) REVOCATION: I understand that I may revoke this OPTIONAL ADVANCE HEALTH-CARE DIRECTIVE at any time, and that if I revoke it, I should promptly notify my supervising health-care provider and any health-care institution where I am receiving care and any others to whom I have given copies of this power of attorney. I understand that I may revoke the designation of an agent either by a signed writing or by personally informing the supervising health-care provider.

(14) SIGNATURES: Sign and date the form here:

_____   _____
(date)   (sign your name)

_____   _____
(address)   (print your name)

_____   _____
(city)   (state)   (your Social Security number)

(Optional) SIGNATURES OF WITNESSES:

First witness   Second witness

_____   _____
(print name)   (print name)

_____   _____
(address)   (address)

_____   _____
(city)   (state)   (city)   (state)

_____   _____
(signature of witness)   (signature of witness)

_____   _____
(date)   (date)

Health Care Proxy

I, _____, (name of principal)
hereby appoint _____
_____ (name, home address, and telephone number of agent) as my health care agent to make any and all health care decisions for me, except to the extent I state otherwise.

This health care proxy shall take effect in the event I become unable to make my own health care decisions.
NOTE: Although not necessary, and neither encouraged nor discouraged, you may wish to state instructions or wishes, and limit your agent's authority. Unless your agent knows your wishes about artificial nutrition and hydration, your agent will not have authority to decide about artificial nutrition and hydration. If you choose to state instructions, wishes, or limits, please do so below:

_____
_____
_____
_____
_____
_____
_____

I direct my agent to make health care decisions in accordance with my wishes and instructions as stated above or as otherwise known to him or her. I also direct my agent to abide by any limitations on his or her authority as stated above or as otherwise known to him or her.

In the event the person I appoint is unable, unwilling or unavailable to act as my health care agent, I hereby appoint _____
_____(name, home address, and telephone number of alternate agent) as my health care agent.

I understand that, unless I revoke it, this proxy will remain in effect indefinitely or until the date or occurrence of the condition I have stated below:

(Please complete the following if you do NOT want this health care proxy to be in effect indefinitely):

This proxy shall expire: _____
_____. (Specify date or condition)

Signature:_____

Address:_____

Date:_____

I declare that the person who signed or asked another to sign this document is personally known to me and appears to be of sound mind and acting willingly and free from duress. He or she signed (or asked another to sign for him or her) this document in my presence and that person signed in my presence. I am not the person appointed as agent by this document.

Witness: _____

Witness: _____

Witness: _____

Declaration Of A Desire For A Natural Death

I, _____, being of sound mind, desire that, as specified below, my life not be prolonged by extraordinary means or be artificial nutrition or hydration if my condition is determined to be terminal and incurable or if I am diagnosed as being in a persistent vegetative state. I am aware and understand that this writing authorizes a physician to withhold or discontinue extraordinary means or artificial nutrition or hydration, in accordance with my specifications set forth below:

(Initial any of the following, as desired):

_____ If my condition is determined to be terminal and incurable, I authorize the following:

_____ My physician may withhold or discontinue extraordinary means only.

_____ In addition to withholding or discontinuing extraordinary means if such means are necessary, my physician may withhold or discontinue either artificial nutrition or hydration, or both.

_____ If my physician determines that I am in a persistent vegetative state, I authorize the following:

_____ My physician may withhold or discontinue extraordinary means only.

_____ In addition to withholding or discontinuing extraordinary means if such means are necessary, my physician may withhold or discontinue either artificial nutrition or hydration, or both.

This the _____ day of _____, _____.

Signature _____

I hereby state that the declarant, _____, being of sound mind, signed the above declaration in my presence and that I am not related to the declarant by blood or marriage and that I do not know or have a reasonable expectation that I would be entitled to any portion of the estate of the declarant under any existing will or codicil of the declarant or as an heir under the Intestate Succession Act if the declarant died on this date without a will. I also state that I am not the declarant's attending physician or an employee of the declarant's attending physician, or an employee of a health facility in which the declarant is a patient or an employee of a nursing home or any group-care home where the declarant resides. I further state that I do not now have any claim against the declarant.

Witness _____
Witness _____

The clerk or assistant clerk, of a notary public may, upon proper proof, certify the declaration as follows:

Certificate

I, _____, Clerk (Assistant Clerk) of Superior Court or Notary Public (circle one as appropriate) for _____ County hereby certify that _____, the declarant, appeared before me and swore to me and to the witnesses in my presence that this instrument is his Declaration Of A Desire For A Natural Death, and that he had willingly and voluntarily made and executed it as his free act and deed for the purposes expressed in it.

I further certify that _____ and _____, witnesses, appeared before me and swore that they witnessed _____, declarant, sign the attached declaration, believing him to be of sound mind; and also swore that at the time they witnessed the declaration (i) they were not related within the third degree to the declarant or to the declarant's spouse, and (ii) they did not know or have a reasonable expectation that they would be entitled to any portion of the estate of the declarant under any existing will of the declarant or codicil thereto then existing or under the Intestate Succession Act as it provided at that time, and (iii) they were not a physician attending the declarant or an employee of an attending physician or an employee of a health facility in which the declarant was a patient or an employee of a nursing home or any group-care home in which the declarant resided, and (iv) they did not have a claim against the declarant. I further certify that I am satisfied as to the genuineness and due execution of the declaration.

This the _____ day of _____, _____.

_____
Clerk (Assistant Clerk) of Superior Court or Notary Public (circle one as appropriate) for the County of
_____

HEALTH CARE DIRECTIVE

I, _____, understand this document allows me to do ONE OR ALL of the following:

PART I: Name another person (called the health care agent) to make health care decisions for me if I am unable to make and communicate health care decisions for myself. My health care agent must make health care decisions for me based on the instructions I provide in this document (Part II), if any, the wishes I have made known to him or her, or my agent must act in my best interest if I have not made my health care wishes known.

AND/OR

PART II: Give health care instructions to guide others making health care decisions for me. If I have named a health care agent, these instructions are to be used by the agent. These instructions may also be used by my health care providers, others assisting with my health care and my family, in the event I cannot make and communicate decisions for myself.

AND/OR

PART III: Allows me to make an organ and tissue donation upon my death by signing a document of anatomical gift.

PART I: APPOINTMENT OF HEALTH CARE AGENT

THIS IS WHO I WANT TO MAKE HEALTH CARE DECISIONS FOR ME IF I AM UNABLE TO MAKE AND COMMUNICATE HEALTH CARE DECISIONS FOR MYSELF (I know I can change my agent or alternate agent at any time and I know I do not have to appoint an agent or an alternate agent)
NOTE: If you appoint an agent, you should discuss this health care directive with your agent and give your agent a copy. If you do not wish to appoint an agent, you may leave Part I blank and go to Part II and/or Part III. None of the following may be designated as your agent: your treating health care provider, a nonrelative employee of your treating health care provider, an operator of a long-term care facility, or a nonrelative employee of a long-term care facility.

When I am unable to make and communicate health care decisions for myself, I trust and appoint _____ to make health care decisions for me. This person is called my health care agent.
Relationship of my health care agent to me: _____
Telephone number of my health care agent: _____
Address of my health care agent: _____

(OPTIONAL) APPOINTMENT OF ALTERNATE HEALTH CARE AGENT: If my health care agent is not reasonably available, I trust and appoint _____ to be my health care agent instead.
Relationship of my alternate health care agent to me: _____
Telephone number of my alternate health care agent: _____
Address of my alternate health care agent: _____

THIS IS WHAT I WANT MY HEALTH CARE AGENT TO BE ABLE TO DO IF I AM UNABLE TO MAKE AND COMMUNICATE HEALTH CARE DECISIONS FOR MYSELF (I know I can change these choices)

My health care agent is automatically given the powers listed below in (A) through (D).
My health care agent must follow my health care instructions in this document or any other instructions I have given to my agent. If I have not given health care instructions, then my agent must act in my best interest.
Whenever I am unable to make and communicate health care decisions for myself, my health care agent has the power to:

(A)   Make any health care decision for me. This includes the power to give, refuse, or withdraw consent to any care, treatment, service, or procedures. This includes deciding whether to stop or not start health care that is keeping me or might keep me alive and deciding about mental health treatment.

(B)   Choose my health care providers.

(C)   Choose where I live and receive care and support when those choices relate to my health care needs.

(D)   Review my medical records and have the same rights that I would have to give my medical records to other people.

If I DO NOT want my health care agent to have a power listed above in (A) through (D) OR if I want to LIMIT any power in (A) through (D), I MUST say that here:

_____
_____
_____

My health care agent is NOT automatically given the powers listed below in (1) and (2). If I WANT my agent to have any of the powers in (1) and (2), I must INITIAL the line in front of the power; then my agent WILL HAVE that power.

_____(1)   To decide whether to donate any parts of my body, including organs, tissues, and eyes, when I die.

_____(2)   To decide what will happen with my body when I die (burial, cremation).

If I want to say anything more about my health care agent's powers or limits on the powers, I can say it here:

_____
_____
_____

PART II: HEALTH CARE INSTRUCTIONS

NOTE: Complete this Part II if you wish to give health care instructions. If you appointed an agent in Part I, completing this Part II is optional but would be very helpful to your agent. However, If you chose not to appoint an agent in Part I, you MUST complete, at a minimum, Part II (B) if you wish to make a valid health care directive.

These are instructions for my health care when I am unable to make and communicate health care decisions for myself. These instructions must be followed (so long as they address my needs).

(A)   THESE ARE MY BELIEFS AND VALUES ABOUT MY HEALTH CARE
        (I know I can change these choices or leave any of them blank)
        I want you to know these things about me to help you make decisions about my health care:

My goals for my health care:

_____
_____

My fears about my health care:

_____
_____

My spiritual or religious beliefs and traditions:

_____
_____

My beliefs about when life would be no longer worth living:

_____
_____

My thoughts about how my medical condition might affect my family:

_____
_____
_____

(B)   THIS IS WHAT I WANT AND DO NOT WANT FOR MY HEALTH CARE
        (I know I can change these choices or leave any of them blank)

Many medical treatments may be used to try to improve my medical condition or to prolong my life. Examples include artificial breathing by a machine connected to a tube in the lungs, artificial feeding or fluids through tubes, attempts to start a stopped heart, surgeries, dialysis, antibiotics, and blood transfusions. Most medical treatments can be tried for a while and then stopped if they do not help.
I have these views about my health care in these situations:
(Note: You can discuss general feelings, specific treatments, or leave any of them blank).

If I had a reasonable chance of recovery and were temporarily unable to make and communicate health care decisions for myself, I would want:

_____
_____
_____

If I were dying and unable to make and communicate health care decisions for myself, I would want:

_____
_____
_____

If I were permanently unconscious and unable to make and communicate health care decisions for myself, I would want:

_____
_____
_____

If I were completely dependent on others for my care and unable to make and communicate health care decisions for myself, I would want:

_____
_____
_____

In all circumstances, my doctors will try to keep me comfortable and reduce my pain. This is how I feel about pain relief if it would affect my alertness or if it could shorten my life:

_____
_____
_____

There are other things that I want or do not want for my health care, if possible:

Who I would like to be my doctor:

_____
_____

Where I would like to live to receive health care:

_____
_____

Where I would like to die and other wishes I have about dying:

_____
_____

My wishes about what happens to my body when I die (cremation, burial):

_____
_____

Any other things:

_____
_____
_____

PART III: MAKING AN ANATOMICAL GIFT

I would like to be an organ donor at the time of my death. I have told my family my decision and ask my family to honor my wishes. I wish to donate the following (initial one statement):

[　　] Any needed organs and tissue.

[　　] Only the following organs and tissue: _____

PART IV: MAKING THE DOCUMENT LEGAL

PRIOR DESIGNATIONS REVOKED. I revoke any prior health care directive.

DATE AND SIGNATURE OF PRINCIPAL
(YOU MUST DATE AND SIGN THIS HEALTH CARE DIRECTIVE)

I sign my name to this Health Care Directive Form on _____ at _____

(date)

_____

(city)

_____

(state)

_____

(you sign here)

(THIS HEALTH CARE DIRECTIVE WILL NOT BE VALID UNLESS IT IS NOTARIZED OR SIGNED BY TWO QUALIFIED WITNESSES WHO ARE PRESENT WHEN YOU SIGN OR ACKNOWLEDGE YOUR SIGNATURE. IF YOU HAVE ATTACHED ANY ADDITIONAL PAGES TO THIS FORM, YOU MUST DATE AND SIGN EACH OF THE ADDITIONAL PAGES AT THE SAME TIME YOU DATE AND SIGN THIS HEALTH CARE DIRECTIVE.)

NOTARY PUBLIC OR STATEMENT OF WITNESSES

This document must be (1) notarized or (2) witnessed by two qualified adult witnesses. The person notarizing this document may be an employee of a health care or long-term care provider providing your care. At least one witness to the execution of the document must not be a health care or long-term care provider providing you with direct care or an employee of the health care or long-term care provider providing you with direct care. None of the following may be used as a notary or witness:

1. A person you designate as your agent or alternate agent;
2. Your spouse;
3. A person related to you by blood, marriage, or adoption;
4. A person entitled to inherit any part of your estate upon your death; or
5. A person who has, at the time of executing this document, any claim against your estate.

Option 1: Notary Public

In my presence on _____ (date), _____ (name of declarant) acknowledged the declarant's signature on this document or acknowledged that the declarant directed the person signing this document to sign on the declarant's behalf.

_____

(Signature of Notary Public)

My commission expires _____, 20____ .

Option 2: Two Witnesses

Witness One:

(1)   In my presence on _____ (date), _____ (name of declarant) acknowledged the declarant's signature on this document or acknowledged that the declarant directed the person signing this document to sign on the declarant's behalf.

(2)   I am at least eighteen years of age.

(3)   If I am a health care provider or an employee of a health care provider giving direct care to the declarant, I must initial this box: [   ].
I certify that the information in (1) through (3) is true and correct.

_____
(Signature of Witness One)

_____
(Address)

Witness Two:

(1)   In my presence on_____(date), _____ (name of declarant) acknowledged the declarant's signature on this document or acknowledged that the declarant directed the person signing this document to sign on the declarant's behalf.

(2)   I am at least eighteen years of age.

(3)   If I am a health care provider or an employee of a health care provider giving direct care to the declarant, I must initial this box: [   ].

I certify that the information in (1) through (3) is true and correct.

_____
(Signature of Witness Two)

_____
(Address)

ACCEPTANCE OF APPOINTMENT OF POWER OF ATTORNEY

I accept this appointment and agree to serve as agent for health care decisions. I understand I have a duty to act consistently with the desires of the principal as expressed in this appointment. I understand that this document gives me authority over health care decisions for the principal only if the principal becomes incapacitated. I understand that I must act in good faith in exercising my authority under this power of attorney. I understand that the principal may revoke this power of attorney at any time in any manner. If I choose to withdraw during the time the principal is competent, I must notify the principal of my decision. If I choose to withdraw when the principal is not able to make health care decisions, I must notify the principal's physician.

_____
(Signature of agent/date)

_____
(Signature of alternate agent/date)

PRINCIPAL'S STATEMENT

I have read a written explanation of the nature and effect of an appointment of a health care agent that is attached to my health care directive.

Dated this _____ day of _____ , 20 _____ .

_____
(Signature of Principal)

STATEMENT AFFIRMING EXPLANATION OF DOCUMENT TO RESIDENT OF LONG-TERM CARE FACILITY. (Only necessary if person is a resident of long-term care facility and Part I is completed appointing an agent. This statement does not need to be completed if the resident has read a written explanation of the nature and effect of an appointment of a health care agent and completed the Principal's Statement above.)
I have explained the nature and effect of this health care directive to _____
(name of principal), who signed this document and who is a resident of _____
(name and city of facility). I am (check one of the following):

    [ ]   A recognized member of the clergy.

    [ ]   An attorney licensed to practice in North Dakota.

    [ ]   A person designated by the district court for the county in which the above-named facility is located.

    [ ]   A person designated by the North Dakota Department of Human Services.

Dated on _____, 20___ .

_____ (Signature)

STATEMENT AFFIRMING EXPLANATION OF DOCUMENT TO HOSPITAL PATIENT OR PERSON BEING ADMITTED TO HOSPITAL. (Only necessary if person is a patient in a hospital or is being admitted to a hospital and Part I is completed appointing an agent. This statement does not need to be completed if the patient or person being admitted has read a written explanation of the nature and effect of an appointment of a health care agent and completed the Principal's Statement above.)

I have explained the nature and effect of this health care directive to _____
(name of principal), who signed this document and who is a patient or is being admitted as a patient of
_____ (name and city of hospital). I am (check one of the following):

    [ ]   An attorney licensed to practice in North Dakota.

    [ ]   A person designated by the hospital to explain the health care directive.

Dated on _____, 20___ .

_____ (Signature)

Declaration

I, _____, being of sound mind, willfully and voluntarily make known my desires regarding my medical care and treatment under the circumstances as indicated below:

_____ 1. If I should be in a terminal condition as defined below, and if I am unable to make decisions regarding my medical treatment, I direct my attending physician to withhold or withdraw life-sustaining treatment and procedures that merely prolong the dying process and are not necessary to my comfort or to alleviate pain. This authorization includes, but is not limited to, the withholding or withdrawal of the following types of medical treatment (subject to any special instructions in paragraph 5 below):

_____ a. Cardiopulmonary resuscitation (CPR) (this includes, but is not limited to, the use of drugs, electric shock, and artificial breathing).

_____ b. Kidney dialysis.

_____ c. Surgery or other invasive procedures.

_____ d. Transfusions of blood or blood products.

_____ e. Drugs and antibiotics.

_____ f. Artificial nutrition and hydration.

_____ g. Other: _____
_____

AS USED IN THIS DOCUMENT, THE TERM "TERMINAL CONDITION" MEANS AN IRREVERSIBLE, INCURABLE, AND UNTREATABLE CONDITION CAUSED BY DISEASE, ILLNESS, OR INJURY FROM WHICH, TO A REASONABLE DEGREE OF MEDICAL CERTAINTY AS DETERMINED IN ACCORDANCE WITH REASONABLE MEDICAL STANDARDS BY THE DECLARANT'S ATTENDING PHYSICIAN AND ONE OTHER PHYSICIAN WHO HAS EXAMINED THE DECLARANT, BOTH OF THE FOLLOWING APPLY:
(1) THERE CAN BE NO RECOVERY.
(2) DEATH IS LIKELY TO OCCUR WITHIN A RELATIVELY SHORT TIME IF LIFE-SUSTAINING TREATMENT IS NOT ADMINISTERED.

_____ 2. If I should be in a permanently unconscious state as defined below, I direct my attending physicians to withhold or withdraw life-sustaining treatment and procedures other than such medical treatment and procedures necessary to my comfort or to alleviate pain. This authorization includes, but is not limited to, the withholding or withdrawal of the following types of medical treatment (subject to any special instructions in paragraph 5 below):

_____ a. Cardiopulmonary resuscitation (CPR) (this includes, but is not limited to, the use of drugs, electric shock, and artificial breathing).

_____ b. Kidney dialysis.

_____ c. Surgery or other invasive procedures.

_____ d. Transfusions of blood or blood products.

_____ e. Drugs and antibiotics.

_____ g. Other: _____

_____ f. Artificial nutrition and hydration. MY ATTENDING PHYSICIAN IS AUTHORIZED TO WITHHOLD OR WITHDRAW NUTRITION AND HYDRATION IF I AM IN A PERMANENTLY UNCONSCIOUS STATE AND IF MY ATTENDING PHYSICIAN

AND AT LEAST ONE OTHER PHYSICIAN WHO HAS EXAMINED ME DETERMINE, TO A REASONABLE DEGREE OF MEDICAL CERTAINTY AND IN ACCORDANCE WITH REASONABLE MEDICAL STANDARDS, THAT NUTRITION OR HYDRATION WILL NOT OR NO LONGER WILL SERVE TO PROVIDE COMFORT TO ME OR ALLEVIATE MY PAIN.

_____
Signature of Declarant

_____   g.   Other: _____
_____
AS USED IN THIS DOCUMENT, THE TERM "PERMANENTLY UNCONSCIOUS STATE" MEANS A STATE OF PERMANENT UNCONSCIOUSNESS IN THE DECLARANT THAT, TO A REASONABLE DEGREE OF MEDICAL CERTAINTY AS DETERMINED IN ACCORDANCE WITH REASONABLE MEDICAL STANDARDS BY THE DECLARANT'S ATTENDING PHYSICIAN AND ONE OTHER PHYSICIAN WHO HAS EXAMINED THE DECLARANT, IS CHARACTERIZED BY BOTH OF THE FOLLOWING:
(1) IRREVERSIBLE UNAWARENESS OF ONE'S BEING AND ENVIRONMENT.
(2) TOTAL LOSS OF CEREBRAL CORTICAL FUNCTIONING, RESULTING IN THE DECLARANT HAVING NO CAPACITY TO EXPERIENCE PAIN OR SUFFERING.

_____   3.   It is my desire that my attending physician notify the following persons, if available, in the event life-sustaining treatment is to be withheld or withdrawn pursuant to this declaration:

_____
_____
_____

_____   4.   I want my life prolonged to the greatest extent possible (subject to any special instructions in paragraph 5 below).

_____   5.   Special instructions (if any)

_____
_____
_____

Signed this _____ day of _____, 200____.

_____
Signature of declarant

Address:_____

_____

Witnesses

The declarant voluntarily signed this document in my presence, and appeared to be of sound mind and not under or subject to duress, fraud, or undue influence. I am an adult; am not related to the declarant by blood, marriage, or adoption; am not the attending physician of the declarant; and am not the administrator of any nursing home in which the declarant is receiving care.

Witness: _____   Witness: _____

Name: _____   Name: _____

Address: _____   Address: _____

_____   _____

State of _____)
County of _____)

    On this _____ day of _____, 200_____, before me, personally appeared _____, the declarant, who is personally known to me or who provided _____ as identification, who signed the foregoing instrument in my presence, and who appeared to be of sound mind and not under or subject to duress, fraud, or undue influence.

_____
Notary Public

Notice to Adult Executing This Document

This is an important legal document. Before executing this document, you should know these facts:

This document gives the person you designate (the attorney in fact) the power to make **most** health care decisions for you if you lose the capacity to make informed health care decisions for yourself. This power is effective only when your attending physician determines that you have lost the capacity to make informed health care decisions for yourself and, notwithstanding this document, as long as you have the capacity to make informed health care decisions for yourself, you retain the right to make all medical and other health care decisions for yourself.

You may include specific limitations in this document on the authority of the attorney in fact to make health care decisions for you.

Subject to any specific limitations you include in this document, if your attending physician determines that you have lost the capacity to make an informed decision on a health care matter, the attorney in fact **generally** will be authorized by this document to make health care decisions for you to the same extent as you could make those decisions yourself, if you had the capacity to do so. The authority of the attorney in fact to make health care decisions for you **generally** will include the authority to give informed consent, to refuse to give informed consent, or to withdraw informed consent to any care, treatment, service, or procedure to maintain, diagnose, or treat a physical or mental condition.

However, even if the attorney in fact has general authority to make health care decisions for you under this document, the attorney in fact **never** will be authorized to do any of the following:

(1)   Refuse or withdraw informed consent to life-sustaining treatment (unless your attending physician and one other physician who examines you determine, to a reasonable degree of medical certainty and in accordance with reasonable medical standards, that either of the following applies:

(a)   You are suffering from an irreversible, incurable, and untreatable condition caused by disease, illness, or injury from which (i) there can be no recovery and (ii) your death is likely to occur within a relatively short time if life-sustaining treatment is not administered, and your attending physician additionally determines, to a reasonable degree of medical certainty and in accordance with reasonable medical standards, that there is no reasonable possibility that you will regain the capacity to make informed health care decisions for yourself.

(b)   You are in a state of permanent unconsciousness that is characterized by you being irreversibly unaware of yourself and your environment and by a total loss of cerebral cortical functioning, resulting in you having no capacity to experience pain or suffering, and your attending physician additionally determines, to a reasonable degree of medical certainty and in accordance with reasonable medical standards, that there is no reasonable possibility that you will regain the capacity to make informed health care decisions for yourself);

(2)   Refuse or withdraw informed consent to health care necessary to provide you with comfort care (except that, if the attorney in fact is not prohibited from doing so under (4) below, the attorney in fact could refuse or withdraw informed consent to the provision of nutrition or hydration to you as described under (4) below). **(You should understand that comfort care is defined in Ohio law to mean artificially or technologically administered sustenance (nutrition) or fluids (hydration) when administered to diminish your pain or discomfort, not to postpone your death, and any other medical or nursing procedure, treatment, intervention, or other measure that would be taken to diminish your pain or discomfort, not to postpone your death. Consequently, if your attending physician were to determine that a previously described medical or nursing procedure, treatment, intervention, or other measure will not or no longer will serve to provide comfort to you or alleviate your pain, then, subject to (4) below, your attorney in fact would be authorized to refuse or withdraw informed consent to the procedure, treatment, intervention, or other measure.)**;

(3)   Refuse or withdraw informed consent to health care for you if you are pregnant and if the refusal or withdrawal would terminate the pregnancy (unless the pregnancy or health care would pose a substantial risk to your life, or unless your attending physician and at least one other physician who examines you determine, to a reasonable degree of medical certainty and in accordance with reasonable medical standards, that the fetus would not be born alive);

(4)   Refuse or withdraw informed consent to the provision of artificially or technologically administered sustenance (nutrition) or fluids (hydration) to you, unless:

(a)   You are in a terminal condition or in a permanently unconscious state.

(b)   Your attending physician and at least one other physician who has examined you determine, to a reasonable degree of medical certainty and in accordance with reasonable medical

standards, that nutrition or hydration will not or no longer will serve to provide comfort to you or alleviate your pain.

(c) **If, but only if, you are in a permanently unconscious state, you authorize the attorney in fact to refuse or withdraw informed consent to the provision of nutrition or hydration to you by doing both of the following in this document:**

(i) **Including a statement in capital letters or other conspicuous type, including, but not limited to, a different font, bigger type, or boldface type, that the attorney in fact may refuse or withdraw informed consent to the provision of nutrition or hydration to you if you are in a permanently unconscious state and if the determination that nutrition or hydration will not or no longer will serve to provide comfort to you or alleviate your pain is made, or checking or otherwise marking a box or line (if any) that is adjacent to a similar statement on this document;**

(ii) **Placing your initials or signature underneath or adjacent to the statement, check, or other mark previously described.**

(d) **Your attending physician determines, in good faith, that you authorized the attorney in fact to refuse or withdraw informed consent to the provision of nutrition or hydration to you if you are in a permanently unconscious state by complying with the requirements of (4)(c)(i) and (ii) above; or,**

(5)   Withdraw informed consent to any health care to which you previously consented, unless a change in your physical condition has significantly decreased the benefit of that health care to you, or unless the health care is not, or is no longer, significantly effective in achieving the purposes for which you consented to its use.

Additionally, when exercising authority to make health care decisions for you, the attorney in fact will have to act consistently with your desires or, if your desires are unknown, to act in your best interest. You may express your desires to the attorney in fact by including them in this document or by making them known to the attorney in fact in another manner.

When acting pursuant to this document, the attorney in fact **generally** will have the same rights that you have to receive information about proposed health care, to review health care records, and to consent to the disclosure of health care records. You can limit that right in this document if you so choose.

Generally, you may designate any competent adult as the attorney in fact under this document. However, you **cannot** designate your attending physician or the administrator of any nursing home in which you are receiving care as the attorney in fact under this document. Additionally, you **cannot** designate an employee or agent of your attending physician, or an employee or agent of a health care facility at which you are being treated, as the attorney in fact under this document, unless either type of employee or agent is a competent adult and related to you by blood, marriage, or adoption, or unless either type of employee or agent is a competent adult and you and the employee or agent are members of the same religious order.

This document has no expiration date under Ohio law, but you may choose to specify a date upon which your durable power of attorney for health care generally will expire. However, if you specify an expiration date and then lack the capacity to make informed health care decisions for yourself on that date, the document and the power it grants to your attorney in fact will continue in effect until you regain the capacity to make informed health care decisions for yourself.

You have the right to revoke the designation of the attorney in fact and the right to revoke this entire document at any time and in any manner. Any such revocation generally will be effective when you express your intention to make the revocation. However, if you made your attending physician aware of this document, any such revocation will be effective only when you communicate it to your attending physician, or when a witness to the revocation or other health care personnel to whom the revocation is communicated by such a witness communicate it to your attending physician.

If you execute this document and create a valid durable power of attorney for health care with it, it will revoke any prior, valid durable power of attorney for health care that you created, unless you indicate otherwise in this document.

This document is not valid as a durable power of attorney for health care unless it is acknowledged before a notary public or is signed by at least two adult witnesses who are present when you sign or acknowledge your signature. No person who is related to you by blood, marriage, or adoption may be a witness. The attorney in fact, your attending physician, and the administrator of any nursing home in which you are receiving care also are ineligible to be witnesses.

If there is anything in this document that you do not understand, you should ask your lawyer to explain it to you.

Advance Directive for Health Care

I, _____, being of sound mind and eighteen (18) years of age or older, willfully and voluntarily make known my desire, by my instructions to others through my living will, or by my appointment of a health care proxy, or both, that my life shall not be artificially prolonged under the circumstances set forth below. I thus do hereby declare:

I. Living Will

a.   If my attending physician and another physician determine that I am no longer able to make decisions regarding my medical treatment, I direct my attending physician and other health care providers, pursuant to the Oklahoma Rights of the Terminally III or Persistently Unconscious Act, to withhold or withdraw treatment from me under the circumstances I have indicated below by my signature. I understand that I will be given treatment that is necessary for my comfort or to alleviate my pain.

b.   If I have a terminal condition:

(1)   I direct that life-sustaining treatment shall be withheld or withdrawn if such treatment would only prolong my process of dying, and if my attending physician and another physician determine that I have an incurable and irreversible condition that even with the administration of life-sustaining treatment will cause my death within six (6) months.

_____ (initials)

(2)   I understand that the subject of the artificial administration of nutrition and hydration (food and water) that will only prolong the process of dying from an incurable and irreversible condition is of particular importance. I understand that if I do not sign this paragraph, artificially administered nutrition and hydration will be administered to me. I further understand that if I sign this paragraph, I am authorizing the withholding or withdrawal of artificially administered nutrition (food) and hydration (water).

_____ (initials)

(3)   I direct that (add other medical directives, if any) _____
_____
_____
_____

_____ (initials)

c.   If I am persistently unconscious:

(1)   I direct that life-sustaining treatment be withheld or withdrawn if such treatment will only serve to maintain me in an irreversible condition, as determined by my attending physician and another physician, in which thought and awareness of self and environment are absent.

_____ (initials)

(2)   I understand that the subject of the artificial administration of nutrition and hydration (food and water) for individuals who have become persistently unconscious is of particular importance. I understand that if I do not sign this paragraph, artificially administered nutrition and hydration will be administered to me. I further understand that if I sign this paragraph, I am authorizing the withholding or withdrawal of artificially administered nutrition (food) and hydration (water).

_____ (initials)

(3)   direct that (add other medical directives, if any) _____

_____

_____

_____

_____ (initials)

II. My Appointment of My Health Care Proxy

a.   If my attending physician and another physician determine that I am no longer able to make decisions regarding my medical treatment, I direct my attending physician and other health care providers pursuant to the Oklahoma Rights of the Terminally Ill or Persistently Unconscious Act to follow the instructions of _____ _____, whom I appoint as my health care proxy. If my health care proxy is unable or unwilling to serve, I appoint _____ as my alternate health care proxy with the same authority. My health care proxy is authorized to make whatever medical treatment decisions I could make if I were able, except that decisions regarding life-sustaining treatment can be made by my health care proxy or alternate health care proxy only as I indicate in the following sections.

b.   If I have a terminal condition:

(1)   I authorize my health care proxy to direct that life-sustaining treatment be withheld or withdrawn if such treatment would only prolong my process of dying and if my attending physician and another physician determine that I have an incurable and irreversible condition that even with the administration of life-sustaining treatment will cause my death within six (6) months.

_____ (initials)

(2)   I understand that the subject of the artificial administration of nutrition and hydration (food and water) is of particular importance. I understand that if I do not sign this paragraph, artificially administered nutrition (food) or hydration (water) will be administered to me. I further understand that if I sign this paragraph, I am authorizing the withholding or withdrawal of artificially administered nutrition and hydration.

_____ (initials)

(3)   I authorize my health care proxy to (add other medical directives, if any)

_____

_____

_____

_____ (initials)

c.   If I am persistently unconscious:

(1)   I authorize my health care proxy to direct that life-sustaining treatment be withheld or withdrawn if such treatment will only serve to maintain me in an irreversible condition, as determined by my attending physician and another physician, in which thought and awareness of self and environment are absent.

_____ (initials)

(2)   I understand that the subject of the artificial administration of nutrition and hydration (food and water) is of particular importance. I understand that if I do not sign this paragraph, artificially administered nutrition (food) and hydration (water) will be administered to me. I further understand that if I sign this paragraph, I am authorizing the withholding and withdrawal of artificially administered nutrition and hydration.

_____ (initials)

(3)   I authorize my health care proxy to (add other medical directives, if any)

_____

_____

_____

_____ (initials)

III. Anatomical Gifts

I direct that at the time of my death my entire body or designated body organs or body parts be donated for purposes of transplantation, therapy, advancement or medical or dental science or research or education pursuant to the provisions of the Uniform Anatomical Gift Act. Death means either irreversible cessation of circulatory and respiratory functions or irreversible cessation of all functions of the entire brain, including the brain stem. I specifically donate:

[ ]   My entire body; or

[ ]   The following body organs or parts:
( ) lungs,   ( ) liver,   ( ) pancreas,   ( ) heart,   ( ) kidneys,
( ) brain,   ( ) skin,   ( ) bones/marrow,   ( ) bloods/fluids,
( ) tissue,   ( ) arteries,   ( ) eyes/cornea/lens,   ( ) glands,
( ) other: _____

_____ (initials)

IV. Conflicting Provisions

I understand that if I have completed both a living will and have appointed a health care proxy, and if there is a conflict between my health care proxy's decision and my living will, my living will shall take precedence unless I indicate otherwise. _____

_____

_____ (initials)

V. General Provisions

a.   I understand that if I have been diagnosed as pregnant and that diagnosis is known to my attending physician, this advance directive shall have no force or effect during the course of my pregnancy.

b.   In the absence of my ability to give directions regarding the use of life-sustaining procedures, it is my intention that this advance directive shall be honored by my family and physicians as the final expression of my legal right to refuse medical or surgical treatment including, but not limited to, the administration of any life-sustaining procedures, and I accept the consequences of such refusal.

c.   This advance directive shall be in effect until it is revoked.

d.   I understand that I may revoke this advance directive at any time.

e.   I understand and agree that if I have any prior directives, and, if I sign this advance directive, my prior directives are revoked.

f.   I understand the full importance of this advance directive and I am emotionally and mentally competent to make this advance directive.

ADVANCE DIRECTIVE

YOU DO NOT HAVE TO FILL OUT AND SIGN THIS FORM

PART A: IMPORTANT INFORMATION ABOUT THIS ADVANCE DIRECTIVE

This is an important legal document. It can control critical decisions about your health care. Before signing, consider these important facts:

Facts About Part B
(Appointing a Health Care Representative)

You have the right to name a person to direct your health care when you cannot do so. This person is called your "health care representative." You can do this by using Part B of this form. Your representative must accept on Part E of this form.

You can write in this document any restrictions you want on how your representative will make decisions for you. Your representative must follow your desires as stated in this document or otherwise made known. If your desires are unknown, your representative must try to act in your best interest. Your representative can resign at any time.

Facts About Part C
(Giving Health Care Instructions)

You also have the right to give instructions for health care providers to follow if you become unable to direct your care. You can do this by using Part C of this form.

Facts About Completing This Form

This form is valid only if you sign it voluntarily and when you are of sound mind. If you do not want an advance directive, you do not have to sign this form.

Unless you have limited the duration of this advance directive, it will not expire. If you have set an expiration date, and you become unable to direct your health care before that date, this advance directive will not expire until you are able to make those decisions again.

You may revoke this document at any time. To do so, notify your representative and your health care provider of the revocation.

Despite this document, you have the right to decide your own health care as long as you are able to do so.

If there is anything in this document that you do not understand, ask a lawyer to explain it to you.

You may sign PART B, PART C, or both parts. You may cross out words that don't express your wishes or add words that better express your wishes. Witnesses must sign PART D.

Print your NAME, BIRTHDATE AND ADDRESS here:

_____
(Name)

_____
(Birthdate)

_____

_____
(Address)

Unless revoked or suspended, this advance directive will continue for:

INITIAL ONE:

__ My entire life

__ Other period (__Years)

PART B: APPOINTMENT OF HEALTH CARE REPRESENTATIVE

I appoint _____ as my health care representative. My representative's address is _____ and telephone number is _____.

I appoint _____ as my alternate health care representative. My alternate's address is _____ and telephone number is _____.

I authorize my representative (or alternate) to direct my health care when I can't do so.

NOTE: You may not appoint your doctor, an employee of your doctor, or an owner, operator or employee of your health care facility, unless that person is related to you by blood, marriage or adoption or that person was appointed before your admission into the health care facility.

1. Limits.

Special Conditions or Instructions:

_____
_____
_____

INITIAL IF THIS APPLIES:

____ I have executed a Health Care Instruction or Directive to Physicians. My
representative is to honor it.

2. Life Support.

"Life support" refers to any medical means for maintaining life, including procedures, devices and medications. If you refuse life support, you will still get routine measures to keep you clean and comfortable.

INITIAL IF THIS APPLIES:

____ My representative MAY decide about life support for me. (If you don't initial this
space, then your representative MAY NOT decide about life support.)

3. Tube Feeding.

One sort of life support is food and water supplied artificially by medical device, known as tube feeding.

INITIAL IF THIS APPLIES:

____ My representative MAY decide about tube feeding for me. (If you don't initial this
space, then your representative MAY NOT decide about tube feeding.)

_____

(Date)

SIGN HERE TO APPOINT A HEALTH CARE REPRESENTATIVE

_____
(Signature of person making appointment)

PART C: HEALTH CARE INSTRUCTIONS

NOTE: In filling out these instructions, keep the following in mind:

• The term "as my physician recommends" means that you want your physician to try life support if your physician believes it could be helpful and then discontinue it if it is not helping your health condition or symptoms.

• "Life support" and "tube feeding" are defined in Part B above.

• If you refuse tube feeding, you should understand that malnutrition, dehydration and death will probably result.

• You will get care for your comfort and cleanliness, no matter what choices you make.

•You may either give specific instructions by filling out Items 1 to 4 below, or you may use the general instruction provided by Item 5.

Here are my desires about my health care if my doctor and another knowledgeable doctor confirm that I am in a medical condition described below:

1. Close to Death. If I am close to death and life support would only postpone the moment of my death:

    A. INITIAL ONE:

    ___ I want to receive tube feeding.

    ___ I want tube feeding only as my physician recommends.

    ___ I DO NOT WANT tube feeding.

    B. INITIAL ONE:

    ___ I want any other life support that may apply.

    ___ I want life support only as my physician recommends.

    ___ I want NO life support.

2. Permanently Unconscious. If I am unconscious and it is very unlikely that I will ever become conscious again:

    A. INITIAL ONE:

    ___ I want to receive tube feeding.

    ___ I want tube feeding only as my physician recommends.

    ___ I DO NOT WANT tube feeding.

B. INITIAL ONE:

___ I want any other life support that may apply.

___ I want life support only as my physician recommends.

___ I want NO life support.

3. Advanced Progressive Illness. If I have a progressive illness that will be fatal and is in an advanced stage, and I am consistently and permanently unable to communicate by any means, swallow food and water safely, care for myself and recognize my family and other people, and it is very unlikely that my condition will substantially improve:

A. INITIAL ONE:

___ I want to receive tube feeding.

___ I want tube feeding only as my physician recommends.

___ I DO NOT WANT tube feeding.

B. INITIAL ONE:

___ I want any other life support that may apply.

___ I want life support only as my physician recommends.

___ I want NO life support.

4. Extraordinary Suffering. If life support would not help my medical condition and would make me suffer permanent and severe pain:

A. INITIAL ONE:

___ I want to receive tube feeding.

___ I want tube feeding only as my physician recommends.

___ I DO NOT WANT tube feeding.

B. INITIAL ONE:

___ I want any other life support that may apply.

___ I want life support only as my physician recommends.

___ I want NO life support.

5. General Instruction.
INITIAL IF THIS APPLIES:

I do not want my life to be prolonged by life support. I also do not want tube feeding as life support. I want my doctors to allow me to die naturally if my doctor and another knowledgeable doctor confirm I am in any of the medical conditions listed in Items 1 to 4 above.

6. Additional Conditions or Instructions.

_____

_____

_____

[Insert description of what you want done.]

7. Other Documents. A "health care power of attorney" is any document you may have signed to appoint a representative to make health care decisions for you.

     INITIAL ONE:

       ___ I have previously signed a health care power of attorney. I want it to remain in effect unless appointed a health care representative after signing the health care power of   attorney.

       ___ I have a health care power of attorney, and I REVOKE IT.

       ___ I DO NOT have a health care power of attorney.

_____

(Date)

SIGN HERE TO GIVE INSTRUCTIONS

_____

(Signature)

PART D: DECLARATION OF WITNESSES

We declare that the person signing this advance directive:

(a) Is personally known to us or has provided proof of identity;

(b) Signed or acknowledged that person's signature on this advance directive in our presence;

(c) Appears to be of sound mind and not under duress, fraud or undue influence;

(d) Has not appointed either of us as health care representative or alternative representative; and

(e) Is not a patient for whom either of us is attending physician.

Witnessed By:

_____   _____

(Signature of Witness/Date   (Printed Name of Witness)

_____   _____

(Signature of Witness/Date   (Printed Name of Witness)

NOTE: One witness must not be a relative (by blood, marriage or adoption) of the person signing this advance directive.

That witness must also not be entitled to any portion of the person's estate upon death. That witness must also not own, operate or be employed at a health care facility where the person is a patient or resident.

PART E: ACCEPTANCE BY HEALTH CARE REPRESENTATIVE

I accept this appointment and agree to serve as health care representative. I understand I must act consistently with the desires of the person I represent, as expressed in this advance directive or otherwise made known to me. If I do not know the desires of the person I represent, I have a duty to act in what I believe in good faith to be that person's best interest. I understand that this document allows me to decide about that person's health care only while that person cannot do so. I understand that the person who appointed me may revoke this appointment. If I learn that this document has been suspended or revoked, I will inform the person's current health care provider if known to me.

_____
(Signature of Health Care Representative/Date)

_____
(Printed name)

_____
(Signature of Alternate Health Care Representative/Date)

_____
(Printed name)

DECLARATION

I, _____, being of sound mind, willfully and voluntarily make this declaration to be followed if I become incompetent. This declaration reflects my firm and settled commitment to refuse life-sustaining treatment under the circumstances indicated below.

I direct my attending physician to withhold or withdraw life-sustaining treatment that serves only to prolong the process of my dying, if I should be in a terminal condition or in a state of permanent unconsciousness.

I direct that treatment be limited to measures to keep me comfortable and to relieve pain, including any pain that might occur by withholding or withdrawing life-sustaining treatment.

In addition, if I am in the condition described above, I feel especially strong about the following forms of treatment:
I ( ) do ( ) do not want cardiac resuscitation.
I ( ) do ( ) do not want mechanical respiration.
I ( ) do ( ) do not want tube feeding or any other artificial or invasive form of nutrition
        (food) or hydration (water).
I ( ) do ( ) do not want blood or blood products.
I ( ) do ( ) do not want any form of surgery or invasive diagnostic tests.
I ( ) do ( ) do not want kidney dialysis.
I ( ) do ( ) do not want antibiotics.
I realize that if I do not specifically indicate my preference regarding any of the forms of treatment listed above, I may receive that form of treatment.

Other instructions:
I ( ) do ( ) do not want to designate another person as my surrogate to make medical treatment decisions for me if I should be incompetent and in a terminal condition or in a state of permanent unconsciousness. Name and address of surrogate (if applicable):

Name and address of substitute surrogate (if surrogate above is unable to serve):

I ( ) do ( ) do not want to make an anatomical gift of all or part of my body, subject to the following limitations, if any:
I made this declaration on the _____ day of _____ (month) (year).

_____   _____
                                        _____
Declarant's signature
                                        _____
                                        Declarant's address
The declarant or the person on behalf of and at the direction of declarant knowingly and voluntarily signed this writing by signature or mark in my presence.

_____   _____
Witness' signature   Witness' signature

_____   _____
Witness' address   Witness' address

DECLARATION

I, _____, being of sound mind willfully and voluntarily make known my desire that my dying shall not be artificially prolonged under the circumstances set forth below, do hereby declare:

If I should have an incurable or irreversible condition that will cause my death within a relatively short time, and if I am unable to make decisions regarding my medical treatment, I direct my attending physician to withhold or withdraw procedures that merely prolong the dying process and are not necessary to my comfort, or to alleviate pain.

This authorization includes ( ) does not include ( ) the withholding or withdrawal of artificial feeding (check only one box above).

Signed this _____ day of _____, 200_____.

_____
Signature

_____
_____
Address

The declarant is personally known to me and voluntarily signed this document in my presence.

_____   _____
Witness   Witness

_____   _____

Statutory Form Durable Power of Attorney for Health Care

WARNING TO PERSON EXECUTING THIS DOCUMENT

This is an important legal document which is authorized by the general laws of this state. Before executing this document, you should know these important facts:

You must be at least eighteen (18) years of age and a resident of the state for this document to be legally valid and binding.

This document gives the person you designate as your agent (the attorney in fact) the power to make health care decisions for you. Your agent must act consistently with your desires as stated in this document or otherwise made known.

Except as you otherwise specify in this document, this document gives your agent the power to consent to your doctor not giving treatment or stopping treatment necessary to keep you alive.

Notwithstanding this document, you have the right to make medical and other health care decisions for yourself so long as you can give informed consent with respect to the particular decision. In addition, no treatment may be given to you over your objection at the time, and health care necessary to keep you alive may not be stopped or withheld if you object at the time.

This document gives your agent authority to consent, to refuse to consent, or to withdraw consent to any care, treatment, service, or procedure to maintain, diagnose, or treat a physical or mental condition. This power is subject to any statement of your desires and any limitation that you include in this document. You may state in this document any types of treatment that you do not desire. In addition, a court can take away the power of your agent to make health care decisions for you if your agent:

(1) Authorizes anything that is illegal,

(2) Acts contrary to your known desires, or

(3) Where your desires are not known, does anything that is clearly contrary to your best interests.

Unless you specify a specific period, this power will exist until you revoke it. Your agent's power and authority ceases upon your death except to inform your family or next of kin of your desire, if any, to be an organ and tissue owner.

You have the right to revoke the authority of your agent by notifying your agent or your treating doctor, hospital, or other health care provider orally or in writing of the revocation.

Your agent has the right to examine your medical records and to consent to their disclosure unless you limit this right in this document.

This document revokes any prior durable power of attorney for health care.

You should carefully read and follow the witnessing procedure described at the end of this form. This document will not be valid unless you comply with the witnessing procedure.

If there is anything in this document that you do not understand, you should ask a lawyer to explain it to you.

Your agent may need this document immediately in case of an emergency that requires a decision concerning your health care. Either keep this document where it is immediately available to your agent and alternate agents or give each of them an executed copy of this document. You may also want to give your doctor an executed copy of this document.

(1) DESIGNATION OF HEALTH CARE AGENT.   I,

_____,

(insert your name and address)

do hereby designate and appoint:

_____

(insert name, address, and telephone number of one individual only as your agent to make health care decisions for you)

(None of the following may be designated as your agent: (1) your treating health care provider, (2) a nonrelative employee of your treating health care provider, (3) an operator of a community care facility, or (4) a nonrelative employee of an operator of a community care facility.) as my attorney in fact (agent) to make health care decisions for me as authorized in this document. For the purposes of this document, "health care decision" means consent, refusal of consent, or withdrawal of consent to any care, treatment, service, or procedure to maintain, diagnose, or treat an individual's physical or mental condition.

(2) CREATION OF DURABLE POWER OF ATTORNEY FOR HEALTH CARE. By this document I intend to create a durable power of attorney for health care.

(3) GENERAL STATEMENT OF AUTHORITY GRANTED. Subject to any limitations in this document, I hereby grant to my agent full power and authority to make health care decisions for me to the same extent that I could make such decisions for myself if I had the capacity to do so. In exercising this authority, my agent shall make health care decisions that are consistent with my desires as stated in this document or otherwise made known to my agent, including, but not limited to, my desires concerning obtaining or refusing or withdrawing life-prolonging care, treatment, services, and procedures and informing my family or next of kin of my desire, if any, to be an organ or tissue donor.

(If you want to limit the authority of your agent to make health care decisions for you, you can state the limitations in paragraph (4) ("Statement of Desires, Special Provisions, and Limitations") below. You can indicate your desires by including a statement of your desires in the same paragraph.)

(4) STATEMENT OF DESIRES, SPECIAL PROVISIONS, AND LIMITATIONS. (Your agent must make health care decisions that are consistent with your known desires. You can, but are not required to, state your desires in the space provided below. You should consider whether you want to include a statement of your desires concerning life-prolonging care, treatment, services, and procedures. You can also include a statement of your desires concerning other matters relating to your health care. You can also make your desires known to your agent by discussing your desires with your agent or by some other means. If there are any types of treatment that you do not want to be used, you should state them in the space below. If you want to limit in any other way the authority given your agent by this document, you should state the limits in the space below. If you do not state any limits, your agent will have broad powers to make health care decisions for you, except to the extent that there are limits provided by law.)

In exercising the authority under this durable power of attorney for health care, my agent shall act consistently with my desires as stated below and is subject to the special provisions and limitations stated below:

(a) Statement of desires concerning life-prolonging care, treatment, services, and procedures:

_____
_____
_____

(b) Additional statement of desires, special provisions, and limitations regarding health care decisions:

_____
_____
_____

(c) Statement of desire regarding organ and tissue donation:

_____
_____
_____

Initial if applicable:

[   ] In the event of my death, I request that my agent inform my family/next of kin of my desire to be an organ and tissue donor, if possible.

(You may attach additional pages if you need more space to complete your statement. If you attach additional pages, you must date and sign EACH of the additional pages at the same time you date and sign this document.)

(5) INSPECTION AND DISCLOSURE OF INFORMATION RELATING TO MY PHYSICAL OR MENTAL HEALTH. Subject to any limitations in this document, my agent has the power and authority to do all of the following:

(a) Request, review, and receive any information, verbal or written, regarding my physical or mental health, including, but not limited to, medical and hospital records.

(b) Execute on my behalf any releases or other documents that may be required in order to obtain this information.

(c) Consent to the disclosure of this information.

(If you want to limit the authority of your agent to receive and disclose information relating to your health, you must state the limitations in paragraph (4) ("Statement of desires, special provisions, and limitations") above.)

(6) SIGNING DOCUMENTS, WAIVERS, AND RELEASES. Where necessary to implement the health care decisions that my agent is authorized by this document to make, my agent has the power and authority to execute on my behalf all of the following:

(a) Documents titled or purporting to be a "Refusal to Permit Treatment" and "Leaving Hospital Against Medical Advice."

(b) Any necessary waiver or release from liability required by a hospital or physician.

(7) DURATION. (Unless you specify a shorter period in the space below, this power of attorney will exist until it is revoked.)

This durable power of attorney for health care expires on _____
_____ (Fill in this space ONLY if you want the authority of your agent to end on a specific date.)

(8) DESIGNATION OF ALTERNATE AGENTS. (You are not required to designate any alternate agents but you may do so. Any alternate agent you designate will be able to make the same health care decisions as the agent you designated in paragraph (1), above, in the event that agent is unable or ineligible to act as your agent. If the agent you designated is your spouse, he or she becomes ineligible to act as your agent if your marriage is dissolved.)

If the person designated as my agent in paragraph (1) is not available or becomes ineligible to act as my agent to make a health care decision for me or loses the mental capacity to make health care decisions for me, or if I revoke that person's appointment or authority to act as my agent to make health care decisions for me, then I designate and appoint the following persons to serve as my agent to make health care decisions for me as authorized in this document, such persons to serve in the order listed below:

(A) First Alternate Agent:

_____
(Insert name, address, and telephone number of first alternate agent.)

(B) Second Alternate Agent:

_____
(Insert name, address, and telephone number of second alternate agent.)

(9) PRIOR DESIGNATIONS REVOKED. I revoke any prior durable power of attorney for health care.

DATE AND SIGNATURE OF PRINCIPAL
(YOU MUST DATE AND SIGN THIS POWER OF ATTORNEY)

I sign my name to this Statutory Form Durable Power of Attorney for Health Care on _____
_____ at _____
                               (Date)
_____, _____.
                (City)   (State)

_____
            (You sign here)

(THIS POWER OF ATTORNEY WILL NOT BE VALID UNLESS IT IS SIGNED BY TWO (2) QUALIFIED WITNESSES WHO ARE PRESENT WHEN YOU SIGN OR ACKNOWLEDGE YOUR SIGNATURE. IF YOU HAVE ATTACHED ANY ADDITIONAL PAGES TO THIS FORM, YOU MUST DATE AND SIGN EACH OF THE ADDITIONAL PAGES AT THE SAME TIME YOU DATE AND SIGN THIS POWER OF ATTORNEY.)

STATEMENT OF WITNESSES

(This document must be witnessed by two (2) qualified adult witnesses. None of the following may be used as a witness:

(1) A person you designate as your agent or alternate agent,

(2) A health care provider,

(3) An employee of a health care provider,

(4) The operator of a community care facility,

(5) An employee of an operator of a community care facility.

You are not required to have this document witnessed by a notary public.

At least one of the witnesses must make the additional declaration set out following the place where the witnesses sign.)

I declare under penalty of perjury that the person who signed or acknowledged this document is personally known to me to be the principal, that the principal signed or acknowledged this durable power of attorney in my presence, that the principal appears to be of sound mind and under no duress, fraud, or undue influence, that I am not the person appointed as attorney in fact by this document, and that I am not a health care provider, an employee of a health care provider, the operator of a community care facility, nor an employee of an operator of a community care facility.

Signature: _____

Residence Address: _____

Print Name: _____

Date: _____

Signature: _____

Residence Address: _____

Print Name: _____

Date: _____

(AT LEAST ONE OF THE ABOVE WITNESSES MUST ALSO SIGN THE FOLLOWING DECLARATION.)

I further declare under penalty of perjury that I am not related to the principal by blood, marriage, or adoption, and, to the best of my knowledge, I am not entitled to any part of the estate of the principal upon the death of the principal under a will now existing or by operation of law.

Signature: _____

Print Name: _____

Signature: _____

Print Name: _____

STATE OF SOUTH CAROLINA
COUNTY OF_____

DECLARATION
OF A DESIRE FOR A
NATURAL DEATH

I,_____, Declarant, being at least eighteen years of age and a resident of and domiciled in the City of _____, County of_____, State of South Carolina, make this Declaration this ____ day of_____, 200_____.

I wilfully and voluntarily make known my desire that no life-sustaining procedures be used to prolong my dying if my condition is terminal or if I am in a state of permanent unconsciousness, and I declare:

If at any time I have a condition certified to be a terminal condition by two physicians who have personally examined me, one of whom is my attending physician, and the physicians have determined that my death could occur within a reasonably short period of time without the use of life-sustaining procedures or if the physicians certify that I am in a state of permanent unconsciousness and where the application of life-sustaining procedures would serve only to prolong the dying process, I direct that the procedures be withheld or withdrawn, and that I be permitted to die naturally with only the administration of medication or the performance of any medical procedure necessary to provide me with comfort care.

INSTRUCTIONS CONCERNING ARTIFICIAL NUTRITION AND HYDRATION

INITIAL ONE OF THE FOLLOWING STATEMENTS
If my condition is terminal and could result in death within a reasonably short time,
_____ I direct that nutrition and hydration BE PROVIDED through any medically indicated means, including medically or surgically implanted tubes.
_____ I direct that nutrition and hydration NOT BE PROVIDED through any medically indicated means, including medically or surgically implanted tubes.

INITIAL ONE OF THE FOLLOWING STATEMENTS
If I am in a persistent vegetative state or other condition of permanent unconsciousness,
_____ I direct that nutrition and hydration BE PROVIDED through any medically indicated means, including medically or surgically implanted tubes.
_____ I direct that nutrition and hydration NOT BE PROVIDED through any medically indicated means, including medically or surgically implanted tubes.

In the absence of my ability to give directions regarding the use of life-sustaining procedures, it is my intention that this Declaration be honored by my family and physicians and any health facility in which I may be a patient as the final expression of my legal right to refuse medical or surgical treatment, and I accept the consequences from the refusal.

I am aware that this Declaration authorizes a physician to withhold or withdraw life-sustaining procedures. I am emotionally and mentally competent to make this Declaration.

APPOINTMENT OF AN AGENT (OPTIONAL)
1. You may give another person authority to revoke this declaration on your behalf. If you wish to do so, please enter that person's name in the space below.
Name of Agent with Power to Revoke:_____
Address:_____
Telephone Number:_____
2. You may give another person authority to enforce this declaration on your behalf. If you wish to do so, please enter that person's name in the space below.
Name of Agent with Power to Enforce: _____
Address:_____
Telephone Number:_____

REVOCATION PROCEDURES

THIS DECLARATION MAY BE REVOKED BY ANY ONE OF THE FOLLOWING METHODS. HOWEVER, A REVOCATION IS NOT EFFECTIVE UNTIL IT IS COMMUNICATED TO THE ATTENDING PHYSICIAN.

    (1)   BY BEING DEFACED, TORN, OBLITERATED, OR OTHERWISE DESTROYED, IN EXPRESSION OF YOUR INTENT TO REVOKE, BY YOU OR BY SOME PERSON IN YOUR PRESENCE AND BY YOUR DIRECTION. REVOCATION BY DESTRUCTION OF ONE OR MORE OF MULTIPLE ORIGINAL DECLARATIONS REVOKES ALL OF THE ORIGINAL DECLARATIONS;

    (2)   BY A WRITTEN REVOCATION SIGNED AND DATED BY YOU EXPRESSING YOUR INTENT TO REVOKE;

    (3)   BY YOUR ORAL EXPRESSION OF YOUR INTENT TO REVOKE THE DECLARATION. AN ORAL REVOCATION COMMUNICATED TO THE ATTENDING PHYSICIAN BY A PERSON OTHER THAN YOU IS EFFECTIVE ONLY IF:

        (a)   THE PERSON WAS PRESENT WHEN THE ORAL REVOCATION WAS MADE;

        (b)   THE REVOCATION WAS COMMUNICATED TO THE PHYSICIAN WITHIN A REASONABLE TIME;

        (c)   YOUR PHYSICAL OR MENTAL CONDITION MAKES IT IMPOSSIBLE FOR THE PHYSICIAN TO CONFIRM THROUGH SUBSEQUENT CONVERSATION WITH YOU THAT THE REVOCATION HAS OCCURRED.

    TO BE EFFECTIVE AS A REVOCATION, THE ORAL EXPRESSION CLEARLY MUST INDICATE YOUR DESIRE THAT THE DECLARATION NOT BE GIVEN EFFECT OR THAT LIFE-SUSTAINING PROCEDURES BE ADMINISTERED;

    (4)   IF YOU, IN THE SPACE ABOVE, HAVE AUTHORIZED AN AGENT TO REVOKE THE DECLARATION, THE AGENT MAY REVOKE ORALLY OR BY A WRITTEN, SIGNED, AND DATED INSTRUMENT. AN AGENT MAY REVOKE ONLY IF YOU ARE INCOMPETENT TO DO SO. AN AGENT MAY REVOKE THE DECLARATION PERMANENTLY OR TEMPORARILY.

    (5)   BY YOUR EXECUTING ANOTHER DECLARATION AT A LATER TIME.

_____

Signature of Declarant

STATE OF _____   AFFIDAVIT

COUNTY OF _____

We, _____ and _____, The undersigned witnesses to the foregoing Declaration, dated the _____ day of _____, 200____, at least one of being first duly sworn, declare to the undersigned authority, on the basis of our best information and belief, that the Declaration was on that date signed by the declarant as and for his DECLARATION OF A DESIRE FOR A NATURAL DEATH in our presence and we, at his request and in his presence, and in the presence of each other subscribe our names as witnesses on that date. The declarant is personally known to us, and we believe him to be of sound mind. Each of us affirms that he is qualified as a witness to this Declaration under the provisions of the South Carolina Death With Dignity Act in that he is not related to the declarant by blood, marriage, or adoption, either as a spouse, lineal ancestor, descendant of the parents of the declarant, or spouse of any of them; nor directly financially responsible for the declarant's medical care; nor entitled to any portion of the declarant's estate upon his decease, whether under any will or as an heir by intestate succession, nor the beneficiary of a life insurance policy of the declarant; nor the declarant's attending physician; nor an employee of the attending physician; nor a person who has a claim against the declarant's decedent's estate as of this time. No more than one of us is an employee of a health facility in which the declarant is a patient. If the declarant is a resident in a hospital or nursing care facility at the date of execution of this Declaration, at least one of us is an ombudsman designated by the State Ombudsman, Office of the Governor.

_____   _____
Witness   Witness

      Subscribed before me by _____, the declarant, and subscribed and sworn to before me by_____, the witnesses, this _____ day of _____, 200_____.

_____
                                       Signature

Notary Public for _____

My commission expires:_____

                                                              SEAL

Health Care Power of Attorney
(SOUTH CAROLINA STATUTORY FORM)

INFORMATION ABOUT THIS DOCUMENT

THIS IS AN IMPORTANT LEGAL DOCUMENT. BEFORE SIGNING THIS DOCUMENT, YOU SHOULD KNOW THESE IMPORTANT FACTS:

1. THIS DOCUMENT GIVES THE PERSON YOU NAME AS YOUR AGENT THE POWER TO MAKE HEALTH CARE DECISIONS FOR YOU IF YOU CANNOT MAKE THE DECISION FOR YOURSELF. THIS POWER INCLUDES THE POWER TO MAKE DECISIONS ABOUT LIFE-SUSTAINING TREATMENT. UNLESS YOU STATE OTHERWISE, YOUR AGENT WILL HAVE THE SAME AUTHORITY TO MAKE DECISIONS ABOUT YOUR HEALTH CARE AS YOU WOULD HAVE.

2. THIS POWER IS SUBJECT TO ANY LIMITATIONS OR STATEMENTS OF YOUR DESIRES THAT YOU INCLUDE IN THIS DOCUMENT. YOU MAY STATE IN THIS DOCUMENT ANY TREATMENT YOU DO NOT DESIRE OR TREATMENT YOU WANT TO BE SURE YOU RECEIVE. YOUR AGENT WILL BE OBLIGATED TO FOLLOW YOUR INSTRUCTIONS WHEN MAKING DECISIONS ON YOUR BEHALF. YOU MAY ATTACH ADDITIONAL PAGES IF YOU NEED MORE SPACE TO COMPLETE THE STATEMENT.

3. AFTER YOU HAVE SIGNED THIS DOCUMENT, YOU HAVE THE RIGHT TO MAKE HEALTH CARE DECISIONS FOR YOURSELF IF YOU ARE MENTALLY COMPETENT TO DO SO. AFTER YOU HAVE SIGNED THIS DOCUMENT, NO TREATMENT MAY BE GIVEN TO YOU OR STOPPED OVER YOUR OBJECTION IF YOU ARE MENTALLY COMPETENT TO MAKE THAT DECISION.

4. YOU HAVE THE RIGHT TO REVOKE THIS DOCUMENT, AND TERMINATE YOUR AGENT'S AUTHORITY, BY INFORMING EITHER YOUR AGENT OR YOUR HEALTH CARE PROVIDER ORALLY OR IN WRITING.

5. IF THERE IS ANYTHING IN THIS DOCUMENT THAT YOU DO NOT UNDERSTAND, YOU SHOULD ASK A SOCIAL WORKER, LAWYER, OR OTHER PERSON TO EXPLAIN IT TO YOU.

6. THIS POWER OF ATTORNEY WILL NOT BE VALID UNLESS TWO PERSONS SIGN AS WITNESSES. EACH OF THESE PERSONS MUST EITHER WITNESS YOUR SIGNING OF THE POWER OF ATTORNEY OR WITNESS YOUR ACKNOWLEDGMENT THAT THE SIGNATURE ON THE POWER OF ATTORNEY IS YOURS.

THE FOLLOWING PERSONS MAY NOT ACT AS WITNESSES:

A. YOUR SPOUSE; YOUR CHILDREN, GRANDCHILDREN, AND OTHER LINEAL DESCENDANTS; YOUR PARENTS, GRANDPARENTS, AND OTHER LINEAL ANCESTORS; YOUR SIBLINGS AND THEIR LINEAL DESCENDANTS; OR A SPOUSE OF ANY OF THESE PERSONS.

B. A PERSON WHO IS DIRECTLY FINANCIALLY RESPONSIBLE FOR YOUR MEDICAL CARE.

C. A PERSON WHO IS NAMED IN YOUR WILL, OR, IF YOU HAVE NO WILL, WHO WOULD INHERIT YOUR PROPERTY BY INTESTATE SUCCESSION.

D. A BENEFICIARY OF A LIFE INSURANCE POLICY ON YOUR LIFE.

E. THE PERSONS NAMED IN THE HEALTH CARE POWER OF ATTORNEY AS YOUR AGENT OR SUCCESSOR AGENT.

F. YOUR PHYSICIAN OR AN EMPLOYEE OF YOUR PHYSICIAN.

G. ANY PERSON WHO WOULD HAVE A CLAIM AGAINST ANY PORTION OF YOUR ESTATE (PERSONS TO WHOM YOU OWE MONEY).

IF YOU ARE A PATIENT IN A HEALTH FACILITY, NO MORE THAN ONE WITNESS MAY BE AN EMPLOYEE OF THAT FACILITY.

7. YOUR AGENT MUST BE A PERSON WHO IS 18 YEARS OLD OR OLDER AND OF SOUND MIND. IT MAY NOT BE YOUR DOCTOR OR ANY OTHER HEALTH CARE PROVIDER THAT IS NOW PROVIDING YOU WITH TREATMENT; OR AN EMPLOYEE OF

YOUR DOCTOR OR PROVIDER; OR A SPOUSE OF THE DOCTOR, PROVIDER, OR EMPLOYEE; UNLESS THE PERSON IS A RELATIVE OF YOURS.

8. YOU SHOULD INFORM THE PERSON THAT YOU WANT HIM OR HER TO BE YOUR HEALTH CARE AGENT. YOU SHOULD DISCUSS THIS DOCUMENT WITH YOUR AGENT AND YOUR PHYSICIAN AND GIVE EACH A SIGNED COPY. IF YOU ARE IN A HEALTH CARE FACILITY OR A NURSING CARE FACILITY, A COPY OF THIS DOCUMENT SHOULD BE INCLUDED IN YOUR MEDICAL RECORD.

1. DESIGNATION OF HEALTH CARE AGENT

I,_____, hereby appoint:
     (Principal)

_____ (Agent)
_____ (Address)
Home Telephone:_____ Work Telephone:_____
as my agent to make health care decisions for me as authorized in this document.

2. EFFECTIVE DATE AND DURABILITY By this document I intend to create a durable power of attorney effective upon, and only during, any period of mental incompetence.

3. AGENT'S POWERS I grant to my agent full authority to make decisions for me regarding my health care. In exercising this authority, my agent shall follow my desires as stated in this document or otherwise expressed by me or known to my agent. In making any decision, my agent shall attempt to discuss the proposed decision with me to determine my desires if I am able to communicate in any way. If my agent cannot determine the choice I would want made, then my agent shall make a choice for me based upon what my agent believes to be in my best interests. My agent's authority to interpret my desires is intended to be as broad as possible, except for any limitations I may state below.

Accordingly, unless specifically limited by Section E, below, my agent is authorized as follows:

A. To consent, refuse, or withdraw consent to any and all types of medical care, treatment, surgical procedures, diagnostic procedures, medication, and the use of mechanical or other procedures that affect any bodily function, including, but not limited to, artificial respiration, nutritional support and hydration, and cardiopulmonary resuscitation;

B. To authorize, or refuse to authorize, any medication or procedure intended to relieve pain, even though such use may lead to physical damage, addiction, or hasten the moment of, but not intentionally cause, my death;

C. To authorize my admission to or discharge, even against medical advice, from any hospital, nursing care facility, or similar facility or service;

D. To take any other action necessary to making, documenting, and assuring implementation of decisions concerning my health care, including, but not limited to, granting any waiver or release from liability required by any hospital, physician, nursing care provider, or other health care provider; signing any documents relating to refusals of treatment or the leaving of a facility against medical advice, and pursuing any legal action in my name, and at the expense of my estate to force compliance with my wishes as determined by my agent, or to seek actual or punitive damages for the failure to comply.

E. The powers granted above do not include the following powers or are subject to the following rules or limitations: _____
_____
_____

4. ORGAN DONATION (INITIAL ONLY ONE)

My agent may _____;   may not _____ consent to the donation of all or any of my tissue or organs for purposes of transplantation.

5. EFFECT ON DECLARATION OF A DESIRE FOR A NATURAL DEATH (LIVING WILL)

I understand that if I have a valid Declaration of a Desire for a Natural Death, the instructions contained in the Declaration will be given effect in any situation to which they are applicable. My agent will have authority to make decisions concerning my health care only in situations to which the Declaration does not apply.

6. STATEMENT OF DESIRES AND SPECIAL PROVISIONS With respect to any Life-Sustaining Treatment, I direct the following: (INITIAL ONLY ONE OF THE FOLLOWING 4 PARAGRAPHS)

(1) _____ GRANT OF DISCRETION TO AGENT. I do not want my life to be prolonged nor do I want life-sustaining treatment to be provided or continued if my agent believes the burdens of the treatment outweigh the expected benefits. I want my agent to consider the relief of suffering, my personal beliefs, the expense involved and the quality as well as the possible extension of my life in making decisions concerning life-sustaining treatment.

OR

(2) _____ DIRECTIVE TO WITHHOLD OR WITHDRAW TREATMENT. I do not want my life to be prolonged and I do not want life-sustaining treatment:

    a. if I have a condition that is incurable or irreversible and, without the administration of life-sustaining procedures, expected to result in death within a relatively short period of time; or

    b. if I am in a state of permanent unconsciousness.

OR

(3) _____ DIRECTIVE FOR MAXIMUM TREATMENT. I want my life to be prolonged to the greatest extent possible, within the standards of accepted medical practice, without regard to my condition, the chances I have for recovery, or the cost of the procedures.

OR

(4) _____ DIRECTIVE IN MY OWN WORDS: _____

_____

_____

7. STATEMENT OF DESIRES REGARDING TUBE FEEDING

With respect to Nutrition and Hydration provided by means of a nasogastric tube or tube into the stomach, intestines, or veins, I wish to make clear that (INITIAL ONLY ONE)

_____ I do not want to receive these forms of artificial nutrition and hydration, and they may be withheld or withdrawn under the conditions given above;

OR

_____ I do want to receive these forms of artificial nutrition and hydration.

IF YOU DO NOT INITIAL EITHER OF THE ABOVE STATEMENTS, YOUR AGENT WILL NOT HAVE AUTHORITY TO DIRECT THAT NUTRITION AND HYDRATION NECESSARY FOR COMFORT CARE OR ALLEVIATION OF PAIN BE WITHDRAWN.

8. SUCCESSORS

If an agent named by me dies, becomes legally disabled, resigns, refuses to act, becomes unavailable, or if an agent who is my spouse is divorced or separated from me, I name the following as successors to my agent, each to act alone and successively, in the order named.

A.   First Alternate Agent: _____
Name: _____
Address: _____
Telephone: _____

B.   Second Alternate Agent:
Name: _____
Address: _____
Telephone: _____

9. ADMINISTRATIVE PROVISIONS

A.   I revoke any prior Health Care Power of Attorney and any provisions relating to health care of any other prior power of attorney.

B.   This power of attorney is intended to be valid in any jurisdiction in which it is presented.

10. UNAVAILABILITY OF AGENT

If at any relevant time the Agent or Successor Agents named herein are unable or unwilling to make decisions concerning my health care, and those decision are to be made by a guardian, by the Probate Court, or by a surrogate pursuant to the Adult Health Care Consent Act, it is my intention that the guardian, Probate Court, or surrogate make those decisions in accordance with my directions as stated in this document.

BY SIGNING HERE I INDICATE THAT I UNDERSTAND THE CONTENT OF THIS DOCUMENT AND THE EFFECT OF THIS GRANT OF POWERS TO MY AGENT.

I sign my name to this Health Care Power of Attorney on this _____ day of _____, _____. My current home address is: _____
_____

Signature: _____

Name: _____

WITNESS STATEMENT

I declare, on the basis of information and belief, that the person who signed or acknowledged this document (the principal) is personally known to me, that he/she signed or acknowledged this Health Care Power of Attorney in my presence, and that he/she appears to be of sound mind and under no duress, fraud, or undue influence. I am not related to the principal by blood, marriage, or adoption, either as a spouse, a lineal ancestor, descendant of the parents of the principal, or spouse of any of them. I am not directly financially responsible for the principal's medical care. I am not entitled to any portion of the principal's estate upon his decease, whether under any will or as an heir by intestate succession, nor am I the beneficiary of an insurance policy on the principal's life, nor do I have a claim against the principal's estate as of this time. I am not the principal's attending physician, nor an employee of the attending physician. No more than one witness is an employee of a health facility in which the principal is a patient. I am not appointed as Health Care Agent or Successor Health Care Agent by this document.

Witness No. 1	Witness No. 2
Date: _____	Date: _____
Signature: _____	Signature: _____
Print Name: _____	Print Name: _____
Residence Address: _____	Residence Address: _____
_____	_____
_____	_____
Telephone: _____	Telephone: _____

LIVING WILL DECLARATION

This is an important legal document. This document directs the medical treatment you are to receive in the event you are unable to participate in your own medical decisions and you are in a terminal condition. This document may state what kind of treatment you want or do not want to receive.

This document can control whether you live or die. Prepare this document carefully. If you use this form, read it completely. You may want to seek professional help to make sure the form does what you intend and is completed without mistakes.

This document will remain valid and in effect until and unless you revoke it. Review this document periodically to make sure it continues to reflect your wishes. You may amend or revoke this document at any time by notifying your physician and other health-care providers. You should give copies of this Document to your physician and your family. This form is entirely optional. If you choose to use this form, please note that the form provides signature lines for you, the two witnesses whom you have selected and a notary public.

TO MY FAMILY, PHYSICIANS, AND ALL THOSE CONCERNED WITH MY CARE:

I, _____, willfully and voluntarily make this declaration as a directive to be followed if I am in a terminal condition and become unable to participate in decisions regarding my medical care.

With respect to any life-sustaining treatment, I direct the following:

(Initial only one of the following optional directives if you agree. If you do not agree with any of the following directives, space is provided below for you to write your own directives).

_____ NO LIFE-SUSTAINING TREATMENT. I direct that no life-sustaining treatment be provided. If life-sustaining treatment is begun, terminate it.

_____ TREATMENT FOR RESTORATION. Provide life-sustaining treatment only if and for so long as you believe treatment offers a reasonable possibility of restoring to me the ability to think and act for myself.

_____ TREAT UNLESS PERMANENTLY UNCONSCIOUS. If you believe that I am permanently unconscious and are satisfied that this condition is irreversible, then do not provide me with life-sustaining treatment, and if life-sustaining treatment is being provided to me, terminate it. If and so long as you believe that treatment has a reasonable possibility of restoring consciousness to me, then provide life-sustaining treatment.

_____ MAXIMUM TREATMENT. Preserve my life as long as possible, but do not provide treatment that is not in accordance with accepted medical standards as then in effect.

(Artificial nutrition and hydration is food and water provided by means of a nasogastric tube or tubes inserted into the stomach, intestines, or veins. If you do not wish to receive this form of treatment, you must initial the statement below which reads: "I intend to include this treatment, among the 'life-sustaining treatment' that may be withheld or withdrawn.")

With respect to artificial nutrition and hydration, I wish to make clear that (Initial only one)

_____ I intend to include this treatment among the "life-sustaining treatment" that may be withheld or withdrawn.

_____ I do not intend to include this treatment among the "life-sustaining treatment" that may be withheld or withdrawn.

(If you do not agree with any of the printed directives and want to write your own, or if you want to write directives in addition to the printed provisions, or if you want to express some of your other thoughts, you can do so here.)

_____

_____

_____

Date: _____   _____

                                        (your signature)

_____   _____

(your address)   (type or print your signature)

The declarant voluntarily signed this document in my presence.

Witness_____   Witness_____

Address _____   Address _____

        On this _____ day of_____, 200_____, the declarant, _____, and witnesses _____, and_____, personally appeared before the undersigned officer and signed the foregoing instrument in my presence. Dated this _____ day of _____, 200_____.

_____

Notary Public
My commission expires: _____

LIVING WILL

I, _____, willfully and voluntarily make known my desire that my dying shall not be artificially prolonged under the circumstances set forth below, and do hereby declare:

If at any time I should have a terminal condition and my attending physician has determined there is no reasonable medical expectation of recovery and which, as a medical probability, will result in my death, regardless of the use or discontinuance of medical treatment implemented for the purpose of sustaining life, or the life process, I direct that medical care be withheld or withdrawn, and that I be permitted to die naturally with only the administration of medications or the performance of any medical procedure deemed necessary to provide me with comfortable care or to alleviate pain.

ARTIFICIALLY PROVIDED NOURISHMENT AND FLUIDS:

By checking the appropriate line below, I specifically:

_____Authorize the withholding or withdrawal of artificially provided food, water or other nourishment or fluids.

_____DO NOT authorize the withholding or withdrawal of artificially provided food, water or other nourishment or fluids.

ORGAN DONOR CERTIFICATION:

Notwithstanding my previous declaration relative to the withholding or withdrawal of life-prolonging procedures, if as indicated below I have expressed my desire to donate my organs and/or tissues for transplantation, or any of them as specifically designated herein, I do direct my attending physician, if I have been determined dead according to Tennessee Code Annotated, § 68-3-501(b), to maintain me on artificial support systems only for the period of time required to maintain the viability of and to remove such organs and/or tissues.

By checking the appropriate line below, I specifically:

_____Desire to donate my organs and/or tissues for transplantation.

_____Desire to donate my _____
(insert specific organs and/or tissues for transplantation)

_____DO NOT desire to donate my organs or tissues for transplantation.

In the absence of my ability to give directions regarding my medical care, it is my intention that this declaration shall be honored by my family and physician as the final expression of my legal right to refuse medical care and accept the consequences of such refusal.

The definitions of terms used herein shall be as set forth in the Tennessee Right to Natural Death Act, Tennessee Code Annotated, § 32-11-103.

I understand the full import of this declaration, and I am emotionally and mentally competent to make this declaration.

In acknowledgment whereof, I do hereinafter affix my signature on this the _____ day of _____, 200____.

_____
Declarant

We, the subscribing witnesses hereto, are personally acquainted with and subscribe our names hereto at the request of the declarant, an adult, whom we believe to be of sound mind, fully aware of the action taken herein and its possible consequence.

We, the undersigned witnesses, further declare that we are not related to the declarant by blood or marriage; that we are not entitled to any portion of the estate of the declarant upon the declarant's decease under any will or codicil thereto presently existing or by operation of law then existing; that we are not the attending physician, an employee of the attending physician or health facility in which the declarant is a patient; and that we are not persons who, at the present time, have a claim against any portion of the estate of the declarant upon the declarant's death.

_____   _____
Witness   Witness

STATE OF TENNESSEE
COUNTY OF _____

    Subscribed, sworn to and acknowledged before me by _____, the declarant, and subscribed and sworn to before me by _____ and _____, witnesses, this _____ day of _____, 200_____.

_____
Notary Public

My Commission Expires: _____

Durable Power of Attorney for Health Care

WARNING TO PERSON EXECUTING THIS DOCUMENT

This is an important legal document. Before executing this document you should know these important facts.

This document gives the person you designate as your agent (the attorney in fact) the power to make health care decisions for you. Your agent must act consistently with your desires as stated in this document.

Except as you otherwise specify in this document, this document gives your agent the power to consent to your doctor not giving treatment or stopping treatment necessary to keep you alive.

Notwithstanding this document, you have the right to make medical and other health care decisions for yourself so long as you can give informed consent with respect to the particular decision. In addition, no treatment may be given to you over your objection, and health care necessary to keep you alive may not be stopped or withheld if you object at the time.

This document gives your agent authority to consent, to refuse to consent, or to withdraw consent to any care, treatment, service, or procedure to maintain, diagnose or treat a physical or mental condition. This power is subject to any limitations that you include in this document. You may state in this document any types of treatment that you do not desire. In addition, a court can take away the power of your agent to make health care decisions for you if your agent: (1) authorizes anything that is illegal; or (2) acts contrary to your desires as stated in this document.

You have the right to revoke the authority of your agent by notifying your agent or your treating physician, hospital or other health care provider orally or in writing of the revocation.

Your agent has the right to examine your medical records and to consent to their disclosure unless you limit this right in this document.

Unless you otherwise specify in this document, this document gives your agent the power after you die to: (1) authorize an autopsy; (2) donate your body or parts thereof for transplant or therapeutic or educational or scientific purposes; and (3) direct the disposition of your remains.

If there is anything in this document that you do not understand, you should ask an attorney to explain it to you.

I, _____

_____ (insert your name and address),

appoint _____

_____ (insert name, address, and telephone number of agent), as my attorney in fact (agent) for health care decisions. I appoint _____

_____(insert name, address, and telephone number of alternate agent), as my alternative agent for health care decisions. I authorize my agent to make health care decisions for me when I am incapable of making my own health care decisions, with all of the authority permitted under the laws of Tennessee, except as may be limited in the following paragraph. I understand the consequences of appointing an agent for health care.

Special Instructions and Limitations: I direct that my agent comply with the following instructions or limitations (if none, write in the word "none"): _____

_____

_____

In addition, I direct that my agent have authority to make decisions regarding the enforcement of my intentions regarding life-prolonging procedures as stated in any living will I have executed or may execute in the future.

Dated:_____   _____

Signature of Principal

WITNESS STATEMENT

I declare under penalty of perjury under the laws of Tennessee that the person who signed this document is personally known to me to be the principal; that the principal signed this durable power of attorney in my presence; that the principal appears to be of sound mind and under no duress, fraud or undue influence; that I am not the person appointed as attorney in fact by this document; that I am not a health care provider, an employee of a health care provider, the operator of a health care institution nor an employee of an operator of a health care institution; that I am not related to the principal by blood, marriage, or adoption; that, to the best of my knowledge, I do not, at the present time, have a claim against any portion of the estate of the principal upon the principal's death; and that, to the best of my knowledge, I am not entitled to any part of the estate of the principal upon the death of the principal under a will or codicil thereto now existing, or by operation of law.

Witness_____   Witness_____

STATE OF TENNESSEE
COUNTY OF _____

Subscribed, sworn to and acknowledged before me by _____
_____, the declarant, and subscribed and sworn to before me by
_____ and _____,
witnesses, this _____ day of _____, _____.

_____

Notary Public

My Commission Expires:_____

DIRECTIVE TO PHYSICIANS AND FAMILY OR SURROGATES

Instructions for completing this document:

This is an important legal document known as an Advance Directive. It is designed to help you communicate your wishes about medical treatment at some time in the future when you are unable to make your wishes known because of illness or injury. These wishes are usually based on personal values. In particular, you may want to consider what burdens or hardships of treatment you would be willing to accept for a particular amount of benefit obtained if you were seriously ill.

You are encouraged to discuss your values and wishes with your family or chosen spokesperson, as well as your physician. Your physician, other health care provider, or medical institution may provide you with various resources to assist you in completing your advance directive. Brief definitions are listed below and may aid you in your discussions and advance planning. Initial the treatment choices that best reflect your personal preferences. Provide a copy of your directive to your physician, usual hospital, and family or spokesperson. Consider a periodic review of this document. By periodic review, you can best assure that the directive reflects your preferences.

In addition to this advance directive, Texas law provides for two other types of directives that can be important during a serious illness. These are the Medical Power of Attorney and the Out-of-Hospital Do-Not-Resuscitate Order. You may wish to discuss these with your physician, family, hospital representative, or other advisers. You may also wish to complete a directive related to the donation of organs and tissues.

DIRECTIVE

I, _____, recognize that the best health care is based upon a partnership of trust and communication with my physician. My physician and I will make health care decisions together as long as I am of sound mind and able to make my wishes known. If there comes a time that I am unable to make medical decisions about myself because of illness or injury, I direct that the following treatment preferences be honored:

If, in the judgment of my physician, I am suffering with a terminal condition from which I am expected to die within six months, even with available life-sustaining treatment provided in accordance with prevailing standards of medical care:

_____ I request that all treatments other than those needed to keep me comfortable be discontinued or withheld and my physician allow me to die as gently as possible; OR

_____ I request that I be kept alive in this terminal condition using available life-sustaining treatment. (THIS SELECTION DOES NOT APPLY TO HOSPICE CARE.)

If, in the judgment of my physician, I am suffering with an irreversible condition so that I cannot care for myself or make decisions for myself and am expected to die without life-sustaining treatment provided in accordance with prevailing standards of care:

_____ I request that all treatments other than those needed to keep me comfortable by discontinued or withheld and my physician allow me to die as gently as possible; OR

_____ I request that I be kept alive in this irreversible condition using available life-sustaining treatment. (THIS SELECTION DOES NOT APPLY TO HOSPICE CARE.)

Additional requests: (After discussion with your physician, you may wish to consider listing particular treatments in this space that you do or do not want in specific circumstances, such as

artificial nutrition and fluids, intravenous antibiotics, etc. Be sure to state whether you do or do not want the particular treatment.) _____
_____
_____

After signing this directive, if my representative or I elect hospice care, I understand and agree that only those treatments needed to keep me comfortable would be provided and I would not be given available life-sustaining treatments.

If I do not have a Medical Power of Attorney, and I am unable to make my wishes known, I designate the following person(s) to make treatment decisions with my physician compatible with my personal values:
1. _____

2. _____

(If a Medical Power of Attorney has been executed, then an agent already has been named and you should not list additional names in this document.)

If the above persons are not available, or if I have not designated a spokesperson, I understand that a spokesperson will be chosen for me following standards specified in the laws of Texas. If, in the judgment of my physician, my death is imminent within minutes to hours, even with the use of all available medical treatment provided within the prevailing standard of care, I acknowledge that all treatments may be withheld or removed except those needed to maintain my comfort. I understand that under Texas law this directive has no effect if I have been diagnosed as pregnant. This directive will remain in effect until I revoke it. No other person may do so.

Signed _____ Date _____

City, County, State of Residence _____

Two competent adult witnesses must sign below, acknowledging the signature of the declarant. The witness designated as Witness 1 may not be a person designated to make a treatment decision for the patient and may not be related to the patient by blood or marriage. This witness may not be entitled to any part of the estate and may not have a claim against the estate of the patient. This witness may not be the attending physician or an employee of the attending physician. If this witness is an employee of a health care facility in which the patient is being cared for, this witness may not be involved in providing direct patient care to the patient. This witness may not be an officer, director, partner, or business office employee of a health care facility in which the patient is being cared for or of any parent organization of the health care facility.
Witness 1 _____ Witness 2 _____

Definitions:

"Artificial nutrition and hydration" means the provision of nutrients or fluids by a tube inserted in a vein, under the skin in the subcutaneous tissues, or in the stomach (gastrointestinal tract).

"Irreversible condition" means a condition, injury, or illness:

(1) that may be treated, but is never cured or eliminated;

(2) that leaves a person unable to care for or make decisions for the person's own self; and

(3) that, without life-sustaining treatment provided in accordance with the prevailing standard of medical care, is fatal.

Explanation: Many serious illnesses such as cancer, failure of major organs (kidney, heart, liver, or lung), and serious brain disease such as Alzheimer's dementia may be considered irreversible early on. There is no cure, but the patient may be kept alive for prolonged periods of time if the patient receives life-sustaining treatments. Late in the course of the same illness, the disease may be considered terminal when, even with treatment, the patient is expected to die. You may wish to consider which burdens of treatment you would be willing to accept in an effort to achieve a particular outcome. This is a very personal decision that you may wish to discuss with your physician, family, or other important persons in your life.

"Life-sustaining treatment" means treatment that, based on reasonable medical judgment, sustains the life of a patient and without which the patient will die. The term includes both life-sustaining medications and artificial life support such as mechanical breathing machines, kidney dialysis treatment, and artificial hydration and nutrition. The term does not include the administration of pain management medication, the performance of a medical procedure necessary to provide comfort care, or any other medical care provided to alleviate a patient's pain.

"Terminal condition" means an incurable condition caused by injury, disease, or illness that according to reasonable medical judgment will produce death within six months, even with available life-sustaining treatment provided in accordance with the prevailing standard of medical care.

Explanation: Many serious illnesses may be considered irreversible early in the course of the illness, but they may not be considered terminal until the disease is fairly advanced. In thinking about terminal illness and its treatment, you again may wish to consider the relative benefits and burdens of treatment and discuss your wishes with your physician, family, or other important persons in your life.

MEDICAL POWER OF ATTORNEY

INFORMATION CONCERNING THE MEDICAL POWER OF ATTORNEY

THIS IS AN IMPORTANT LEGAL DOCUMENT. BEFORE SIGNING THIS DOCUMENT, YOU SHOULD KNOW THESE IMPORTANT FACTS:

Except to the extent you state otherwise, this document gives the person you name as your agent the authority to make any and all health care decisions for you in accordance with your wishes, including your religious and moral beliefs, when you are no longer capable of making them yourself. Because "health care" means any treatment, service, or procedure to maintain, diagnose, or treat your physical or mental condition, your agent has the power to make a broad range of health care decisions for you. Your agent may consent, refuse to consent, or withdraw consent to medical treatment and may make decisions about withdrawing or withholding life-sustaining treatment. Your agent may not consent to voluntary inpatient mental health services, convulsive treatment, psychosurgery, or abortion. A physician must comply with your agent's instructions or allow you to be transferred to another physician.

Your agent's authority begins when your doctor certifies that you lack the competence to make health care decisions.

Your agent is obligated to follow your instructions when making decisions on your behalf. Unless you state otherwise, your agent has the same authority to make decisions about your health care as you would have had.

It is important that you discuss this document with your physician or other health care provider before you sign it to make sure that you understand the nature and range of decisions that may be made on your behalf. If you do not have a physician, you should talk with someone else who is knowledgeable about these issues and can answer your questions. You do not need a lawyer's assistance to complete this document, but if there is anything in this document that you do not understand, you should ask a lawyer to explain it to you.

The person you appoint as agent should be someone you know and trust. The person must be 18 years of age or older or a person under 18 years of age who has had the disabilities of minority removed. If you appoint your health or residential care provider (e.g., your physician or an employee of a home health agency, hospital, nursing home, or residential care home, other than a relative), that person has to choose between acting as your agent or as your health or residential care provider; the law does not permit a person to do both at the same time.

You should inform the person you appoint that you want the person to be your health care agent. You should discuss this document with your agent and your physician and give each a signed copy. You should indicate on the document itself the people and institutions who have signed copies. Your agent is not liable for health care decisions made in good faith on your behalf.

Even after you have signed this document, you have the right to make health care decisions for yourself as long as you are able to do so and treatment cannot be given to you or stopped over your objection. You have the right to revoke the authority granted to your agent by informing your agent or your health or residential care provider orally or in writing or by your execution of a subsequent medical power of attorney. Unless you state otherwise, your appointment of a spouse dissolves on divorce.

This document may not be changed or modified. If you want to make changes in the document, you must make an entirely new one.

You may wish to designate an alternate agent in the event that your agent is unwilling, unable, or ineligible to act as your agent. Any alternate agent you designate has the same authority to make health care decisions for you.

THIS POWER OF ATTORNEY IS NOT VALID UNLESS IT IS SIGNED IN THE PRESENCE OF TWO COMPETENT ADULT WITNESSES. THE FOLLOWING PERSONS MAY NOT ACT AS ONE OF THE WITNESSES:

(1) the person you have designated as your agent;

(2) a person related to you by blood or marriage;

(3) a person entitled to any part of your estate after your death under a will or codicil executed by you or by operation of law;

(4) your attending physician;

(5) an employee of your attending physician;

(6) an employee of a health care facility in which you are a patient if the employee is providing direct patient care to you or is an officer, director, partner, or business office employee of the health care facility or of any parent organization of the health care facility; or

(7) a person who, at the time this power of attorney is executed, has a claim against any part of your estate after your death.

MEDICAL POWER OF ATTORNEY DESIGNATION OF HEALTH CARE AGENT

I, _____(insert your name), appoint:
Name: _____
Address:_____
Phone: _____

as my agent to make any and all health care decisions for me, except to the extent I state otherwise in this document. This medical power of attorney takes effect if I become unable to make my own health care decisions and this fact is certified in writing by my physician.

LIMITATIONS ON THE DECISION-MAKING AUTHORITY OF MY AGENT ARE AS FOLLOWS:
_____
_____
_____

DESIGNATION OF ALTERNATE AGENT.

(You are not required to designate an alternate agent but you may do so. An alternate agent may make the same health care decisions as the designated agent if the designated agent is unable or unwilling to act as your agent. If the agent designated is your spouse, the designation is automatically revoked by law if your marriage is dissolved.)

If the person designated as my agent is unable or unwilling to make health care decisions for me, I designate the following persons to serve as my agent to make health care decisions for me as authorized by this document, who serve in the following order:

A.   First Alternate Agent
        Name: _____
        Address: _____
        Phone: _____

B.   Second Alternate Agent
        Name: _____
        Address: _____
        Phone: _____

The original of this document is kept at: _____
_____
_____

The following individuals or institutions have signed copies:
        Name: _____
        Address: _____
        Phone: _____

        Name: _____
        Address: _____
        Phone: _____

DURATION.

I understand that this power of attorney exists indefinitely from the date I execute this document unless I establish a shorter time or revoke the power of attorney. If I am unable to make health care decisions for myself when this power of attorney expires, the authority I have granted my agent continues to exist until the time I become able to make health care decisions for myself.

(IF APPLICABLE) This power of attorney ends on the following date:

_____

PRIOR DESIGNATIONS REVOKED.

I revoke any prior medical power of attorney.

ACKNOWLEDGMENT OF DISCLOSURE STATEMENT.

I have been provided with a disclosure statement explaining the effect of this document. I have read and understand that information contained in the disclosure statement.

(YOU MUST DATE AND SIGN THIS POWER OF ATTORNEY.)

I sign my name to this medical power of attorney on _____ day of _____(month, year) at _____
(City and State)

_____
(Signature)

_____
(Printed Name)

STATEMENT OF FIRST WITNESS.

I am not the person appointed as agent by this document. I am not related to the principal by blood or marriage. I would not be entitled to any portion of the principal's estate on the principal's death. I am not the attending physician of the principal or an employee of the attending physician. I have no claim against any portion of the principal's estate on the principal's death. Furthermore, if I am an employee of a health care facility in which the principal is a patient, I am not involved in providing direct patient care to the principal and am not an officer, director, partner, or business office employee of the health care facility or of any parent organization of the health care facility.

Signature: _____

Printed Name: _____   Date: _____

Address: _____

SIGNATURE OF SECOND WITNESS.

Signature: _____

Printed Name: _____   Date: _____

Address: _____

DIRECTIVE TO PHYSICIANS AND PROVIDERS OF MEDICAL SERVICES

(Pursuant to Section 75-2-1104, UCA)

This directive is made this _____ day of _____, 200_____.

1.   I, _____, being of sound mind, willfully and voluntarily make known my desire that my life not be artificially prolonged by life-sustaining procedures except as I may otherwise provide in this directive.

2.   I declare that if at any time I should have an injury, disease, or illness, which is certified in writing to be a terminal condition or persistent vegetative state by two physicians who have personally examined me, and in the opinion of those physicians the application of life-sustaining procedures would serve only to unnaturally prolong the moment of my death and to unnaturally postpone or prolong the dying process, I direct that these procedures be withheld or withdrawn and my death be permitted to occur naturally.

3.   I expressly intend this directive to be a final expression of my legal right to refuse medical or surgical treatment and to accept the consequences from this refusal which shall remain in effect notwithstanding my future inability to give current medical directions to treating physicians and other providers of medical services.

4.   I understand that the term "life-sustaining procedure" includes artificial nutrition and hydration and any other procedures that I specify below to be considered life-sustaining but does not include the administration of medication or the performance of any medical procedure which is intended to provide comfort care or to alleviate pain:_____

_____

5.   I reserve the right to give current medical directions to physicians and other providers of medical services so long as I am able, even though these directions may conflict with the above written directive that life-sustaining procedures be withheld or withdrawn.

6.   I understand the full import of this directive and declare that I am emotionally and mentally competent to make this directive.

_____   _____
Declarant's signature   City, County, and State of Residence

We witnesses certify that each of us is 18 years of age or older and each personally witnessed the declarant sign or direct the signing of this directive; that we are acquainted with the declarant and believe him to be of sound mind; that the declarant's desires are as expressed above; that neither of us is a person who signed the above directive on behalf of the declarant; that we are not related to the declarant by blood or marriage nor are we entitled to any portion of declarant's estate according to the laws of intestate succession of this state or under any will or codicil of declarant; that we are not directly financially responsible for declarant's medical care; and that we are not agents of any health care facility in which the declarant may be a patient at the time of signing this directive.

_____   _____
Signature of Witness   Signature of Witness

_____   _____

Special Power of Attorney

I, _____ , of _____ ,
this _____ day of _____ , _____ , being of sound mind,
willfully and voluntarily appoint _____ ,
of _____ , as my agent and
attorney-in-fact, without substitution, with lawful authority to execute a directive on my
behalf under Section 75-2-1105, governing the care and treatment to be administered to
or withheld from me at any time after I incur an injury, disease, or illness which renders
me unable to give current directions to attending physicians and other providers of
medical services.

I have carefully selected my above-named agent with confidence in the belief
that this person's familiarity with my desires, beliefs, and attitudes will result in directions
to attending physicians and providers of medical services which would probably be the
same as I would give if able to do so.

This power of attorney shall be and remain in effect from the time my attending
physician certifies that I have incurred a physical or mental condition rendering me
unable to give current directions to attending physicians and other providers of medical
services as to my care and treatment.

_____
Signature of Principal

State of _____)
County of _____)

On the _____ day of _____ , _____ , personally
appeared before me _____ , who duly
acknowledged to me that he has read and fully understands the foregoing power of
attorney, executed the same of his own volition and for the purposes set forth, and that
he was acting under no constraint or undue influence whatsoever.

_____
Notary Public

My commission expires: Residing at: _____

_____

Durable Power of Attorney for Health Care

INFORMATION CONCERNING THE DURABLE POWER OF ATTORNEY FOR HEALTH CARE

THIS IS AN IMPORTANT LEGAL DOCUMENT. BEFORE SIGNING THIS DOCUMENT, YOU SHOULD KNOW THESE IMPORTANT FACTS:

Except to the extent you state otherwise, this document gives the person you name as your agent the authority to make any and all health care decisions for you when you are no longer capable of making them yourself. "Health care" means any treatment, service or procedure to maintain, diagnose or treat your physical or mental condition. Your agent therefore can have the power to make a broad range of health care decisions for you. Your agent may consent, refuse to consent, or withdraw consent to medical treatment and may make decisions about withdrawing or withholding life-sustaining treatment.

You may state in this document any treatment you do not desire or treatment you want to be sure you receive. Your agent's authority will begin when your doctor certifies that you lack the capacity to make health care decisions. You may attach additional pages if you need more space to complete your statement.

Your agent will be obligated to follow your instructions when making decisions on your behalf. Unless you state otherwise, your agent will have the same authority to make decisions about your health care as you would have had.

It is important that you discuss this document with your physician or other health care providers before you sign it to make sure that you understand the nature and range of decisions which may be made on your behalf. If you do not have a physician, you should talk with someone else who is knowledgeable about these issues and can answer your questions. You do not need a lawyer's assistance to complete this document, but if there is anything in this document that you do not understand, you should ask a lawyer to explain it to you.

The person you appoint as agent should be someone you know and trust and must be at least 18 years old. If you appoint your health or residential care provider (e.g. your physician, or an employee of a home health agency, hospital, nursing home, or residential care home, other than a relative), that person will have to choose between acting as your agent or as you health or residential care provider; the law does not permit a person to do both at the same time.

You should inform the person you appoint that you want him or her to be your health care agent. You should discuss this document with your agent and your physician and give each a signed copy. You should indicate on the document itself the people and institutions who will have signed copies. Your agent will not be liable for health care decisions for yourself as long as you are able to do so, and treatment cannot be given to you or stopped over your objection. You have the right to revoke the authority granted to your agent by informing him or her or your health care provider orally or in writing.

This document may not be changed or modified. If you want to make changes in the document you must make an entirely new one.

You may wish to designate an alternate agent in the event that your agent is unwilling, unable or ineligible to act as your agent. Any alternate agent you designate will have the same authority to make health care decisions for you.

THIS POWER OF ATTORNEY WILL NOT BE VALID UNLESS IT IS SIGNED IN THE PRESENCE OF TWO (2) OR MORE QUALIFIED WITNESSES WHO MUST BOTH BE PRESENT WHEN YOU SIGN OR ACKNOWLEDGE YOUR SIGNATURE. THE FOLLOWING PERSONS MAY NOT ACT AS WITNESSES:

— the person you have designated as your agent;
— your health or residential care provider or one of their employees;
— your spouse;
— your lawful heirs or beneficiaries named in your will or a deed;
— creditors or persons who have a claim against you.

I, _____ , hereby appoint _____
_____ as my agent to make any and all health care decisions for me, except to the extent I state otherwise in this document. This durable power of attorney for health care shall take effect in the event I become unable to make my own health care decisions.

(a) **STATEMENT OF DESIRES, SPECIAL PROVISIONS, AND LIMITATIONS REGARDING HEALTH CARE DECISIONS.**

Here you may include any specific desires or limitations you deem appropriate, such as when or what life-sustaining measures should be withheld; directions whether to continue or discontinue artificial nutrition and hydration; or instructions to refuse any specific types of treatment that are inconsistent with your religious beliefs or unacceptable to you for any reason.

_____
_____
_____
_____

(attach additional pages as necessary)

(b) **THE SUBJECT OF LIFE-SUSTAINING TREATMENT IS OF PARTICULAR IMPORTANCE.** For your convenience in dealing with that subject, some general statements concerning the withholding or removal of life-sustaining treatment are set forth below.

IF YOU AGREE WITH ONE OF THESE STATEMENTS, YOU MAY INCLUDE THE STATEMENT IN THE BLANK SPACE ABOVE:

- If I suffer a conditions from which there is no reasonable prospect of regaining my ability to think and act for myself, I want only care directed to my comfort and dignity, and authorize my agent to decline all treatment (including artificial nutrition and hydration) the primary purpose of which is to prolong my life.
- If I suffer a condition from which there is no reasonable prospect of regaining my ability to think and act for myself, I want care directed to my comfort and dignity and also want artificial nutrition and hydration if needed, but authorize my agent to decline all other treatment the primary purpose of which is to prolong my life.
- I want my life sustained by any reasonable medical measures, regardless of my condition.

In the event the person I appoint above is unable, unwilling or unavailable to act as my health care agent, I hereby appoint _____ of _____ as alternate agent.

I hereby acknowledge that I have been provided with a disclosure statement explaining the effect of this document. I have read and understand the information contained in the disclosure statement.

The original of this document will be kept at _____
_____ and the following persons and institutions will have signed copies:
_____
_____

In witness whereof, I have hereunto signed my name this _____ day of _____ ,
_____ .

_____
Signature

I declare that the principal appears to be of sound mind and free from duress at the time the durable power of attorney for health care is signed and that the principal has affirmed that he or she is aware of the nature of the document and is signing it freely and voluntarily.

Witness: _____ Address: _____

Witness: _____ Address: _____

State of ombudsman, hospital representative or other authorized person (to be signed only if the principal is in or is being admitted to a hospital, nursing home or residential care home):

I declare that I have personally explained the nature and effect of this durable power of attorney to the principal and that the principal understands the same.

Date: _____

Name:_____ Address: _____

Terminal Care Document

To my family, my physician, my lawyer, my clergyman. To any medical facility in whose care I happen to be. To any individual who may become responsible for my health, welfare or affairs.

Death is as much a reality as birth, growth, maturity and old age—it is the one certainty of life. If the time comes when I, _____, can no longer take part in decisions of my own future, let this statement stand as an expression of my wishes, while I am still of sound mind.

If the situation should arise in which I am in a terminal state and there is no reasonable expectation of my recovery, I direct that I be allowed to die a natural death and that my life not be prolonged by extraordinary measures. I do, however, ask that medication be mercifully administered to me to alleviate suffering even though this may shorten my remaining life.

This statement is made after careful consideration and is in accordance with my strong convictions and beliefs. I want the wishes and directions here expressed carried out to the extent permitted by law. Insofar as they are not legally enforceable, I hope that those to whom this will is addressed will regard themselves as morally bound by these provisions.

Signed: _____

Date: _____

Witness: _____   Witness: _____

Copies of this request have been given to:

_____

_____

_____

ADVANCE MEDICAL DIRECTIVE

I, _____, willfully and voluntarily make known my desire and do hereby declare: If at any time my attending physician should determine that I have a terminal condition where the application of life-prolonging procedures would serve only to artificially prolong the dying process, I direct that such procedures be withheld or withdrawn, and that I be permitted to die naturally with only the administration of medication or the performance of any medical procedure deemed necessary to provide me with comfort care or to alleviate pain (OPTION: I specifically direct that the following procedures or treatments be provided to me: _____)

In the absence of my ability to give directions regarding the use of such life-prolonging procedures, it is my intention that this advance directive shall be honored by my family and physician as the final expression of my legal right to refuse medical or surgical treatment and accept the consequences of such refusal.

OPTION: APPOINTMENT OF AGENT (CROSS THROUGH IF YOU DO NOT WANT TO APPOINT AN AGENT TO MAKE HEALTH CARE DECISIONS FOR YOU.)
I hereby appoint _____ (primary agent), of _____
_____
(address and telephone number), as my agent to make health care decisions on my behalf as authorized in this document. If _____ (primary agent) is not reasonably available or is unable or unwilling to act as my agent, then I appoint _____
_____ (successor agent), of _____
_____
(address and telephone number), to serve in that capacity.

I hereby grant to my agent, named above, full power and authority to make health care decisions on my behalf as described below whenever I have been determined to be incapable of making an informed decision about providing, withholding or withdrawing medical treatment. The phrase "incapable of making an informed decision" means unable to understand the nature, extent and probable consequences of a proposed medical decision or unable to make a rational evaluation of the risks and benefits of a proposed medical decision as compared with the risks and benefits of alternatives to that decision, or unable to communicate such understanding in any way. My agent's authority hereunder is effective as long as I am incapable of making an informed decision.

The determination that I am incapable of making an informed decision shall be made by my attending physician and a second physician or licensed clinical psychologist after a personal examination of me and shall be certified in writing. Such certification shall be required before treatment is withheld or withdrawn, and before, or as soon as reasonably practicable after, treatment is provided, and every 180 days thereafter while the treatment continues.

In exercising the power to make health care decisions on my behalf, my agent shall follow my desires and preferences as stated in this document or as otherwise known to my agent. My agent shall be guided by my medical diagnosis and prognosis and any information provided by my physicians as to the intrusiveness, pain, risks, and side effects associated with treatment or nontreatment. My agent shall not authorize a course of treatment which he knows, or upon reasonable inquiry ought to know, is contrary to my religious beliefs or my basic values, whether expressed orally or in writing. If my agent cannot determine what treatment choice I would have made on my own behalf, then my agent shall make a choice for me based upon what he believes to be in my best interests.

OPTION: POWERS OF MY AGENT (CROSS THROUGH ANY LANGUAGE YOU DO NOT WANT AND ADD ANY LANGUAGE YOU DO WANT.)

The powers of my agent shall include the following:

A. To consent to or refuse or withdraw consent to any type of medical care, treatment, surgical procedure, diagnostic procedure, medication and the use of mechanical or other procedures that affect any bodily function, including, but not limited to, artificial respiration, artificially administered nutrition and hydration, and cardiopulmonary resuscitation. This authorization specifically includes the power to consent to the administration of dosages of pain-relieving medication in excess of recommended dosages in an amount sufficient to relieve pain, even if such medication carries the risk of addiction or inadvertently hastens my death;

B. To request, receive, and review any information, verbal or written, regarding my physical or mental health, including but not limited to, medical and hospital records, and to consent to the disclosure of this information;

C. To employ and discharge my health care providers;

D. To authorize my admission to or discharge (including transfer to another facility) from any hospital, hospice, nursing home, adult home or other medical care facility for services other than those for treatment of mental illness requiring admission procedures provided in Article 1 (§ 37.2-800 et seq.) of Chapter 8 of Title 37.2; and

E. To take any lawful actions that may be necessary to carry out these decisions, including the granting of releases of liability to medical providers.

Further, my agent shall not be liable for the costs of treatment pursuant to his authorization, based solely on that authorization.

OPTION: APPOINTMENT OF AN AGENT TO MAKE AN ANATOMICAL GIFT OR ORGAN, TISSUE OR EYE DONATION (CROSS THROUGH IF YOU DO NOT WANT TO APPOINT AN AGENT TO MAKE AN ANATOMICAL GIFT OR ANY ORGAN, TISSUE OR EYE DONATION FOR YOU.)

Upon my death, I direct that an anatomical gift of all of my body or certain organ, tissue or eye donations may be made pursuant to Article 2 (§ 32.1-289 et seq.) of Chapter 8 of Title 32.1 and in accordance with my directions, if any. I hereby appoint _____ as my agent, of _____ (address and telephone number), to make any such anatomical gift or organ, tissue or eye donation following my death. I further direct that: _____ (declarant's directions concerning anatomical gift or organ, tissue or eye donation).

This advance directive shall not terminate in the event of my disability.

By signing below, I indicate that I am emotionally and mentally competent to make this advance directive and that I understand the purpose and effect of this document.

_____
(Date)

_____
(Signature of Declarant)

The declarant signed the foregoing advance directive in my presence. I am not the spouse or a blood relative of the declarant.

(Witness) _____

(Witness) _____

HEALTH CARE DIRECTIVE

Directive made this _____ day of _____ (month, year).

I, _____, having the capacity to make health care decisions, willfully, and voluntarily make known my desire that my dying shall not be artificially prolonged under the circumstances set forth below, and do hereby declare that:

(a) If at any time I should be diagnosed in writing to be in a terminal condition by the attending physician, or in a permanent unconscious condition by two physicians, and where the application of life-sustaining treatment would serve only to artificially prolong the process of my dying, I direct that such treatment be withheld or withdrawn, and that I be permitted to die naturally. I understand by using this form that a terminal condition means an incurable and irreversible condition caused by injury, disease, or illness, that would within reasonable medical judgment cause death within a reasonable period of time in accordance with accepted medical standards, and where the application of life-sustaining treatment would serve only to prolong the process of dying. I further understand in using this form that a permanent unconscious condition means an incurable and irreversible condition in which I am medically assess within reasonable medical judgment as having no reasonable probability of recovery from an irreversible coma or a persistent vegetative state.

(b) In the absence of my ability to give directions regarding the use of such life-sustaining treatment, it is my intention that this directive shall be honored by my family and physician(s) as the final expression of my legal right to refuse medical or surgical treatment and I accept the consequences of such refusal. If another person is appointed to make these decisions for me, whether through a durable power of attorney or otherwise, I request that the person be guided by this directive and any other clear expressions of my desires.

(c) If I am diagnosed to be in a terminal condition or a permanent unconscious condition (check one):

      _____ I DO want to have artificially provided nutrition and hydration.
      _____ I DO NOT want to have artificially provided nutrition and hydration.

(d) If I have been diagnosed as pregnant and that diagnosis is known to my physician, this directive shall have no force or effect during the course of my pregnancy.

(e) I understand the full import of this directive and I am emotionally and mentally capable to make the health care decisions contained in this directive.

(f) I understand that before I sign this directive, I can add to or delete from or otherwise change the wording of this directive and that I may add to or delete from this directive at any time and that any changes shall be consistent with Washington state law or federal constitutional law to be legally valid.

(g) It is my wish that every part of this directive be fully implemented. If for any reason any part is held invalid it is my wish that the remainder of my directive be implemented.

Signed_____

_____
City, County, and State of Residence

The declarer has been personally known to me and I believe him or her to be capable of making health care decisions.

Witness_____
Witness_____

STATE OF WEST VIRGINIA
LIVING WILL

Living will made this _____day of _____(month, year).
I,_____, being of sound mind, willfully and voluntarily declare that I want my wishes to be respected if I am very sick and not able to communicate my wishes for myself. In the absence of my ability to give directions regarding the use of life-prolonging medical intervention, it is my desire that my dying shall not be prolonged under the following circumstances:

If I am very sick and not able to communicate my wishes for myself and I am certified by one physician, who has personally examined me, to have a terminal condition or to be in a persistent vegetative state (I am unconscious and am neither aware of my environment nor able to interact with others), I direct that life-prolonging medical intervention that would serve solely to prolong the dying process or maintain me in a persistent vegetative state be withheld or withdrawn. I want to be allowed to die naturally and only be given medications or other medical procedures necessary to keep me comfortable. I want to receive as much medication as is necessary to alleviate my pain.

I give the following SPECIAL DIRECTIVES OR LIMITATIONS: (Comments about tube feedings, breathing machines, cardiopulmonary resuscitation, dialysis and mental health treatment may be placed here. My failure to provide special directives or limitations does not mean that I want or refuse certain treatments.) _____
_____

It is my intention that this living will be honored as the final expression of my legal right to refuse medical or surgical treatment and accept the consequences resulting from such refusal.
I understand the full import of this living will.

_____
Signed

_____

_____
Address

I did not sign the principal's signature above for or at the direction of the principal. I am at least eighteen years of age and am not related to the principal by blood or marriage, entitled to any portion of the estate of the principal to the best of my knowledge under any will of principal or codicil thereto, or directly financially responsible for principal's medical care. I am not the principal's attending physician or the principal's medical power of attorney representative or successor medical power of attorney representative under a medical power of attorney.

_____   _____
Witness   Date

_____   _____
Witness   Date

_____
STATE OF

_____
COUNTY OF

I, _____, a Notary Public of said County, do certify that
_____, as principal, and_____
and _____, as witnesses, whose names are signed to the writing
above bearing date on the _____ day of _____, 20_____,have this day
acknowledged the same before me.
Given under my hand this _____ day of _____, 20_____.

My commission expires:_____

_____
Notary Public

State of West Virginia
Medical Power of Attorney

The Person I Want to Make Health Care Decisions For Me When I Can't Make Them for Myself

Dated: _____, 20_____

I, _____,
(Insert your name and address)

hereby appoint as my representative to act on my behalf to give, withhold or withdraw informed consent to health care decisions in the event that I am not able to do so myself.

The person I choose as my representative is:

_____
(Insert the name, address, area code and telephone number of the person you wish to designate as your representative)

The person I choose as my successor representative is: If my representative is unable, unwilling or disqualified to serve, then I appoint:

_____
(Insert the name, address, area code and telephone number of the person you wish to designate as your successor representative)

This appointment shall extend to, but not be limited to, health care decisions relating to medical treatment, surgical treatment, nursing care, medication, hospitalization, care and treatment in a nursing home or other facility, and home health care. The representative appointed by this document is specifically authorized to be granted access to my medical records and other health information and to act on my behalf to consent to, refuse or withdraw any and all medical treatment or diagnostic procedures, or autopsy if my representative determines that I, if able to do so, would consent to, refuse or withdraw such treatment or procedures. Such authority shall include, but not be limited to, decisions regarding the withholding or withdrawal of life-prolonging interventions.

I appoint this representative because I believe this person understands my wishes and values and will act to carry into effect the health care decisions that I would make if I were able to do so, and because I also believe that this person will act in my best interest when my wishes are unknown. It is my intent that my family, my physician and all legal authorities be bound by the decisions that are made by the representative appointed by this document, and it is my intent that these decisions should not be the subject of review by any health care provider or administrative or judicial agency.

It is my intent that this document be legally binding and effective and that this document be taken as a formal statement of my desire concerning the method by which any health care decisions should be made on my behalf during any period when I am unable to make such decisions.

In exercising the authority under this medical power of attorney, my representative shall act consistently with my special directives or limitations as stated below.

I am giving the following SPECIAL DIRECTIVES OR LIMITATIONS ON THIS POWER: (Comments about tube feedings, breathing machines, cardiopulmonary resuscitation and dialysis may be placed here. My failure to provide special directives or limitations does not mean that I want or refuse certain treatments.)

THIS MEDICAL POWER OF ATTORNEY SHALL BECOME EFFECTIVE ONLY UPON MY INCAPACITY TO GIVE, WITHHOLD OR WITHDRAW INFORMED CONSENT TO MY OWN MEDICAL CARE.

_____
(Signature of the Principal)

I did not sign the principal's signature above. I am at least eighteen years of age and am not related to the principal by blood or marriage. I am not entitled to any portion of the estate of the principal or to the best of my knowledge under any will of the principal or codicil thereto, or legally responsible for the costs of the principal's medical or other care. I am not the principal's attending physician, nor am I the representative or successor representative of the principal.

Witness: _____ DATE: _____

Witness: _____ DATE: _____

STATE OF _____
COUNTY OF _____

I, _____, a Notary Public of said _____ County, do certify that _____, as principal, and _____ and _____, as witnesses, whose names are signed to the writing above bearing date on the _____ day of _____, 20_____, have this day acknowledged the same before me.

Given under my hand this _____ day of _____, 20_____.

My commission expires: _____.

_____
(Notary Public)

DECLARATION TO PHYSICIANS

I, _____, being of sound mind, voluntarily state my desire that my dying may not be prolonged under the circumstances specified in this document. Under those circumstances, I direct that I be permitted to die naturally. If I am unable to give directions regarding the use of life-sustaining procedures or feeding tubes, I intend that my family and physician honor this document as the final expression of my legal right to refuse medical or surgical treatment.

1. If I have a TERMINAL CONDITION, as determined by 2 physicians who have personally examined me, I do not want my dying to be artificially prolonged and I do not want life-sustaining procedures to be used. In addition, the following are my directions regarding the use of feeding tubes (check only one):

        ___ YES, I want feeding tubes used if I have a terminal condition.
        ___ NO, I do not want feeding tubes used if I have a terminal condition.
If you have not checked either box, feeding tubes will be used.

2. If I am in a PERSISTENT VEGETATIVE STATE, as determined by 2 physicians who have personally examined me, the following are my directions regarding the use of life-sustaining procedures:

        ___ YES, I want life-sustaining procedures used if I am in a persistent vegetative state.
        ___ NO, I do not want life-sustaining procedures used if I am in a persistent vegetative state.
If you have not checked either box, life-sustaining procedures will be used.

3. If I am in a PERSISTENT VEGETATIVE STATE, as determined by 2 physicians who have personally examined me, the following are my directions regarding the use of feeding tubes:

        ___ YES, I want feeding tubes used if I am in a persistent vegetative state.
        ___ NO, I do not want feeding tubes used if I am in a persistent vegetative state.
If you have not checked either box, feeding tubes will be used.

If you are interested in more information about the significant terms used in this document, see section 154.01 of the Wisconsin Statutes or the information accompanying this document.

ATTENTION: You and the 2 witnesses must sign the document at the same time.

Signed _____   Date _____

Address _____   Date of birth _____

_____

I believe that the person signing this document is of sound mind. I am an adult and am not related to the person signing this document by blood, marriage, or adoption. I am not entitled to and do not have a claim on any portion of the person's estate and am not otherwise restricted by law from being a witness.

Witness signature _____   Date signed _____

Print name _____

Witness signature _____   Date signed _____

Print name _____

DIRECTIVES TO ATTENDING PHYSICIAN

1.   This document authorizes the withholding or withdrawal of life-sustaining procedures or of feeding tubes when 2 physicians, one of whom is the attending physician, have personally examined and certified in writing that the patient has a terminal condition or is in a persistent vegetative state.

2.   The choices in this document were made by a competent adult. Under the law, the patient's stated desires must be followed unless you believe that withholding or withdrawing life-sustaining procedures or feeding tubes would cause the patient pain or reduced comfort and that the pain or discomfort cannot be alleviated through pain relief measures. If the patient's stated desires are that life-sustaining procedures or feeding tubes be used, this directive must be followed.

3.   If you feel that you cannot comply with this document, you must make a good faith attempt to transfer the patient to another physician who will comply. Refusal or failure to make a good faith attempt to do so constitutes unprofessional conduct.

4.   If you know that the patient is pregnant, this document has no effect during her pregnancy.

* * * * *

The person making this living will may use the following space to record the names of those individuals and health care providers to whom he or she has given copies of this document:

_____
_____
_____
_____

Power of Attorney for Health Care

NOTICE TO PERSON MAKING THIS DOCUMENT

YOU HAVE THE RIGHT TO MAKE DECISIONS ABOUT YOUR HEALTH CARE. NO HEALTH CARE MAY BE GIVEN TO YOU OVER YOUR OBJECTION, AND NECESSARY HEALTH CARE MAY NOT BE STOPPED OR WITHHELD IF YOU OBJECT.

BECAUSE YOUR HEALTH CARE PROVIDERS IN SOME CASES MAY NOT HAVE HAD THE OPPORTUNITY TO ESTABLISH A LONG-TERM RELATIONSHIP WITH YOU, THEY ARE OFTEN UNFAMILIAR WITH YOUR BELIEFS AND VALUES AND THE DETAILS OF YOUR FAMILY RELATIONSHIPS. THIS POSES A PROBLEM IF YOU BECOME PHYSICALLY OR MENTALLY UNABLE TO MAKE DECISIONS ABOUT YOUR HEALTH CARE.

IN ORDER TO AVOID THIS PROBLEM, YOU MAY SIGN THIS LEGAL DOCUMENT TO SPECIFY THE PERSON WHOM YOU WANT TO MAKE HEALTH CARE DECISIONS FOR YOU IF YOU ARE UNABLE TO MAKE THOSE DECISIONS PERSONALLY. THAT PERSON IS KNOWN AS YOUR HEALTH CARE AGENT. YOU SHOULD TAKE SOME TIME TO DISCUSS YOUR THOUGHTS AND BELIEFS ABOUT MEDICAL TREATMENT WITH THE PERSON OR PERSONS WHOM YOU HAVE SPECIFIED. YOU MAY STATE IN THIS ANY TYPES OF HEALTH CARE THAT YOU DO OR DO NOT DESIRE, AND YOU MAY LIMIT THE AUTHORITY OF YOUR HEALTH CARE AGENT. IF YOUR HEALTH CARE AGENT IS UNAWARE OF YOUR DESIRES WITH RESPECT TO A PARTICULAR HEALTH CARE DECISION, HE OR SHE IS REQUIRED TO DETERMINE WHAT WOULD BE IN YOUR BEST INTERESTS IN MAKING THE DECISION.

THIS IS AN IMPORTANT LEGAL DOCUMENT. IT GIVES YOUR AGENT BROAD POWERS TO MAKE HEALTH CARE DECISIONS FOR YOU. IT REVOKES ANY PRIOR POWER OF ATTORNEY FOR HEALTH CARE THAT YOU MAY HAVE MADE. IF YOU WISH TO CHANGE YOUR POWER OF ATTORNEY FOR HEALTH CARE, YOU MAY REVOKE THIS DOCUMENT AT ANY TIME BY DESTROYING IT, BY DIRECTING ANOTHER PERSON TO DESTROY IT IN YOUR PRESENCE, BY SIGNING A WRITTEN AND DATED STATEMENT OR BY STATING THAT IT IS REVOKED IN THE PRESENCE OF TWO WITNESSES. IF YOU REVOKE, YOU SHOULD NOTIFY YOUR AGENT, YOUR HEALTH CARE PROVIDERS AND ANY OTHER PERSON TO WHOM YOU HAVE GIVEN A COPY. IF YOUR AGENT IS YOUR SPOUSE AND YOUR MARRIAGE IS ANNULLED OR YOU ARE DIVORCED AFTER SIGNING THIS DOCUMENT, THE DOCUMENT IS INVALID.

YOU MAY ALSO USE THIS DOCUMENT TO MAKE OR REFUSE TO MAKE AN ANATOMICAL GIFT UPON YOUR DEATH. IF YOU USE THIS DOCUMENT TO MAKE OR REFUSE TO MAKE AN ANATOMICAL GIFT, THIS DOCUMENT REVOKES ANY PRIOR DOCUMENT OF GIFT THAT YOU MAY HAVE MADE. YOU MAY REVOKE OR CHANGE ANY ANATOMICAL GIFT THAT YOU MAKE BY THIS DOCUMENT BY CROSSING OUT THE ANATOMICAL GIFT PROVISION IN THIS DOCUMENT.

DO NOT SIGN THIS DOCUMENT UNLESS YOU CLEARLY UNDERSTAND IT.

IT IS SUGGESTED THAT YOU KEEP THE ORIGINAL OF THIS DOCUMENT ON FILE WITH YOUR PHYSICIAN.

POWER OF ATTORNEY FOR HEALTH CARE

Document made this _____ day of _____ (month), _____ (year).

CREATION OF POWER OF ATTORNEY FOR HEALTH CARE

I, _____
(print name, address and date of birth), being of sound mind, intend by this document to create a power of attorney for health care. My executing this power of attorney for health care is voluntary. Despite the creation of this power of attorney for health care, I expect to be fully informed about and allowed to participate in any health care decision for me, to the extent that I am able. For the purposes of this document, "health care decision" means an informed decision to accept, maintain, discontinue or refuse any care, treatment, service or procedure to maintain, diagnose or treat my physical or mental condition. In addition, I may, by this document, specify my wishes with respect to making an anatomical gift upon my death.

DESIGNATION OF HEALTH CARE AGENT

If I am no longer able to make health care decisions for myself, due to my incapacity, I hereby designate

_____
_____ (print name, address and telephone number) to be my health care agent for the purpose of making health care decisions on my behalf. If he or she is ever unable or unwilling to do so, I hereby designate _____
_____ (print name, address and telephone number) to be my alternate health care agent for the purpose of making health care decisions on my behalf. Neither my health care agent nor my alternate health care agent whom I have designated is my health care provider, an employee of my health care provider, an employee of a health care facility in which I am a patient or a spouse of any of those persons, unless he or she is also my relative. For purposes of this document, "incapacity" exists if 2 physicians or a physician and a psychologist who have personally examined me sign a statement that specifically expresses their opinion that I have a condition that means that I am unable to receive and evaluate information effectively or to communicate decisions to such an extent that I lack the capacity to manage my health care decisions. A copy of that statement must be attached to this document.

GENERAL STATEMENT OF AUTHORITY GRANTED

Unless I have specified otherwise in this document, if I ever have incapacity I instruct my health care provider to obtain the health care decision of my health care agent, if I need treatment, for all of my health care and treatment. I have discussed my desires thoroughly with my health care agent and believe that he or she understands my philosophy regarding the health care decisions I would make if I were able. I desire that my wishes be carried out through the authority given to my health care agent under this document.

If I am unable, due to my incapacity, to make a health care decision, my health care agent is instructed to make the health care decision for me, but my health care agent should try to discuss with me any specific proposed health care if I am able to communicate in any manner, including by blinking my eyes. If this communication cannot be made, my health care agent shall base his or her decision on any health care choices that I have expressed prior to the time of the decision. If I have not expressed a health care choice about the health care in question and communication cannot be made, my health care agent shall base his or her health care decision on what he or she believes to be in my best interest.

LIMITATIONS ON MENTAL HEALTH TREATMENT

My health care agent may not admit or commit me on an inpatient basis to an institution for mental diseases, an intermediate care facility for the mentally retarded, a state treatment facility or a treatment facility. My health care agent may not consent to experimental mental health research or psychosurgery, electro-convulsive treatment or drastic mental health treatment procedures for me.

ADMISSION TO NURSING HOMES OR COMMUNITY-BASED RESIDENTIAL FACILITIES

My health care agent may admit me to a nursing home or community-based residential facility for short-term stays for recuperative care or respite care.

If I have checked "Yes" to the following, my health care agent may admit me for a purpose other than recuperative care or respite care, but if I have checked "No" to the following, my health care agent may not so admit me:

1. A nursing home - Yes ____   No ____
2. A community-based residential facility - Yes ____   No ____

If I have not checked either "Yes" or "No" immediately above, my health care agent may admit me only for short-term stays for recuperative care or respite care.

PROVISION OF A FEEDING TUBE

If I have checked "Yes" to the following, my health care agent may have a feeding tube withheld or withdrawn from me, unless my physician has advised that, in his or her professional judgment, this will cause me pain or will reduce my comfort. If I have checked "No" to the following, my health care agent may not have a feeding tube withheld or withdrawn from me.

My health care agent may not have orally ingested nutrition or hydration withheld or withdrawn from me unless the provision of the nutrition or hydration is medically contraindicated.

Withhold or withdraw a feeding tube - Yes ___   No ___

If I have not checked either "Yes" or "No immediately above, my health care agent may not have a feeding tube withdrawn from me.

HEALTH CARE DECISIONS FOR PREGNANT WOMEN

If I have checked "Yes" to the following, my health care agent may make health care decisions for me even if my health care agent knows I am pregnant. If I have checked "No" to the following, my health care agent may not make health care decisions for me if my health care agent knows I am pregnant.

Health care decision if I am pregnant - Yes ___   No ___

If I have not checked either "Yes" or "No" immediately above, my health care agent may not make health care decisions for me if my health care agent knows I am pregnant.

STATEMENT OF DESIRES, SPECIAL PROVISIONS, OR LIMITATIONS

In exercising authority under this document, my health care agent shall act consistently with my following stated desires, if any, and is subject to any special provisions or limitations that I specify. The following are specific desires, provisions or limitations that I wish to state:

_____

_____

_____

INSPECTION AND DISCLOSURE OF INFORMATION
RELATING TO MY PHYSICAL OR MENTAL HEALTH

Subject to any limitations in this document, my health care agent has the authority to do all of the following:

(a) Request, review and receive any information, oral or written, regarding my physical or mental health, including medical and hospital records.

(b) Execute on my behalf any documents that may be required in order to obtain this information.

(c) Consent to the disclosure of this information.

(The principal and the witnesses all must sign the document at the same time.)
SIGNATURE OF PRINCIPAL

(person creating the power of attorney for health care)

Signature _____   Date _____

(The signing of this document by the principal revokes all previous powers of attorney for health care documents.)

STATEMENT OF WITNESSES

I know the principal personally and I believe him or her to be of sound mind and at least 18 years of age. I believe that his or her execution of this power of attorney for health care is voluntary. I am at least 18 years of age, am not related to the principal by blood, marriage or adoption and am not directly financially responsible for the principal's health care. I am not a health care provider who is serving the principal at this time, an employee of the health care provider, other than a chaplain or a social worker, of an inpatient health care facility in which the declarant is a patient. I am not the principal's health care agent. To the best of my knowledge, I am not entitled to and do not have a claim on the principal's estate.

Witness No. 1:

Print Name _____   Date _____

Address _____

_____

Signature _____

Witness No. 2:

Print Name _____   Date _____

Address _____

_____

Signature _____

STATEMENT OF HEALTH CARE AGENT AND ALTERNATE HEALTH CARE AGENT

I understand that _____ (name of principal) has designated me to be his or her health care agent or alternate health care agent if he or she is ever found to have incapacity and unable to make health care decisions himself or herself. _____ (name of principal) has discussed his or her desires regarding health care decisions with me.

Agent's signature _____

Address _____

_____

Alternate's signature _____

Address _____

_____

Failure to execute a power of attorney for health care document under chapter 155 of the Wisconsin Statutes creates no presumption about the intent of any individual with regard to his or her health care decisions.

This power of attorney for health care is executed as provided in chapter 155 of the Wisconsin Statutes.

ANATOMICAL GIFTS (optional)

Upon my death:

____ I wish to donate only the following organs or parts (specify the organs or parts): _____

_____

____ I wish to donate any needed organ or part.

____ I with to donate my body for anatomical study if needed.

____ I refuse to make an anatomical gift. (If this revokes a prior commitment that I have made to make an anatomical gift to a designated donee, I will attempt to notify the donee to which or to whom I agreed to donate.)

Failing to check any of the lines immediately above creates no presumption about my desire to make or refuse to make an anatomical gift.

Signature _____   Date _____

DECLARATION

NOTICE

This document has significant medical, legal and possible ethical implications and effects. Before you sign this document, you should become completely familiar with these implications and effects. The operation, effects and implications of this document may be discussed with a physician, a lawyer and a clergyman of your choice.

Declaration made this _____ day of _____ (month, year). I, _____, being of sound mind, willfully and voluntarily make known my desire that my dying shall not be artificially prolonged under the circumstances set forth below, do hereby declare:

If at any time I should have an incurable injury, disease or other illness certified to be a terminal condition by two (2) physicians who have personally examined me, one (1) of whom shall be my attending physician, and the physicians have determined that my death will occur whether or not life-sustaining procedures are utilized and where the application of life-sustaining procedures would serve only to artificially prolong the dying process, I direct that such procedures be withheld or withdrawn, and that I be permitted to die naturally with only the administration of medication or the performance of any medical procedure deemed necessary to provide me with comfort care.

If, in spite of this declaration, I am comatose or otherwise unable to make treatment decisions for myself, I HEREBY designate _____ to make treatment decisions for me.

In the absence of my ability to give directions regarding the use of life-sustaining procedures, it is my intention that this declaration shall be honored by my family and physician(s) and agent as the final expression of my legal right to refuse medical or surgical treatment and accept the consequences from this refusal. I understand the full import or this declaration and I am emotionally and mentally competent to make this declaration.

Signed_____

City, County and State of Residence_____

The declarant has been personally known to me and I believe him or her to be of sound mind. I did not sign the declarant's signature above for or at the direction of the declarant. I am not related to the declarant by blood or marriage, entitled to any portion of the estate of the declarant according to the laws of intestate succession or under any will of the declarant or codicil thereto, or directly financially responsible for declarant's medical care.

Witness_____

Witness_____

Advance Health Care Directive
Explanation

You have the right to give instructions about your own health care. You also have the right to name someone else to make health care decisions for you. This form lets you do either or both of these things. It also lets you express your wishes regarding donation of organs and the designation of your supervising health care provider. If you use this form, you may complete or modify all or any part of it. You are free to use a different form.

Part 1 of this form is a power of attorney for health care. Part 1 lets you name another individual as agent to make health care decisions for you if you become incapable of making your own decisions or if you want someone else to make those decisions for you now even though you are still capable.

You may also name an alternate agent to act for you if your first choice is not willing, able or reasonably available to make decisions for you. Unless related to you, your agent may not be an owner, operator or employee of a residential or community care facility at which you are receiving care.

Unless the form you sign limits the authority of your agent, your agent may make all health care decisions for you. This form has a place for you to limit the authority of your agent. You need not limit the authority of your agent if you wish to rely on your agent for all health care decisions that may have to be made. If you choose not to limit the authority of your agent, your agent will have the right to:

(a) Consent or refuse consent to any care, treatment, service or procedure to maintain, diagnose or otherwise affect a physical or mental condition;

(b) Select or discharge health care providers and institutions;

(c) Approve or disapprove diagnostic tests, surgical procedures, programs of medication and orders not to resuscitate; and

(d) Direct the provision, withholding or withdrawal of artificial nutrition and hydration and all other forms of health care.

Part 2 of this form lets you give specific instructions about any aspect of your health care. Choices are provided for you to express your wishes regarding the provision, withholding or withdrawal of treatment to keep you alive, including the provision of artificial nutrition and hydration, as well as the provision of pain relief. Space is also provided for you to add to the choices you have made or for you to write out any additional wishes.

Part 3 of this form lets you express an intention to donate your bodily organs and tissues following your death.

Part 4 of this form lets you designate a supervising health care provider to have primary responsibility for your health care.

After completing this form, sign and date the form at the end. This form must either be signed before a notary public or, in the alternative, be witnessed by two (2) witnesses. Give a copy of the signed and completed form to your physician, to any other health care providers you may have, to any health care institution at which you are receiving care, and to any health care agents you have named. You should talk to the person you have named as agent to make sure that he or she understands your wishes and is willing to take the responsibility.

You have the right to revoke this advance health care directive or replace this form at any time.

* * * * * * * * * * * * * * * * * * * *

PART 1
POWER OF ATTORNEY FOR HEALTH CARE

(1) DESIGNATION OF AGENT: I designate the following individual as my agent to make health care decisions for me:

_____
(name of individual you choose as agent)

_____
(address)   (city)   (state)   (zip code)

_____
(home phone)   (work phone)

OPTIONAL: If I revoke my agent's authority or if my agent is not willing, able or reasonably available to make a health care decision for me, I designate as my first alternate agent:

_____
(name of individual you choose as first alternate agent)

_____
(address)   (city)   (state)   (zip code)

_____
(home phone)   (work phone)

OPTIONAL: If I revoke the authority of my agent and first alternate agent or if neither is willing, able or reasonably available to make a health care decision for me, I designate as my second alternate agent:

_____
(name of individual you choose as second alternate agent)

_____
(address)   (city)   (state)   (zip code)

_____
(home phone)   (work phone)

(2) AGENT'S AUTHORITY: My agent is authorized to make all health care decisions for me, including decisions to provide, withhold or withdraw artificial nutrition and hydration and all other forms of health care to keep me alive, except as I state here:

_____
_____
_____
(Add additional sheets if needed.)

(3) WHEN AGENT'S AUTHORITY BECOMES EFFECTIVE: My agent's authority becomes effective when my supervising health care provider determines that I lack the capacity to make my own health care decisions unless I initial the following box. If I initial this box [   ], my agent's authority to make health care decisions for me takes effect immediately.

(4) AGENT'S OBLIGATION: My agent shall make health care decisions for me in accordance with this power of attorney for health care, any instructions I give in Part 2 of this form, and my other wishes to the extent known to my agent. To the extent my wishes are unknown, my agent shall make health care decisions for me in accordance with what my agent determines to be in my best interest. In determining my best interest, my agent shall consider my personal values to the extent known to my agent.

(5) NOMINATION OF GUARDIAN: If a guardian of my person needs to be appointed for me by a court, (please initial one):

[   ]   I nominate the agent(s) whom I named in this form in the order designated to act as guardian.

[   ]   I nominate the following to be guardian in the order designated:

_____
_____
_____

[   ]   I do not nominate anyone to be guardian.

PART 2
INSTRUCTIONS FOR HEALTH CARE

Please strike any wording that you do not want.

(6) END-OF-LIFE DECISIONS: I direct that my health care providers and others involved in my care provide, withhold or withdraw treatment in accordance with the choice I have initialed below:

[   ]   (a) Choice Not To Prolong Life
I do not want my life to be prolonged if (i) I have an incurable and irreversible condition that will result in my death within a relatively short time, (ii) I become unconscious and, to a reasonable degree of medical certainty, I will not regain consciousness, or (iii) the likely risks and burdens of treatment would outweigh the expected benefits, OR

[   ]   (b) Choice To Prolong Life
I want my life to be prolonged as long as possible within the limits of generally accepted health care standards.

(7) ARTIFICIAL NUTRITION AND HYDRATION: Artificial nutrition and hydration must be provided, withheld or withdrawn in accordance with the choice I have made in paragraph (6) unless I initial the following box. If I initial this box [   ], artificial nutrition must be provided regardless of my condition and regardless of the choice I have made in paragraph (6). If I initial this box [   ], artificial hydration must be provided regardless of my condition and regardless of the choice I have made in paragraph (6).

(8) RELIEF FROM PAIN: Except as I state in the following space, I direct that treatment for alleviation of pain or discomfort be provided at all times:

_____
_____

(9) OTHER WISHES: (If you do not agree with any of the optional choices above and wish to write your own, or if you wish to add to the instructions you have given above, you may do so here.) I direct that:

_____
_____
(Add additional sheets if needed.)

PART 3
DONATION OF ORGANS AT DEATH
(OPTIONAL)

(10) Upon my death (initial applicable box):
[   ]   (a) I give my body, or
[   ]   (b) I give any needed organs, tissues or parts, or
[   ]   (c) I give the following organs, tissues or parts only

_____

[   ]   (d) My gift is for the following purposes (strike any of the following you do not want):
          (i) Any purpose authorized by law;
          (ii) Transplantation;
          (iii) Therapy;
          (iv) Research;
          (v) Medical education.

(11) I designate the following physician as my primary physician:

_____
(name of physician)

_____
(address)   (city)   (state)   (zip code)

_____
(phone)

If the physician I have designated above is not willing, able or reasonably available to act as my primary physician, I designate the following as my primary physician:

_____
(name of physician)

_____
(address)   (city)   (state)   (zip code)

_____
(phone)

* * * * * * * * * * * * * * * * * * *

(12) EFFECT OF COPY: A copy of this form has the same effect as the original.

(13) SIGNATURES: Sign and date the form here:

_____   _____
(sign your name)   (date)

_____
(print your name)

_____
(address)

_____
(city)   (state)

(Optional) SIGNATURES OF WITNESSES:

First witness

_____   _____
(print name)   (address)

_____   _____
(signature of witness)   (city)   (state)

_____
(date)

Second witness

_____   _____
(print name)   (address)

_____   _____
(signature of witness)   (city)   (state)

_____
(date)

_____
(Signature of notary public in lieu of witnesses)

_____
(date)

Standard Notary Page

State of _____   )

County of _____   )

On this _____ day of _____, 200_____, before me, personally appeared _____, principal, and _____ and _____, witnesses, who are personally known to me or who provided _____ _____ _____ as identification, and signed the foregoing instrument in my presence.

_____

Notary Public

My Commission expires:

Statement of Desires and Location of Property & Documents

I, _____ , am signing this document as the expression of my desires as to the matters stated below, and to inform my family members or other significant persons of the location of certain property and documents in the event of any emergency or of my death.

1.   **Funeral Desires.** It is my desire that the following arrangements be made for my funeral and disposition of remains in the event of my death (state if you have made any arrangements, such as pre-paid burial plans, cemetery plots owned, etc.):

    ❏   Burial at _____

    _____ .

    ❏   Cremation at _____

    _____ .

    ❏   Other specific desires: _____

    _____ .

    _____ .

2.   **Minor Children.** I have the following minor child(ren): _____
_____ . The following are my desires concerning the custody, education, and rearing of said minor child(ren): _____
_____
_____
_____
_____
_____ .

3.   **Pets.** I have the following pet(s): _____
_____ . The following are my desires concerning the care of said pet(s): _____
_____
_____ .

4.   **Notification.** I would like the following person(s) notified in the event of emergency or death (give name, address, and phone number):
_____
_____
_____
_____
_____ .

5.   **Location of Documents.** The following is a list of important documents, and their location:

    ❏   Last Will and Testament, dated _____ . Location: _____

    _____

❑   Durable Power of Attorney, dated _____. Location: _____

_____ .

❑   Living Will, dated _____. Location: _____

_____

❑   Deed(s) to real estate (describe property location and location of deed):

_____

_____

_____

❑   Title(s) to vehicles (cars, boats, etc.) (Describe vehicle, its location, and location of title, registration, or other documents):

_____

_____

_____

_____

❑   Life insurance policies (list name, address, & phone number of insurance company and insurance agent, policy number, and location of policy):

_____

_____

_____

❑   Other insurance policies (list type, company, & agent, policy number, and location of policy):

_____

_____

_____

_____

_____

❏   Other: (list other documents such as stock certificates, bonds, certificates of deposit, etc., and their location):

_____

_____

_____

_____

6.   **Location of Assets.** In addition to items readily visible in my home or listed above, I have the following assets:

❏   Safe deposit box located at _____, box number _____.
Key located at: _____.

❏   Bank accounts (list name & address of bank, type of account, and account number):

_____

❏   Other (describe the item and give its location):

_____

_____

_____

_____

_____

_____

7.   Other desires or information (state any desires or provide any information not given above; use additional sheets of paper if necessary):

_____

_____

_____

_____

_____

Dated: _____

_____
Signature

Addendum to Living Will

I, _____, hereby execute this addendum to
the _____ ("Living Will"),
executed by me on _____, 200____. The sole purpose of this addendum is to
more fully express my wishes regarding my medical treatment. If any or all of the terms of this addendum
are determined to be invalid, my living will shall remain in effect. My desires regarding my medical care
and treatment are as indicated below:

_____ 1. If I should have an incurable or irreversible condition that will cause my death within a
relatively short time without the administration of artificial life support procedures or
treatment, and if I am unable to make decisions regarding my medical treatment, I direct
my attending physician to withhold or withdraw procedures that merely prolong the dying
process and are not necessary to my comfort or to alleviate pain. This authorization
includes, but is not limited to, the withholding or withdrawal of the following types of
medical treatment (subject to any special instructions in paragraph 5 below):

_____ a. Artificial feeding and hydration.
_____ b. Cardiopulmonary resuscitation (this includes, but is not limited to, the use
of drugs, electric shock, and artificial breathing).
_____ c. Kidney dialysis.
_____ d. Surgery or other invasive procedures.
_____ e. Drugs and antibiotics.
_____ f. Transfusions of blood or blood products.
_____ g. Other: _____
_____

_____ 2. If I should be in an irreversible coma or persistent vegetative state that my physician
reasonably believes to be irreversible or incurable, I direct my attending physician to
withhold or withdraw medical procedures and treatment other than such medical
procedures and treatment necessary to my comfort or to alleviate pain. This authorization
includes, but is not limited to, the withholding or withdrawal of the following types of
medical treatment (subject to any special instructions in paragraph 5 below):

_____ a. Artificial feeding and hydration.
_____ b. Cardiopulmonary resuscitation (this includes, but is not limited to, the use
of drugs, electric shock, and artificial breathing).
_____ c. Kidney dialysis.
_____ d. Surgery or other invasive procedures.
_____ e. Drugs and antibiotics.
_____ f. Transfusions of blood or blood products.
_____ g. Other: _____
_____

_____ 3. If I should have a medical condition where I am unable to communicate my desires as to
treatment and my physician determines that the burdens of treatment outweigh the
expected benefits, I direct my attending physician to withhold or withdraw medical
procedures and treatment other than such medical procedures and treatment necessary
to my comfort or to alleviate pain This authorization includes, but is not limited to, the
withholding or withdrawal of the following types of medical treatment (subject to any
special instructions in paragraph 5 below):

_____ a. Artificial feeding and hydration.
_____ b. Cardiopulmonary resuscitation (this includes, but is not limited to, the use
of drugs, electric shock, and artificial breathing).
_____ c. Kidney dialysis.

_____ d. Surgery or other invasive procedures.

_____ e. Drugs and antibiotics.

_____ f. Transfusions of blood or blood products.

_____ g. Other: _____

_____

_____ 4. I want my life prolonged to the greatest extent possible (subject to any special instructions in paragraph 5 below).

_____ 5. I specifically DO NOT want the governor, state legislature, President of the United States, United States Congress, or any other individual, group, body, or agency of any local, state, or federal legislative or executive branch of government to be involved in any manner in the decision-making regarding my medical treatment, or the withholding or withdrawal of medical treatment. I specifically DO NOT want the following person(s) to be involved in any manner in the decision-making regarding my medical treatment, or the withholding or withdrawal of medical treatment: _____.

_____ 6. Special instructions (if any) _____

_____

_____

_____

Signed this _____ day of _____, 200____.

_____

Signature

Address: _____

_____

Each of the undersigned hereby witnesses the foregoing signature of the declarant, and attests that the declarant is personally known to me, that I believe the declarant to be of sound mind, and that the declarant voluntarily signed this document in my presence. I further attest that I am at least 18 years of age; that I am not related to the declarant by blood, marriage, or adoption; that I do not have a claim against any portion of the estate of the declarant; that I am not entitled to any portion of the declarant's estate by any will or codicil or by operation of law; that I am not the attending physician, nor an employee of the attending physician, of the declarant; that I am not employed by, an agent of, or a patient in, a health facility in which the declarant is a patient; that I am not directly responsible for the financial affairs or medical care of the declarant; that I did not sign this document on behalf of the declarant; and that I am not the declarant's health care representative or successor health care representative under a health care power of attorney.

Witness: _____   Witness: _____

Name: _____   Name: _____

Address: _____   Address: _____

Durable Power of Attorney for Health Care

1.   Appointment of Agent. I, _____ , appoint _____ , as my agent for health care decisions (called "Agent" in the rest of this document). If my Agent shall be unable or unwilling to make decisions pursuant to this Durable Power of Attorney for Health Care, I appoint as my alternate Agent _____ . I specifically DO NOT want the governor, state legislature, President of the United States, United States Congress, or any other individual, group, body, or agency of any local, state, or federal legislative or executive branch of government to be involved in any manner in the decision-making regarding my medical treatment, or the withholding or withdrawal of medical treatment. I specifically DO NOT want the following person(s) to be involved in any manner in the decision-making regarding my medical treatment, or the withholding or withdrawal of medical treatment: _____ _____ .

2.   Effective Date and Durability. My Agent may only act if I am unable to participate in making decisions regarding my medical treatment. My attending physician and another physician or licensed psychologist shall determine, after examining me, when I am unable to participate in making my own medical decisions. This designation is suspended during any period when I regain the ability to participate in my own medical treatment decisions. I intend this document to be a Durable Power of Attorney for Health Care and it shall survive my disability or incapacity.

3.   Agent's Powers. I grant my Agent full authority to make decisions for me. In making such decisions, he or she should follow my expressed wishes, either written or oral, regarding my medical treatment. If my Agent cannot determine the choice I would want based on my written or oral statements, then he or she shall choose for me based on what he or she believes to be in my best interests. I direct that my Agent comply with the following instructions or limitations: _____ _____ .

4.   Life-sustaining Treatment. (CHOOSE ONLY ONE.) I understand that I do not have to choose any of the instructions regarding life-sustaining treatment listed below. If I choose one, I will place a check mark by the choice and sign below my choice. If I sign one of the choices listed below, I direct that reasonable measures be taken to keep me comfortable and to relieve pain.

[ ]   **CHOICE 1**: Life-sustaining treatment: I grant discretion to my Agent.

I do not want life-sustaining treatment (including artificial delivery of food and water except for artificial delivery of food and water) if any of the following medical conditions exist:

a.   I am in an irreversible coma or persistent vegetative state.

b.   I am terminally ill, and life-sustaining procedures would only serve to artificially delay my death.

c.   My medical condition is such that burdens of treatment outweigh the expected benefits. In making this determination, I want my Patient Advocate to consider relief of my suffering, the expenses involved, and the quality of life, if prolonged.

I expressly authorize my Agent to make decisions to withhold or withdraw treatment which would allow me to die, and I acknowledge such decisions could or would allow my death.

Signed: _____

OR

[ ]   **CHOICE 2**: Life-sustaining treatment: withhold treatment only if I am in a coma or persistent vegetative state.

I want life-sustaining treatment (____including artificial delivery of food and water ____except for artificial delivery of food and water) unless I am in a coma or persistent vegetative state that my physician reasonably believes to be irreversible. Once my physician has reasonably concluded that I will remain unconscious for the rest of my life, I do not want life-sustaining treatment to be provided or continued.

I expressly authorize my Agent to make decisions to withhold or withdraw treatment which would allow me to die, and I acknowledge such decisions could or would allow my death.

Signed: _____

OR

[ ]   **CHOICE 3**: Directive for maximum treatment.

I want my life to be prolonged to the greatest extent possible consistent with sound medical practice without regard to my condition, the chances I have for recovery, or the cost of the procedures, and I direct life-sustaining treatment to be provided in order to prolong my life.

Signed: _____

5.   Protection of third parties who rely on the instructions of my Agent. No person or entity that relies in good faith on the instructions of my Agent pursuant to this document, without actual notice that this power has been revoked or amended, shall incur any liability to me or to my estate. If I am unable to participate in making decisions for my care and there is no Agent to act for me, I request that the instructions I have given in this document be followed and be considered conclusive evidence of my wishes.

6.   Administrative provisions. I revoke any prior durable powers of attorney for health care that I may have executed to the extent that, and only to the extent that, they grant powers and authority within the scope of the powers granted to the Agent appointed in this document.

The document shall be governed by _____ law. However, I intend for this durable power of attorney for health care to be honored in any jurisdiction where it is presented and for such jurisdiction to refer to _____ law to interpret and determine the validity and enforceability of this document.

Photocopies of this signed power of attorney shall be treated as original counterparts.

I am providing these instructions voluntarily and have not been required to give them to obtain treatment or to have care withheld or withdrawn. I am at least eighteen years of age and of solid mind.

Dated: _____   _____
                                        Signature

WITNESS STATEMENT

I declare that the person who signed this Durable Power of Attorney for Health Care did so in my presence and appears to be of sound mind and under no duress, fraud or undue influence. I am not the husband or wife, parent, child, grandchild, brother or sister of the person who signed this document. Further, I am not his or her presumptive heir and to the best of my knowledge, I am not a beneficiary to his or her will at the time of witnessing. I am not the Agent, the physician or an employee of the life or health insurance provider for the person signing this document. Nor am I an employee of the health care facility or home for the aged where the person signing this document resides or is being treated.

Dated: _____   _____
                                        (signature)
                                        Name: _____
                                        Address: _____
                                        _____

Dated: _____   _____
                                        (signature)
                                        Name: _____
                                        Address: _____
                                        _____

State of _____)
County of _____)

On this _____ day of _____, _____, before me personally appeared _____, principal, and _____ and _____, witnesses, who are personally known to me or who produced _____ _____ as identification, and signed the foregoing instrument in my presence.

                                        _____
                                        Notary Public
                                        My Commission Expires:

Affidavit of Attorney in Fact

STATE OF   )
)
COUNTY OF   )

      Before me, the undersigned authority, personally appeared _____ ("Affiant"), who swore or affirmed that:

      1. Affiant is the attorney in fact named in the _____ _____(title of document) executed by _____ ("Principal") on _____ (date).

      2. This _____ (title of document) is currently exercisable by Affiant. The principal is domiciled in _____ (insert name of state, territory, or foreign country).

      3. To the best of the Affiant's knowledge after diligent search and inquiry:

          a. The Principal is not deceased; and

          b. The Principal has not partially nor completely revoked or suspended the _____ _____ (title of document); and

          c. There has been no partial or complete termination by adjudication of incapacity or incompetence, by the occurrence of an event referenced in the _____ (title of document), nor any suspension by initiation of proceedings to determine incapacity or to appoint a guardian.

      4. Affiant agrees not to exercise any powers granted by the _____ _____ (title of document) if Affiant attains knowledge that it has been partially or completely revoked, terminated, or suspended; or is no longer valid because of the death or adjudication of incapacity or incompetence of the Principal.

                                                     _____
                                                     (Affiant)

      Sworn to (or affirmed) and subscribed before me this _____ day of _____, 20___, by _____ (name of person making statement).

Index

About the Author

Edward A. Haman received his law degree in 1978 from the University of Toledo College of Law. As a student, he served as coordinator of the law school's Client Counseling Competition team, and as editor of the law school's legal journal, *Discovery*. He also has a bachelor of arts degree from Western Michigan University, with a major in communication and minors in accounting and general business.

Since graduating from law school, he has practiced law in three states. In Hawaii, Mr. Haman was engaged in general private practice, initially as a sole practitioner, then with a small law firm emphasizing family law, real estate, and business law. This included trial practice, as well as criminal appellate work before the Supreme Court of Hawaii and the U.S Court of Appeals in San Francisco. In Michigan, he served as a Circuit Court domestic relations hearing officer. After moving to Florida in 1986, he spent several years as an attorney for the Florida social services agency, handling a variety of legal matters, including cases involving the abuse and neglect of children, the elderly, and the disabled; public health matters; child support enforcement; welfare fraud; and the licensing of assisted living facilities, nursing homes, and other health care facilities. Mr. Haman has also engaged in private practice in area such as real estate, family law, and probate.

Since 1987, Mr. Haman has authored and co-authored numerous self-help law books, including *The Complete Bankruptcy Guide*, *File Your Own Divorce*, and *The Complete Prenuptial Agreement Kit*. In connection with the self-help law books, he has been a guest on numerous radio programs, and has appeared on the Fox News Channel. He has also written several articles for *The Florida Keystone Series*, a legal publication for attorneys. Currently residing in Tampa, Florida, Mr. Haman continues to write books, and also volunteers as a support group facilitator for the Alzheimer's Association. In his spare time, he enjoys traveling, kayaking, snow skiing, hiking, and mountaineering.

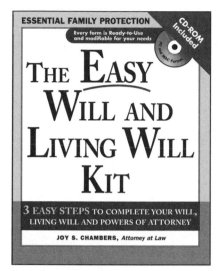
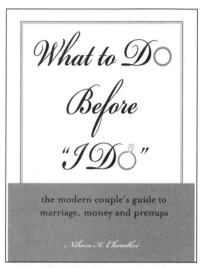
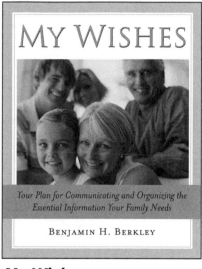

Sphinx® Publishing's National Titles
Valid in All 50 States

LEGAL SURVIVAL IN BUSINESS

The Complete Book of Corporate Forms (2E)	$29.95
The Complete Hiring and Firing Handbook	$19.95
The Complete Limited Liability Kit	$24.95
The Complete Partnership Book	$24.95
The Complete Patent Book	$26.95
The Complete Patent Kit	$39.95
The Entrepreneur's Internet Handbook	$21.95
The Entrepreneur's Legal Guide	$26.95
Financing Your Small Business	$16.95
Fired, Laid-Off or Forced Out	$14.95
Form Your Own Corporation (5E)	$29.95
The Home-Based Business Kit	$14.95
How to Buy a Franchise	$19.95
How to Form a Nonprofit Corporation (3E)	$24.95
How to Register Your Own Copyright (5E)	$24.95
HR for Small Business	$14.95
Incorporate in Delaware from Any State	$26.95
Incorporate in Nevada from Any State	$24.95
The Law (In Plain English)® for Restaurants	$16.95
The Law (In Plain English)® for Small Business	$19.95
The Law (In Plain English)® for Writers	$14.95
Making Music Your Business	$18.95
Minding Her Own Business (4E)	$14.95
Most Valuable Business Legal Forms You'll Ever Need (3E)	$21.95
Profit from Intellectual Property	$28.95
Protect Your Patent	$24.95
The Small Business Owner's Guide to Bankruptcy	$21.95
Start Your Own Law Practice	$16.95
Tax Power for the Self-Employed	$17.95
Tax Smarts for Small Business	$21.95
Your Rights at Work	$14.95

LEGAL SURVIVAL IN COURT

Attorney Responsibilities & Client Rights	$19.95
Crime Victim's Guide to Justice (2E)	$21.95
Legal Research Made Easy (4E)	$24.95
Winning Your Personal Injury Claim (3E)	$24.95

LEGAL SURVIVAL IN REAL ESTATE

The Complete Kit to Selling Your Own Home	$18.95
The Complete Book of Real Estate Contracts	$18.95
Essential Guide to Real Estate Leases	$18.95
Homeowner's Rights	$19.95
How to Buy a Condominium or Townhome (2E)	$19.95
How to Buy Your First Home (2E)	$14.95
How to Make Money on Foreclosures	$16.95
The Mortgage Answer Book	$14.95
Sell Your Own Home Without a Broker	$14.95
The Weekend Landlord	$16.95
The Weekend Real Estate Investor	$14.95
Working with Your Homeowners Association	$19.95

LEGAL SURVIVAL IN SPANISH

Cómo Comprar su Primera Casa	$8.95
Cómo Conseguir Trabajo en los Estados Unidos	$8.95
Cómo Hacer su Propio Testamento	$16.95
Cómo Iniciar su Propio Negocio	$8.95
Cómo Negociar su Crédito	$8.95
Cómo Organizar un Presupuesto	$8.95
Cómo Solicitar su Propio Divorcio	$24.95
Guía de Inmigración a Estados Unidos (4E)	$24.95
Guía de Justicia para Víctimas del Crimen	$21.95
Guía Esencial para los Contratos de Arrendamiento de Bienes Raices	$22.95
Inmigración y Ciudadanía en los EE.UU. Preguntas y Respuestas	$16.95
Inmigración a los EE.UU. Paso a Paso (2E)	$24.95
Manual de Beneficios del Seguro Social	$18.95
El Seguro Social Preguntas y Respuestas	$16.95
¡Visas! ¡Visas! ¡Visas!	$9.95

LEGAL SURVIVAL IN PERSONAL AFFAIRS

101 Complaint Letters That Get Results	$18.95
The 529 College Savings Plan (2E)	$18.95
The 529 College Savings Plan Made Simple	$7.95
The Alternative Minimum Tax	$14.95
The Antique and Art Collector's Legal Guide	$24.95
The Childcare Answer Book	$12.95
Child Support	$18.95
The Complete Book of Insurance	$18.95
The Complete Book of Personal Legal Forms	$24.95
The Complete Credit Repair Kit	$19.95
The Complete Legal Guide to Senior Care	$21.95
The Complete Personal Bankruptcy Guide	$21.95
Credit Smart	$18.95
The Easy Will and Living Will Kit	$16.95
Fathers' Rights	$19.95
File Your Own Divorce (6E)	$24.95
The Frequent Traveler's Guide	$14.95
Gay & Lesbian Rights (2E)	$21.95
Grandparents' Rights (4E)	$24.95
How to Parent with Your Ex	$12.95
How to Write Your Own Living Will (4E)	$18.95
How to Write Your Own Premarital Agreement (3E)	$24.95
The Infertility Answer Book	$16.95
Law 101	$16.95
Law School 101	$16.95
The Living Trust Kit	$21.95
Living Trusts and Other Ways to Avoid Probate (3E)	$24.95
Make Your Own Simple Will (4E)	$26.95
Mastering the MBE	$16.95
Money and Divorce	$14.95
My Wishes	$21.95
Nursing Homes and Assisted Living Facilities	$19.95
Power of Attorney Handbook (6E)	$24.95
Quick Cash	$14.95
Seniors' Rights	$19.95
Sexual Harassment in the Workplace	$18.95
Sexual Harassment: Your Guide to Legal Action	$18.95
Sisters-in-Law	$16.95
The Social Security Benefits Handbook (4E)	$18.95
Social Security Q&A	$12.95
Starting Out or Starting Over	$14.95
Teen Rights (and Responsibilities) (2E)	$14.95
Unmarried Parents' Rights (and Responsibilities)(3E)	$16.95
U.S. Immigration and Citizenship Q&A	$18.95
U.S. Immigration Step by Step (2E)	$24.95
U.S.A. Immigration Guide (5E)	$26.95
What They Don't Teach You in College	$12.95
What to Do—Before "I DO"	$14.95
The Wills and Trusts Kit (2E)	$29.95
Win Your Unemployment Compensation Claim (2E)	$21.95
Your Right to Child Custody, Visitation and Support (3E)	$24.95